P9-CJS-218

Advance Praise

for *Morning Meetings with Jesus!*

Morning Meetings with Jesus: 180 Devotions for Teachers provides an enormous amount of encouragement and guidance, not only for teachers but for everyone who has a life full of daily challenges. I think the readers will look to each day's "morning meeting" with anticipation and hope.

—Benjamin S. Carson Sr., MD,
Director of Pediatric Neurosurgery
Professor of Neurological Surgery, Oncology,
Plastic Surgery, and Pediatrics

Written by one who has walked in your footsteps, this powerful devotional reveals the heart of a fellow teacher who saw the classroom as an opportunity to make an eternal impact on the lives of students. Susan's honest reflections and practical applications will inspire and encourage you.

—Steven C. Babbitt, Director, Publishing Services
Association of Christian Schools International
Colorado Springs, Colorado

This work is Spirit-inspired and wisdom-based. Each day's devotion has urged me on in my work. Jesus is the greatest teacher, and we have so much to learn from him. Many teachers could be helped and encouraged by this book—in parochial, private, and public schools.

—Robert Chapman III, President,
Calvary Lutheran Church & School
Retired Professor of Education
Loyola University, Baltimore, Maryland

morning meetings
with Jesus
180 devotions
for teachers

SUSAN O'CARROLL DRAKE

Foreword by Tony Campolo

JUDSON PRESS
PUBLISHERS SINCE 1824
VALLEY FORGE, PA

Library of Congress Cataloging-in-Publication Data

Drake, Susan O'Carroll.
    Morning meetings with Jesus : 180 devotions for teachers / Susan O'Carroll Drake. — 1st ed.
        p. cm.
    ISBN 978-0-8170-1526-8 (pbk. : alk. paper) 1.Teachers—Prayers and devotions. I. Title.
    BV4596.T43D73 2007
    242'.68—dc22
                                                    2007035099

First Printing, 2008.

*To Professor Jesus, Master Teacher,
lover of my soul and model of
excellence for all humankind.*

Contents

Foreword

Teachers are a heroic people, especially those who teach in public schools. When politicians, parents, and average citizens criticize public education and blame teachers because children aren't learning in school today as we did a generation or two ago, people simply demonstrate that they are unaware of how things have changed.

Today's teachers can no longer count on support from parents. It isn't just a lack of parental involvement in homework either. When I was a boy, if my mother or father came to school, I trembled, knowing my parent would side with the teacher and that I was in serious trouble. In contrast, when parents arrive at school today, too often it means trouble for the administration and the classroom teacher rather than for the pupil. No doubt every teacher has some horror story about a confrontation with a disgruntled parent.

Second, today's typical American youngster watches television from four to six hours a day—a great departure from previous generations. When television consumes time that should be spent on homework, the learning process is significantly hampered. What's more, as many sociologists will point out, what television teaches as an alternative is that information must be entertaining—and catered to increasingly shorter attention spans. No wonder teachers are often confronted with students who seem to be bored or turned off by the educational process.

Added to these factors are other challenges related to America's poor overall nutrition, increased transience among school-aged children (especially in our cities), and families in transition because of divorce and remarriage. Then there are the sheer financial straits in which many public school systems find themselves—particularly in rural and inner-city settings where poverty means the tax base is low but the needs of the students are high.

Consider that in the suburban township where my university is located the school board spends approximately $18,000 per student annually while just nine miles away, the Philadelphia school board allots just $8,000 per student each year. Money may not be everything in education, but when, because of lack of funding, students have to study in classrooms wherein the ceiling plaster is crumbling, textbooks are out-of-date, and computers are unavailable, we have to recognize that money *does* make a difference.

All children are created by God to be equal and they should be educated that way. That's why my friend David Hornbeck, the former superintendent of schools in the city of Philadelphia, has initiated a program called "Prepare The Future" (www.prepare thefuture.org). He is working for legislation at the state level that would provide adequate funding for under-resourced schools. (You can support this effort by contacting David at 731 Colorado Street, Baltimore, MD 21210.)

David sees his work as a Christian calling—just as the author of this book, Susan O'Carroll Drake, sees teaching itself as a Christian ministry. Teachers in general are among the least respected and underpaid professionals in our nation. Yet their investment in the lives of our children, in the future of our country and the world, has never been more vital. They need the support of politicians, parents, community, and media—and they need the words of encouragement contained in this candid and compassionate book of devotions.

Some Christians dismiss the value of public education as secular and therefore hostile to our faith. But Susan Drake embraces the spiritual potential of public school education. She recognizes what many people do not: that God will never be absent from the schools as long as prayerful people of faith are walking the halls and ministering through example and education in the classroom. In her *Morning Meetings with Jesus,* she exhorts her fellow teachers to heed the words of Francis of Assisi who once said, "Preach the Gospel at all times, and when necessary use words."

Christian teachers can so live their lives before their students and colleagues that something of Christ is revealed and the message of God's love is clearly communicated. We need teachers who will do this—and teachers need a book such as this one to exhort their spirits to learn first from Jesus and to strengthen their hearts in the ministry of teaching.

Author Susan O'Carroll Drake is a veteran teacher from an inner-city school. In the devotional thoughts collected in this book, she shares with candor and humor her own challenges, the challenges of her students, and how her morning meetings with the Master Teacher sustained her in the teaching ministry. In these pages, fellow teachers will find a spirit of compassion, empathy, and encouragement as they carry out their duties, looking to Jesus' life and teaching for wisdom, understanding, comfort, and hope.

Tony Campolo
President, Evangelical Association
for the Promotion of Education (EAPE)
Professor Emeritus, Eastern University
St. Davids, Pennsylvania

Preface

Teaching is one of the most important career paths imaginable in our society, and yet it is, perhaps, one of the most discouraging due to hassles and lack of recognition. *Morning Meetings with Jesus: 180 Devotions for Teachers* provides an enormous amount of encouragement and guidance, not only for teachers but for everyone who has a life full of daily challenges. I think the readers will look to each day's "morning meeting" with anticipation and hope.

Benjamin S. Carson Sr., M.D.
Director of Pediatric Neurosurgery
Professor of Neurological Surgery, Oncology,
Plastic Surgery, and Pediatrics
Johns Hopkins University Hospital

Acknowledgments

Special thanks for years of encouragement, editing and correcting, the great stories you gave me and for so many prayers—Wuzzy and George (mom and dad), Lorraine, Diane, Kelly, Fiona, Tammi, Seana, my entire house church, my teaching colleagues and mentors (you know who you are), Riley and Wolfie. Special thanks to my husband, Chuck, who issued a challenge and gave me the chance to take it.

Introduction

I remember one Sunday when a church lady, learning that I was a high school biology teacher, approached me after worship, sniffing, "Really—a public school teacher! I say, have you considered the mission field?" At the time I was intimidated and angered. After all, whether we teach in the city, the suburbs, or a rural community, whether we choose public, private, or parochial schools—all teachers are positioned for ministry to our students, their families, and our colleagues. My urban public school seemed just as worthy as any mission field I could imagine. I wish I'd had the sense to reply, "Oh, yes. I *have* considered it. In fact, I *am* already on a mission!"

Some of us are made for the job of teaching in challenging settings because we enjoy the daily adrenaline rush, facing the obstacles head-on and hoping for the chance to make a difference. Others are returning to serve the community in which we grew up, wanting to offer the next generation the same opportunities we ourselves received through quality public school education. Some teachers work in difficult districts because of limited employment options or the financial benefits provided by loan forgiveness. Whatever our reasons for teaching and for working on the mission field we do, once we recognize that we are in this ministry for the long haul, we need to find ways to survive *and* thrive.

One source of my survival was the incredibly talented and gracious individuals who made up my school's science department. Drawing on the examples and the support of ten generous, wise, and esteemed colleagues lent me perspective, assistance, and humor. Leaning on my family, my Lord, and my faith, I managed to survive *and* thrive. I knew that, ultimately, God alone could ensure my well-being and peace of mind. I yearned to be closer to him. I looked for a devotional that might help me in that quest, wanting a guide that would tie together teaching-related, day-to-day issues with relevant Scriptures and practical spiritual challenges. Many devotional books were available to me, but none quite met my needs. Many devotional guides developed specifically for teachers lacked Scripture references or consisted of sweet stories, poems, and trite advice. I also learned that few teacher devotions dealt with the nitty-gritty issues that many public school teachers encounter. One morning, after reading an inspirational story detailing the events that led to a gracious and oh-so-successful Christian teacher receiving a bright, crisp apple from delightful little Johnny, I was more frustrated and angered than closer to God. On that day, I began recording my teaching experiences and vowed to put them to use someday. The result is the daily guide you now hold.

These 180 devotions are designed to be used by Christian teachers on student contact days. Although non-Christian educators might find them useful, the content is more specific to those who want to follow Jesus in their teaching and lives. The topics are arranged in an order that takes into account the seasonal concerns relevant to most educators. For example, initial devotions deal with issues concerning teacher confidence, fear, and mission assurance. Topics positioned toward the end of the book approach issues relating to endurance, spiritual reward, and discipline. Feel free to skip around.

Read this book with your Bible at hand. Each devotion offers a recommended Scripture reading and a verse to ponder. Most also include an anecdote taken from my public school teaching experience. A few of the anecdotes relate to lessons learned outside the classroom, referencing other experiences in the changing landscape of my life: family life, parenting, physical fitness, and relational issues. Regardless of the anecdote's origin, the theme of Jesus as Master Teacher is revisited in each devotion.

A discussion follows, ending with a suggested prayer that includes a challenge or focus. I hope you will find the entries brief yet provocative. Although individual events presented within devotions may not be typical of those encountered by every Christian educator in every public setting, the anecdotes speak to universal teaching issues to which most teachers can relate. My experience in a somewhat challenging urban setting may not match your experience, but you may find this guide useful whether you work in a public, private, parochial, or home-school venue. Regardless of your mission, if you are a Christian teacher, you already know that you need guidance, inspiration, strength, wisdom, and Jesus—a model worth emulating. I pray that this devotional helps you find all these as you continue in your teaching journey. Enjoy, and God bless!

Fall Term

Back to School

1

Walk Like Jesus

SUGGESTED SCRIPTURE READING: 1 John 2:1-6

VERSE DU JOUR: *Whoever claims to live in him must walk as Jesus did.* (1 John 2:6)

During my student teaching, I was incredibly impressed by the classroom presence of my mentor, Lorraine. The kids respected her, and she was the master of the classroom. I somehow became convinced that part of her effectiveness was related to her high heels. As Lorraine observed each student's work and patrolled the classroom, her sturdy heels made an impressive clicking sound. I wanted my heels to sound just like that. I finally found the right brand of high-heeled shoes and made the big investment. Sure enough, soon I was clicking my way to teaching stardom. I didn't consciously seek to imitate the shoe-clicking style, but I'd watched Lorraine so much (and she was so cool) that I couldn't help wanting to be just like her. Colleagues have told me that they've had similar experiences with their mentors, men or women.

Perhaps that is how it can work with us as we try to imitate the life of Jesus. The more we watch him and learn his ways, the more we will become like him. We will never *be* Jesus, but we can come closer to his perfection. In attempting to imitate Jesus, we must better understand him: his values, his mission, his compassion for others, and issues that motivated him to action. The Scriptures tell us that if we claim to be Christians, we must walk like Jesus did. Is this some kind of joke? Or is this seemingly impossible dictate attainable? More than a mere form of flattery, our imitation of Jesus is the way we mark ourselves as his own.

Years later, I realized that I not only wear and click my heels just like Lorraine did, but I've also adopted many of her other ways. My voice has the same inflection and even the same tone when I want to convey enthusiasm to the class or when I want to get the students' attention. I write my class notes in the way she did, lecture in the same style, and even set up my lab cart using Lorraine's system. I learned so much more than I ever could have imagined just by watching her. My reflection on this phenomenon taught me that when we spend time watching someone we admire, imitation becomes second nature. If you want to be more like Jesus and you don't want your transformation to feel like a chore, why not try spending more time with him today?

PRAYER: Jesus, I want to be near you, and I yearn to imitate your ways. Help me to walk like you.

2
Called by Your Name

SUGGESTED SCRIPTURE READING: John 20:1-16

VERSE DU JOUR: *Jesus said to her, "Mary."* (John 20:16)

"Josh, put down the scalpel NOW!" I barked when I saw Josh's "weapon" pushed up against his lab partner's abdomen. Recognizing that I was talking to him, Josh reluctantly lowered the scalpel—and his partner was visibly relieved. I'm convinced that if I hadn't yet known Josh's name, there could've been big trouble in my classroom that day. After all, it was still early enough in the semester that the scalpels were quite sharp.

Aren't we better teachers and communicators when we know and use names? Isn't it better to hear your name than "Hey, you!"? Don't you respond more quickly when you hear your name? Also, I'm more comfortable in an unfamiliar crowd if even one person knows me by name. Turns out, the master Teacher knew the power inherent in names and demonstrated how to use them.

When Jesus wanted to recruit some roughnecks by the Sea of Galilee, he quickly got their attention by calling out their names. When Jesus wanted to comfort his friends, Jesus called to them by name. Jesus also knew the calming effect of hearing one's own name. In John 20, Jesus referred to Mary Magdalene as "woman." Because she remained frightened, Jesus spoke her name.

Perhaps because Jesus knew the power held within a name, he went so far as to rename several disciples. Jesus assigned the name Peter, which means "the rock," to one of his closest friends. Imagine the honor of having Jesus give you a name that indicates such confidence!

When discussing how the disciples were to pray, Jesus told them to ask of God anything in God's name, thereby emphasizing the power of his own name. When Jesus retrieved his decaying friend from death's claws, he did so by calling, "Lazarus, come out!" (John 11:43). There is no doubt to whom Jesus is speaking, nor is there any question of Jesus' authority over death.

Teachers are inundated with a plethora of names that they have to learn: names of new students, parents, colleagues, and administrators. To some, remembering names comes naturally, but others need to work to learn and remember so many names. Because they know how important it is to know every student, even memory-challenged educators do eventually learn names. Once we know and use a student's name, we have the ability to deal better with discipline problems and to communicate more effectively. Like Jesus, we can use names to gain attention, to comfort, and to instruct. Be assured that the effort you expend on the process will be well worth it and that mastering the process is consistent with the teaching methods of our Lord.

PRAYER: Help me learn and remember all these names. Give me your power, and sharpen my memory. Please help me to use these names so that through my teaching I can glorify you.

3
To See What Jesus Sees

SUGGESTED SCRIPTURE READING: Matthew 9:35-38

VERSE DU JOUR: *Therefore, as God's chosen people, holy and dearly loved, clothe yourselves with compassion, kindness, humility, gentleness and patience.* (Colossians 3:12)

All five of the sample tubes flew to the floor, and then I heard the crunch of the shattered glass under Adam's feet. How could he drop all the test tubes and then walk into the glass? "Watch what you're doing! You just dropped all the samples for your lab group. Your carelessness is going to cost your whole group. Get the broom and start the clean-up. What is wrong with you today?" As Adam looked at me, I saw a cloud pass over his face. I was tired and in no mood for his foolishness. Usually, he would goof around; he had a knack for distracting the other students, but today Adam's carelessness was unacceptable.

After a grueling tour through the towns and villages of dusty Galilee, Jesus saw a crowd that wanted his attention. He not only saw them, but the Scriptures tell us that he felt compassion for them. Rather than run away to soak his tired feet and grab a good meal, Jesus chose to focus his attentions on those for whom he had come. Jesus chose to share himself and ignore his own fatigue.

Jesus' compassion was motivated by a sense that these people were harassed and helpless. Could he see it in their eyes, or by the tatters in their clothing? Did they verbally share their desperation, or did Jesus see it in their behavior? I often feel harassed and helpless, and I'm glad that Jesus has compassion on me. He is the Shepherd with whom I am never truly helpless.

After class, Adam found me alone in my office. "I just wanted you to know why I messed up today, Mrs. Drake," he said in an unusually quiet voice. "I had nowhere to go last night and had to sleep in a dumpster. It was really cold, and I didn't get much rest. I guess that's why I made a stupid mistake. I'm sorry."

I was sorry, too. I had let my own fatigue and frustration dictate my mood and my actions. Rather than showing this young man compassion, I had spoken to him with words of harsh judgment. Once I knew more about Adam's carelessness, I realized my own carelessness. I did not show Adam the compassion that Jesus constantly shows me. How many times do I get so caught up in the hectic demands of my schedule that I choose to forego compassion? The next time a student's carelessness disturbs you, why not follow it with a small act of kindness or a bit of patience? A small act of kindness can shout the message of Jesus' love.

PRAYER: Today I choose to be like you. I choose to follow you and want to see what you see. Let me show kindness and patience to all my students. Now, please go with me and give me your vision and your strength!

4

Fishing for People

SUGGESTED SCRIPTURE READING: Mark 1:14-20

VERSE DU JOUR: *And Jesus said to them, "Follow me and I will make you fishers for people."* (Mark 1:17, NRSV)

Their hulking frames filling the doorway, my posse growled their commands to the squirming freshman initiates who listened with fear and curiosity. "Mess with Mrs. Drake, and you mess with us. Don't let us find out you bein' bad!" Trying hard to look detached, I waved off my friends—the few tough guys who had made it through my class in years past and who now looked out for my welfare. Our strange and special bond was now working in my favor. I didn't have too many of these advocates, but they definitely were a powerful force in the inner-city school zone.

Jesus, in his desire to teach his disciples—and a rag-tag lot they were—used an analogy. These fishermen understood all about fishing, so Jesus taught them by focusing on a topic with which they were comfortable and familiar. Jesus effectively roused their interest, so much so that they abandoned all that they knew to follow him. Fishers for people, indeed! At another time, Jesus hit them with the largest catch of fish they had ever seen and used the miracle to illustrate the catch that would ultimately be brought in by these disciples.

Notice that Jesus chose only twelve to follow him. Jesus could have chosen at least a hundred—thereby ensuring his safety. Also, Jesus might have gotten better press and appeared to be more important if he were attended by a large entourage. But Jesus planned to change history and bank the entire success of his mission on a few people. And with those few, Jesus did change the world—they started a church that changed the earth forever. Jesus' mission was a success because he invested wisely and personally in those people. The disciples would never be the same again; they became influential people because they had seen the power of the living Lord!

Jesus started with twelve. Could you change your world by starting with one? If you show the love of Jesus to one kid this year, this semester, or this week, couldn't you positively affect human history? Think of the potential you wield over the long term. You have the potential to change the world. Human history shows us that the love of Jesus and his influence was not limited to the disciples. Instead, the love of our Lord is passed on and multiplied many times over.

PRAYER: Lord, please give me the foresight to see those whom you have chosen to put before me. Let me show you to them, one at a time. Let me not despair, but rather let me be used to pass on your hope to the world, one student at a time.

5

Fear Be Gone!

SUGGESTED SCRIPTURE READING: 1 John 4:7-18

VERSE DU JOUR: *There is no fear in love. But perfect love drives out fear, because fear has to do with punishment. The one who fears is not made perfect in love.* (1 John 4:18)

Could the buzz in the hallways be true? Everyone was talking about the sniper who was supposedly outside the school. Sure, our high school had made the news last week when one student "accidentally" stabbed another student with a hunting knife during band class, but this was a new week. Some of the more prudent students had been hesitant to walk across the grounds to get to their next classes. Then the administrators issued the lock-down command.

You have to wonder under exactly what kind of circumstances Jesus taught about love casting out fear. Maybe it was one of the days when the religious zealots were chasing him, hoping to get a chance to stone him or throw him into jail? Perhaps Jesus had narrowly escaped from a throng of admirers who had tried to rip apart his cloak? It could have worried him that the travel budget was already tight yet the bottoms of his sandals were wearing a little thin. Perhaps his best friends doubted Jesus or were talking behind his back?

We're not sure about the circumstances of that day, but we are certain of his words. Jesus says that perfect love casts out all fear—not just a little bit of our fear or half of our worries, but all of our fear. Jesus understands fear, and he speaks to all our fears, whether about your safety, finances, or reputation. Jesus cares about the fear that stems from your upcoming observation or the anxiety caused by the growing pile of papers to grade that is taking over your desk and your life. He wants to take the fear that slows us down and steals our joy and banish it.

Students were finally allowed to leave their classrooms and move through the inner halls. "Was there really some lunatic sniper outside?" we asked our department head. "I'm not sure what's up," he said. "There was some talk at our department meeting about a SWAT team near the grounds. Let's see." At that he opened the door and pushed our colleague, Andy, through the outside door to check and give us an "all clear." And so, the matter was settled by experimental method.

I'm thankful that you and I have a Protector who is worthy of our trust; Jesus reminds us that our protection is from above—thank God! He will take care of our safety and our fear. The next time you feel fear, realize that this normal human emotion may be completely rational, but also remember that God and the angels are protecting and watching over you.

PRAYER: Lord, because you have placed me here, I believe that you will protect me and direct me. Please transform my fear into love and my worries into joy.

6

The Power of One

SUGGESTED SCRIPTURE READING: Luke 15:1-10

VERSE DU JOUR: *"In the same way, I tell you, there is rejoicing in the presence of the angels of God over one sinner who repents."* (Luke 15:10)

My patience was nearly spent. It was my first year in a new school, a much tougher place than I was used to. My resolve was dwindling. I was becoming frightened by my charges. Then, I looked up from my desk to see a student who remained after everyone else had left for lunch. Her name was Tanya, and she seemed to be the one good student who'd been misplaced in a challenging group. I didn't know much about her but sensed that she was intelligent and frustrated. She simply said, "Ms. Drake, I know you're having a hard time with the kids in my class. They're trying to drive you out, like they drove out the other teachers. They don't know any better. I'm gonna get them in line for you; we need you to stay. I appreciate what you are trying to do here. I just got a job and want to use my first paycheck to take you out to lunch. Will you go with me?"

It took a good week before I could schedule lunch at the local pizzeria with Tanya. Our meal was short and hectic but sweet. I had a student who wanted to be a friend and an ally. I took our meeting as a sign that I should stay put here because maybe I *could* make a difference. Even if I made a difference for only one student, maybe it would be worth it . . .

Jesus uses the analogy of the lost coin to describe the importance of one lost soul. He tells us that the angels rejoice over one sinner redeemed. Sometimes all it takes for us, too, to see redemption in our work is reaching or being reached by one. One student can make the difference in the world, in your world, or in eternity. One friend can make the difference in a life.

Tanya did work hard to turn around the atmosphere in that classroom. She put her own reputation and safety on the line by defending me. Tanya was not afraid to chastise even the toughest thugs for their horrendous behavior. Tanya's bravery and allegiance supported me more than any principal or administrative support program could have. Tanya helped me show the class that I did care and that I was in for the duration.

Although Tanya's assistance in changing the atmosphere in the classroom yielded phenomenal results for the students, it was I who benefited the most. Her friendship reinforced my resolve and allowed me the patience to watch my mission unfold. It was because of Tanya that I did not lose hope and was eventually able to see the good around me. It took was just one person to turn me around. You may be that person to someone else today!

PRAYER: Lord, I am just one. Thank you for showing me the difference that one person can make. Help me remember that if my whole life is spent helping one of your own, my life is not spent in vain.

7

The Invisibles

SUGGESTED SCRIPTURE READING: Luke 7:36-48

VERSE DU JOUR: *Then he turned toward the woman and said to Simon, "Do you see this woman?"* (Luke 7:44)

Colin continually tested the classroom limits. He tested all of my limits, too. I found myself alternating between protecting him from the other students and wanting to punch him. He was a scrawny, pasty-skinned, pimply boy who sat quietly in a corner near the back of the room. Colin was so ignored by the other students in this specially identified at-risk class that I honestly wondered whether they even saw him.

It wasn't too late into the semester that Colin made himself visible. He began a routine that focused on showcasing his brilliance by frequent know-it-all comments. Colin indulged in annoying new habits, too: poking other students, constantly drumming his pencil, attempting to move class discussions off-topic and frequently sharing inane facts with the class. Once he began this new behavior, Colin *was* noticed by those around him—but the response was not what he had anticipated. The other students were quick to make Colin the brunt of all their jokes and frequently harassed him.

When Jesus came to earth, he noticed people and saw their value and their needs. He gave to others his attention and did not walk on by. Jesus made people feel visible, and it must have frustrated him that others failed to do the same. It seems that Jesus took special pains to show his attention to those whom others failed to notice or those whom others ignored: the poor, the lonely, and the powerless. Notice how he pointedly asks Simon, "Do you see this woman?"

I often wondered why Colin purposely drew attention to himself, when doing so only led to humiliation. If he had sat alone quietly, he could have avoided countless episodes of grief and harassment. I finally realized that Colin was willing to do anything to be noticed. Perhaps his attention-seeking behavior demonstrates a fact of human nature: we fear invisibility more than we dread humiliation.

Fortunately, Colin was not harmed physically by his classmates, and I eventually was able to praise some of his more positive traits. After gaining a bit of positive attention, Colin's previously obnoxious behavior evolved to a more bearable shtick. I came to appreciate his strengths and potential. Some students, like Colin, need just a thimbleful of attention to change their worlds. And by changing the world of one child, we can change the world. How many of your students may feel unaccepted or invisible to those around them? How many people do you know who might feel lost in the crowd or insignificant in the grand scheme of life?

PRAYER: Lord, I am ready to change the world for you. Give me the insight and the courage to notice someone today. Let me demonstrate your hope by showing someone that he or she is visible and special.

8

Reveille

SUGGESTED SCRIPTURE READING: Mark 1:35-39

VERSE DU JOUR: *Very early in the morning, while it was still dark, Jesus got up, left the house and went off to a solitary place, where he prayed.* (Mark 1:35)

The covers are so warm and cozy, yet the alarm won't stop. I try to open my eyes, but they stick together. Forcing myself out of bed, I stumble over to the sink, feel around for a washcloth, and apply cold water to my face. Ah, now my eyes open, and I see the covers as they slowly rise and fall. I look at my husband, still happily in dreamland, and think, "This is torture. It's five o'clock, still very dark, and time to get going. How dare he keep sleeping! I should find some cold water for him . . ."

Obviously, I have some unresolved sleep issues; if I don't have at least eight hours of sleep each night, I am not my normal fun-loving self. Every school-day morning I find myself calculating the number of hours of sleep that I've gotten. Did I get enough sleep to think clearly, or am I going to be a little slow today? Sometimes late at night, worried that I'll be tired the next day, I stress out, wasting the time for sleep that I do have. "Why," I have often asked myself, "did I enter a profession in which early mornings and often late nights are a mandate? Exactly what *was* I thinking?"

We don't know the sleep requirements of Jesus, but we do know that like other teachers, he wisely used the hours of the early morning. Jesus knew the purpose of his mission on earth, and one of the reasons that he came to earth (by his own accounting) was to teach. Jesus knew that his time on this earth was limited and that keeping a direct line to God would help him to accomplish his goals. So, we are told, very early in the morning, while it was still dark, Jesus got up and went outside by himself to pray. Here is a man who is God yet gets up before everyone else does—to pray! I've done well if I get to work on time with my hair dry and a few minutes to check my lab prep and my lesson plan. Jesus didn't get up just early enough so that he could review the itinerary and lesson plans for the day. He got up early enough so that he had uninterrupted time to pray.

A search of Old Testament teachers and leaders reveals that God's prophets were also in the habit of early rising. In Genesis and Exodus, numerous references discuss the early risings of Abraham and Moses. Joshua and Samuel, King Hezekiah, Absalom, Jeremiah, and King David were apparently also early risers. A little groggy self-pity might be normal, but never forget that your early rising puts you in a category of great company. It was another early riser, Mary Magdalene, whose presence at the tomb in the wee hours of the morning made her the first witness of Jesus' resurrection. Imagine the difference in the text and in the life of Mary if she had slept in that morning!

PRAYER: Help me find the rest that I need. Thank you for your willingness to meet me in the morning.

9

Soul Gunk

SUGGESTED SCRIPTURE READING: Romans 6:15-23

VERSE DU JOUR: *For the wages of sin is death, but the gift of God is eternal life in Christ Jesus our Lord.* (Romans 6:23)

Following two days of mind-numbing in-service instruction, we were allowed to visit our classrooms to prepare for the first day of school. When I'd left for summer break, I'd left my classroom spotless, and I expected to find it somewhere close to the same condition. Imagine my surprise when I found the remains of summer school: filthy walls, scattered dirty desks, and sticky gunk of unknown origin all over the floors. Ben, our department head, and Ron, an ex-Marine turned science teacher, came running when they heard my screams of anguish. Ben called the head janitor, who explained that because of a short-staffed crew, the floors weren't scheduled to be cleaned until sometime mid-year.

"We've got to clean this up *now!*" Ben declared. So Ben, Ron, and I traipsed down to the janitors' closet, where we found mops, buckets and, wonder of wonders, a floor buffing machine. Thanks to the U.S. Marine Corps, Ron was quite familiar with the buffer. He briefed me on how to operate it before leaving me to check the status of his classroom. I'd seen these used plenty of times before and was looking forward to some power-tool fun. How hard could it be? Ron had no sooner left than my comedy of errors began. Somehow, during the excitement of seeing this beast work and experiencing its hand-numbing vibrations, I had managed to advance the speed lever. I was no longer controlling the buffer— it was controlling me. The buffer pulled me in circles and from one end of the floor to the other. I was hitting walls, pulling muscles, completely out of control.

Jesus recognized the severity of sin and the consequences it brings. Because he loved greatly, Jesus also sacrificed greatly; he wants to free us from sin's evil grip and its ugliness. The ultimate sacrifice of Jesus' death conquered sin once and for all; through the Holy Spirit, Jesus continues to counsel and comfort his followers. Jesus has promised us his presence and his grace. God's grace is not just about forgiveness but about positive change and growth. If we allow him to do it, Jesus will help us become new and continue to help us remain clean.

"Release the control lever, Sue!" Ron yelled over the machine's roar. He must've heard the commotion from three doors down. Soon, Ben and Ron returned to help. Two hours, three mops, and one buffer later, my floor gleamed as never before. The unidentified gunk was gone! Just as I needed my colleagues to help me get rid of the gunk, we need Jesus to help clean up the consequences of our sin. Jesus taught that when we try to control our lives without him, we are helpless. Jesus knows that sin can control us rather than the other way around. He not only forgives our sins but also continues to say, "Pass me the mop and bucket. Let's get rid of this mess!" Are you ready to accept his offer?

PRAYER: Jesus, please forgive my sins; take away the stuff that clouds my soul. Help me avoid evil by turning from temptation and toward you.

10

Confidence to Continue

SUGGESTED SCRIPTURE READING: Hebrews 11 (especially vv. 1-3)

VERSE DU JOUR: *What is faith? It is the confident assurance that what we want is going to happen. It is the certainty that what we hope for is waiting for us, even though we cannot see it up ahead.* (Hebrews 11:1, TLB)

The teachers left the meeting in a somber mood. The local gang-crime unit of police officers had come with a special program intended to acquaint us with gang-related signs and behavior. "As the neighborhood has become increasingly gang-infiltrated, it's become more important for teachers to work with us," they explained. "As early as 1995, one third of all students surveyed reported presence of gangs in their schools. You can imagine the percentage of gang infiltration today," the officers warned. We learned to watch for predominant colors in a student's wardrobe, specific sports-team paraphernalia that may be gang-associated, which letters kids cross out in their written assignments, and various hand signals. We were also warned by these officers to report any doodling or student work containing the number 187—something to do with the California penal code for homicide being listed as code number 187. Great, I thought. I've seen several of those lately. Between my ever-increasing job responsibilities and the risks surrounding me, I felt vulnerable and my confidence was shaken. How could I keep doing this job?

Jesus equates faith with confidence. When the disciples are scared stupid by a storm that threatens their safety and their lives, Jesus calms the storm and returns the boat to a horizontal position before chiding them: "Why are you so afraid? Do you still have no faith?" (Mark 4:40). In The Living Bible, the word *confidence* is used in place of the word *faith*. Could we then postulate that faith is confidence and that confidence is a gift from God? If I ask God for the faith required to believe wholeheartedly in him, can I not ask him for the confidence to continue in a challenging and dangerous job? If Jesus can calm the seas and the winds, he can give me the confidence and ability to calm thirty-five hormone-laden teenagers. If God can give the strength to defeat armies, God can help me get through my most difficult classes and will give me the courage to teach the students who otherwise would have me running scared.

The letter to the Hebrews recounts for us the many famous faithful of God. Hebrews 11 describes how faith allowed mere mortals to win battles, overthrow kingdoms, and escape death. Some believers were given great power in battle; they made whole armies turn and run. Although some of God's faithful were beaten, laughed at, whipped, or killed, the Scripture assures us that all God's faithful eventually experience fulfilled promises.

Our confidence is based on our faith in Jesus. Jesus not only protects us from a child scribbling 187s on a paper but also saves us from eternal separation from God. Faith enables us to go wherever we are meant to go and do whatever we are meant to do. Faith gives us confidence and demonstrates our connection to God. Why not ask for increased faith today?

PRAYER: Jesus, thank you for the gift of faith. Give me faith to believe your promises and the confidence to do what I must.

11

Roller-Coaster Ride

SUGGESTED SCRIPTURE READING: Ecclesiastes 3:1–15

VERSE DU JOUR: *Jesus Christ is the same yesterday and today and forever.* (Hebrews 13:8)

Running frantically down the hallway, I duck into the faculty restroom. I'm so nervous. I don't know what to expect today. My stomach is churning, and my thoughts are racing. Although I'm excited about the lesson I've planned, I'm also filled with dread. A mere eight hours later, although I should be exhausted, I feel energized, and my mood has changed: "The students are great. I'm starting to understand them and think I'm communicating effectively. I know that I am where I am supposed to be. I can't believe that I am getting paid to do this," I think at day's end as I bounce into my car.

The next day my tune changes: "I am so exhausted. These kids are sucking the life out of me; they are so disrespectful and don't appreciate a thing I do for them. I'm so tired of the filthy language and never finding a parent around, much less a parent who cares to take some responsibility for these brats. The gang bangers are shooting signs across the room and scaring the decent kids. I didn't have any time to eat lunch, and I'm ready to quit this wasteland of a job."

Jesus no doubt experienced similar roller-coaster rides of emotion. He must have relished the excitement on the day he taught and fed five thousand people yet felt a bitter low after outrunning the crowd bent on killing him for his teaching. Jesus taught that although our feelings and our circumstances might fluctuate, God is always the same. Jesus taught that God does not measure our success by how we feel but by our connection to him. Jesus knew that human emotions can deceive and that our feelings are not as important as what we do about them.

Seasoned teachers know that it is normal to experience the fluctuating emotions that accompany a highly public and stressful role. But expecting these feelings doesn't necessarily make handling them any easier. What does make handling our changing circumstances and varying emotions easier is to understand that our feelings do not always reflect reality. God's reality is different from what we often feel. God will neither judge you for how you feel nor change his feelings toward you. God will love you today and tomorrow. God will never leave you, never disrespect you, and never harm you. God is the one constant in our otherwise changing world.

PRAYER: Lord, let me see my emotions as what they are. Let me use them as signals to elicit change instead of letting them use me. Let me feel your presence today instead of the negative emotions that slow me down.

12

Precious Names

SUGGESTED SCRIPTURE READING: Mark 9:33-41

VERSE DU JOUR: *"Whoever welcomes one of these little children in my name welcomes me; and whoever welcomes me does not welcome me but the one who sent me."* (Mark 9:37)

I'd checked my mailbox and the pouch outside the classroom door and spoken with my supervisor. It was the first day of a new class, and the attendance lists were still unavailable. The class bell sounded as I nervously surveyed the entering students. Would I have enough seats? The late bell rang before an office assistant hand-delivered the roster sheet. I had time to notice the final number of students listed and that was about all. The class was packed. It was time to begin, so with one eye scanning the list and another looking out to the assembled crowd, I began roll call.

Concerned that I hadn't previewed the student names (I prefer to practice pronunciation ahead of time), I breezed through the first few names. Then I hit one that was unfamiliar; the first name of the next student was listed as LaTrine. I hesitated and started to sweat. I finally blurted out the name, only to be advised by its owner that, although the spelling was correct, the name was to be pronounced La Trine ah. I continued down the list until I hit another stumper. The next child's name was Dung! My butchering of that one also led to correction: the D is pronounced with a blend of the sounds made by D, N, and Y. I needed a lot of work on that one.

Jesus, along with the rest of the first-century world, recognized the great importance of names. In the New Testament alone, the word *name* is referenced 169 times. That number does not even take into account variations of the word. Jesus renamed his disciples to better reflect their new missions while repeatedly teaching of the power yielded by his own name. He used his own name to identify himself, to validate his godly identity, and to drive out demons.

Jesus knew that the most precious sound to any human is the sound of one's own name. I am sure Dung and LaTrine would agree. Whether we are amused, puzzled, or enchanted with another's name matters not; we should still recognize the precious nature and the value of each and every name. Dung turned out to be a favorite student of mine and an influential leader within school society. Dung not only served as an excellent academic role model but also frequently volunteered to interpret English and Vietnamese to newly immigrated students. Many of these students owed their academic success to Dung. LaTrine also held a special place within the classroom and within my heart. She had a kind heart and an infectious laugh. Can you welcome each student on your list today in the name of Jesus?

PRAYER: Jesus, I lift my praise to your wonderful name. Please let me see each name on my class list as a precious person and a valuable gift from you.

13

Samson's Strength

SUGGESTED SCRIPTURE READING: Judges 16:23-30

VERSE DU JOUR: *Then Samson prayed to the LORD, "O Sovereign LORD, remember me. O God, please strengthen me just once more."* (Judges 16:28)

"I hate you and hope you die soon," said the note scribbled on white loose-leaf paper that was stuck under the windshield wipers of my car. Why, oh why, did this have to be on my windshield? Who did I tick off today, and how did I do such a good job of it?

To these questions I had no solid answers. Relieved that at least the message was not permanently etched in the car's paint and hopeful that it might have been a case of mistaken car identity (it wasn't addressed to me by name, was it?), I threw my overstuffed briefcase into the cargo area and peeled out of the parking lot.

Remember the story of Samson? The Lord's strong man served as a leader and judge of Israel for twenty years. His body was a sight of wonder—probably like Arnold Schwarzenegger in the early days. Though he was strong, this guy was something else. Expected to deliver the Israelites from the Philistines, he instead arranged to marry a Philistine woman, visited with a Philistine prostitute, and had an illicit affair with Delilah, yet another Philistine woman, who was his undoing. Samson was captured by his enemies before realizing at last that the source of his great strength was the Lord. While being tortured and mocked by his captors, Samson called out to God. "One last time, please, God, give me the strength again!" God heard his cry and granted his request. The pillars that Samson pulled down destroyed him and the entire mocking crowd.

Even the best teachers are mocked and harassed. It even happened to Jesus. It's not a personal thing but comes along with the teaching territory. Sometimes, however, a call to our all-powerful God is in order. Or, as my friend Diane suggests, perhaps I should've prayed while ordering a bulletproof vest. But seriously, when is the last time that you have called out for God's help, deliverance, or strength? God's offer of assistance is not an empty one. God answers our cries for help time and time again. Samson had sinned against God repeatedly. Yet Samson was still one of God's own, and God answered Samson's cry. If you are one of God's children, why won't he deliver you?

I didn't meet an untimely end the afternoon I found that note. God will not withhold divine wisdom or strength from us. We just need to ask.

PRAYER: Lord, deliver me from the trials that I will face today. Please help me as I accomplish your plans for my life. I beg you for strength and understanding.

14

Rear Guard

SUGGESTED SCRIPTURE READING: Isaiah 52:1-12

VERSE DU JOUR: *But you will not leave in haste or go in flight; for the LORD will go before you, the God of Israel will be your rear guard.* (Isaiah 52:12)

Two usually giggly girls walked cowering and tentatively toward me. Then one literally pushed the other into my office. As Tia came closer, I saw that her beautiful brown eyes were open wide but her pupils were pinpoint tiny. Her hands and her voice were shaking as she approached. Tears began to fall as Tia whispered, "I am so scared. I'm afraid to even tell you." Knowing that she hadn't quite been herself during class, I suspected a problem, maybe a family issue or other personal dilemma. I was not ready for Tia's next words: "I kept shaking and was really scared during lab today. I thought you should know why. I saw Tony drop a gun on the floor. It fell out of his jacket and landed right next to my lab stool. You didn't see it because he grabbed it and hid it really fast. He knows that I saw it. I'm scared and don't want to come to class anymore. If he finds out that I told you . . ."

I was shocked. Tony was one of my favorite students. I was equally thankful that I hadn't seen the gun. I would have most likely caused a scene and precipitated a shooting. I gave Tia a hug and told her not to worry. Sure.

God makes it clear that we need not fear what is ahead of us or what is behind us. God knows about every detail on this earth, even about the things that we can't see or feel. God has us covered and will watch our backs. Perhaps it is cognizance of this kind of watchful protection that allowed Jesus to do the audacious things he did. Did his radical style and confident demeanor stem from believing this promise? Jesus could not have accomplished his mission if he had been compromised or incapacitated by fear.

Before the day was done, I learned that Tony had been apprehended for possession of a weapon: it was a 357 magnum loaded with hollow-tip bullets. In addition, he was carrying a fair amount of reefer and was stoned out of his mind. I wondered how I could be such a poor judge of character. Tony seemed well-behaved and respectful; I had met to work with him after school several times. I started to shake as I considered several scenarios that blessedly did not occur and realized that God may have blinded my eyes to that gun for my own protection.

I now know that fear is a normal part of a teacher's reality; whether you fear facing the crowds of parents on back-to-school night or fear for your life. In light of this, I urge you to try something new today. When you read Isaiah 52:1-12, in the place of "Israel" or "Zion," insert your name. Notice the insistent reminder that God will comfort the people now and will return for them later. God has promised to go before you and to be your rear guard. So never forget that God has you covered and may return sooner than you think.

PRAYER: Lord, let me recognize that you go before *and* behind me.

15

Honeymoon Over?

SUGGESTED SCRIPTURE READING: John 2:1-16

VERSE DU JOUR: *Now I know that the LORD saves his anointed; he answers him from his holy heaven with the saving owner of his right hand.* (Psalm 20:6)

It's the third week of school, and I adore my next class. The students are filing in now. They are respectful, quiet, and attentive; every student seems interested in what I have to say. Wait a minute—what's going on? As I finish the attendance sheet, I notice not one but two latecomers sneak through the door and slide into their seats. Several students are loudly talking, and I hear snickers in the back row as a wadded paper flies past me.

Maybe 50 percent of the students are ready to begin class. How disappointing.

In marriage and in teaching, it is sad to find that the honeymoon is over. I vividly remember the shock I experienced following my marital honeymoon. I found myself working by day, sorting wash by night, and wondering how I fell for the marriage deal. "So, this is like a date that won't end. He just isn't going home." At least I was warned about the feelings I might have after my wedding and honeymoon were over. But nobody warned me about the feelings I would experience with every new class when inevitably that honeymoon would be over.

It appears that even Jesus experienced a honeymoon period at the beginning of his ministry. His was a very short honeymoon, followed by a sudden switch to the stark realities of his mission. Jesus' formal ministry began when he started to gather his disciples. The chosen disciples seem to have gladly and without question dropped everything and faithfully followed him. So far, so good . . . Jesus followed this auspicious beginning with his first and probably most popular miracle—changing water into wine at a wedding feast. He may have been the most popular and appreciated guest at that wedding. People were probably clapping Jesus on the back and looking at him with amazement and wonder. "Who is this guy?" they thought. "He is so cool! We have *got* to hang out with him!"

How quickly his honeymoon must have ended. The next big public appearance for Jesus was no less dramatic but didn't win him any points for popularity. This time, he was furiously whipping the sales people who were set up in the temple. You can bet that the temple guards and the priests weren't affectionately patting his back after that one!

We will all experience some form of disappointment when our honeymoon is over. When the newness and the novelty of you as an amazing and interesting teacher wears off and the students start to show their natural behaviors, it is time to start real life, time to teach and bring out the best in your students and in yourself. It is time to rely on the Lord who knows about honeymoon beginnings and rough endings. Can you trust him to help you today?

PRAYER: Thank you for understanding my predicament; my wine has turned to whine. I am thankful that although my teaching honeymoon may be over, your power, protection, and blessing are not. Teach me to bring out the best in my students and myself.

16
Asking for Courage

SUGGESTED SCRIPTURE READING: Joshua 1:1-8

VERSE DU JOUR: *Keep alert, stand firm in your faith, be courageous, be strong.* (1 Corinthians 16:13, NRSV)

It's going to take more than caffeine to get myself into school this morning. It's going to take courage, and I feel more like a lamb than a lion. Like a lamb on the way to slaughter, that is. Several rough characters that I encountered in the hall yesterday made it clear that they do not like me. I asked them to move their foul mouths away from my doorway; apparently they don't take criticism well. When they finally left, I thought I heard one say something about how I should pay. These guys looked pretty tough, and judging by the way they talk to each other, I'm guessing they can be mean. I'm not sure how they intend to proceed. I don't even know their names, which puts me in a predicament, since it's hard to report five big, trash-talking students; their type are all over the place. Who knows if they are even official students?

Jesus was a man of great resolve and courage. He taught his followers about courage by his example and was also well versed in the lives of the biblical prophets. Joshua was one of those Old Testament prophets; he was the prophet known for leading the Jews to the Promised Land. Joshua was the leader who marched his army around the walls of Jericho with nothing but pottery jars and trumpets to stand up against a fortified city of trained fighters. Talk about a man of courage! And yet, throughout the Book of Joshua, over and over we read of God telling Joshua to be unafraid and to be of good courage. Why do you suppose that God kept reminding Joshua to be courageous? Was it because Joshua was already so brave or because Joshua was scared to death and needed some courage?

Heiresses don't pray for money, but people who are destitute and spiraling into debt do. A man with a head of thick, lustrous hair doesn't pray for hair; it is the balding who pray for their follicles to fill. It seems that people ask God, and they should ask him, for what they don't have.

So, other than donning a bulletproof vest or calling in sick, perhaps there is something else I should do. Seems I should start praying for courage. Ralph Waldo Emerson (1801–1882) once said, "A hero is no braver than an ordinary man, but he is braver five minutes longer." I guess I'll get moving and take today five minutes at a time. I'm no hero but can relate to Joshua. How amazing that a man who initially lacked courage is part of God's Hall of Fame. Can you take comfort in knowing that God will provide you with courage and protection?

PRAYER: Go ahead of me and behind me today, Lord. I want to be strong and courageous but don't feel like either. Please give me courage and strength as I go into my classroom.

17

Seventy Times Seven

SUGGESTED SCRIPTURE READING: Matthew 18:21-35

VERSES DU JOUR: *Then Peter came to Jesus and asked, "Lord, how many times shall I forgive my brother when he sins against me? Up to seven times?" Jesus answered, "I tell you, not seven times, but seventy-seven times."* (Matthew 18:21-22)

I stood astounded. The room that just moments ago had been buzzing with activity was now completely silent. Jaws dropped, and eyes widened. The nerve of this student! I had been giving him extra tutoring. I had placed him in a lab group with supportive, smart students. He was given every chance to excel. But there, in the middle of class, he looked right at me and said, "F— you!" I was so angry I couldn't speak (a rare state for me), and even a week later I was in no mood to forgive him. As soon as school let out that day, I marched to the administrative offices, determined that suspension was the least he would pay. Even now, years later, I can still remember the event, down to the subtle nuances of the aftermath. I think I've finally forgiven him for his audacity and his anger, but I haven't forgotten.

Jesus understands how difficult it can be for us to forgive. Hanging in shame and agony on the cross, he asked God to forgive those who were killing him. I don't know about you, but while I'm being offended, I am in no mood to forgive anyone for anything. Yet our Lord asks God to forgive his murderers while being killed! If that isn't a model of ultimate forgiveness, what is? And Jesus continues to forgive all of us who continue to disobey his Word. He had already forgiven me seventy times seven even before I hit forty! Imagine how many times he will have forgiven me before my death. Jesus asks us to forgive others for their offensive behavior, just as he has forgiven us. Essentially, Jesus tells us that we should have no limits on how many times we forgive another soul, including students. Jesus also explains that following his forgiveness, the offending sin is forgotten. Imagine. The Creator, who designed the complexities of the human brain and every other wonder, is able and willing to forget.

I was not so quick to forgive that boy who had so galled me. As time went on, my anger increased, my teaching was hampered, and I was distracted. Admittedly, I did dole out some consequences, but my offender returned from his three-day suspension rejuvenated, rested, and well-versed in daytime television. It wasn't until after he returned that I forgave him and my concentration was restored. The lesson I needed to remember is that when we forgive others, God promises to forgive us. Additionally, when we forgive others, our unhealthy anger is replaced with nourishing joy. Perhaps Jesus orders us to forgive for the sake of others and for the protection of our emotional and physical health.

The next time a student angers you, I urge you to follow through on any necessary discipline and immediately follow that action with a prayer for the offending student. You will probably need to force yourself to pray for him or her, but you can ask God to help you forgive even if you don't yet feel forgiving. Ask God for release from your anger, and you will be blessed!

PRAYER: Forgive me my trespasses as I forgive those who have trespassed against me.

18

A Holy Mission

SUGGESTED SCRIPTURE READING: Ephesians 2:1-10

VERSE DU JOUR: *For we are God's workmanship, created in Christ Jesus to do good works, which God prepared in advance for us to do.* (Ephesians 2:10)

I made my way through the sweltering hallways, amid the crude and cursing crowds. I was exhausted well before noon and needed, yet again, to visit the makeshift administrative office. I was fed up with everything: the disrespectful attitude of the students, the vulgar speech surrounding me, the dingy appearance of my surroundings, and my sense of powerlessness. I was sick of this school and its students. I wanted out. "It's time to re-open my application to the greener pastures of the suburban school that called me yesterday," I thought. Mostly, though, I was thinking judgmental, evil thoughts about my most challenging students, and my spirit was anything but holy.

This is the mission for which God has prepared you. Do you sometimes wonder if it was God's call you heard or a flash of insanity? Do you sometimes lose focus and direction? Jesus knew the purpose for his visit here on earth. Jesus always kept the importance of his mission in focus. He did not become sidetracked by the minutia and inconveniences that threatened to deter him.

The importance of Jesus' holy mission took precedence even over his own will. Awaiting the end, Jesus was able to say, "Not my will but yours, Father." The commitment to his mission and his love for God gave Jesus the strength to endure the most excruciating of all known suffering. Jesus also demonstrated an incredible peace about his place on earth. No storm could rattle Jesus, and no person could intimidate him. This same Jesus is the one who has chosen you, ransomed you, and designed you for your mission. Perhaps just knowing that God wants you where you are will offer you peace and strength.

Do you believe that God sometimes speaks to us through flashes of insight or thought? I believe so, because while I stood near the entry desk of that makeshift administrative office, I felt simultaneously rebuked and offered insight of brilliant clarity. It was as if time were on hold while God said, "I need you here to feed my sheep. They are my sheep, and I love them. You, too, must love them and serve them." I felt deep shame for the hostility in my heart and for my judgmental thoughts. At the same time, I immediately felt great peace as God's vision for my mission became clear. I was to remain here, and I had better make the best of it.

Perhaps you won't need a similar unusual experience, but you can rely on the Scriptures to assure you that God has a plan for you and is using you. Your teaching position is more than a job; it is a holy mission. You need not walk the hallways with a bullhorn announcing, "Yo! Check me out. Here I am, the teacher on a holy mission from God." (Indeed, if you were to do so, your mission might be prematurely terminated.) Will you accept your mission?

PRAYER: Jesus, help me to shake off the bad days and remember the goodness and mercy that you have shown to me. Do not let my spirit be broken when all looks grim. Remind me of my mission.

19

Spinning Yarns

SUGGESTED SCRIPTURE READING: Matthew 13:31-52

VERSE DU JOUR: *He said to them, "Therefore every teacher of the law who has been instructed about the kingdom of heaven is like the owner of a house who brings out of his storeroom new treasures as well as old."* (Matthew 13:52)

Every student who has ever taken my introductory biology class knows about the time I nearly died in the Grand Canyon. If they were absent the day I used the story to illustrate the biological process of dehydration synthesis, they heard about it later from their classmates.

In a nutshell: Teacher and boyfriend drive to Grand Canyon and decide to hike to the bottom—in one day. Both laugh at tourists perched on descending donkeys while ignoring ranger warnings and rapidly increasing temperatures. When water supply is gone and temperatures exceed 120 degrees F, teacher is stung in the calf by red hornet. She starts to panic and prays for deliverance. Soon after prayer, clouds roll in to cover sun and a German-speaking mystery man suddenly approaches. Without being asked to share, the man offers the rapidly dehydrating duo a life-saving portion of his ample water supply. This gracious, generous man sprints off into the setting sun before the two reach canyon rim . . . Of course, I told the story with greater detail and plenty of drama, with what some might call exaggeration. Truly, though, this tale required no embellishment.

Jesus was a brilliant storyteller who could masterfully spin a yarn that entertained and taught a lesson. Jesus used stories to illustrate ideas that were hard to explain and difficult to comprehend. The parables and metaphors Jesus employed were so applicable and memorable that they are repeated to this day. Even those who are unschooled in biblical literature often can recall many of Jesus' stories and lessons, including those of the lost sheep, the wise and foolish builders, the prodigal son, the good Samaritan, the lost coin, the valuable pearl, the hidden treasure, the mustard seed, and the lamp under a bowl. Jesus knew the teaching power of stories and had an impressive repertoire.

The dramatized version of the canyon story was not as dry as the encapsulated version. In the classroom version, I acted out my stumbling, desperate descent and the horror of the hornet's sting, complete with moans of pain and whimpering whines. I also emphasized how much, at our most pathetic point, I would've paid for one lousy donkey . . .

I had so much fun telling the story and watching the students' reactions that year after year I looked forward to the dehydration lesson. To my recollection, following this lesson, none of my students ever forgot the meaning of dehydration or its biological relevance. Your experiences and adventures are treasures that can be woven into lasting lessons. What stories do you have to tell?

PRAYER: Thank you for the stories you have given me, Jesus. Please teach me how to use my experiences and my adventures to better teach my students.

20
Never Say Never

SUGGESTED SCRIPTURE READING: John 13:1-10

VERSE DU JOUR: *The human mind plans the way, but the LORD directs the steps.* (Proverbs 16:9, NRSV)

"Oh, we're gonna be on the news tonight!" the students raucously laughed as they piled out of the classroom door. The air smelled of excitement mingled with curiosity and a touch of anxiety as the emergency alarm continued to clamor. No one was sure why it didn't stop. Usually that meant that this was not just a drill. Seasoned staff members were herding students away from the building and across the street. Lined up against the curb and straining to see what was causing the disturbance, students began to cluster together. A loud voice echoed over the crowds, "Drake, get in the group." Not wanting to disobey but also sensitive to the upset around me, I nonchalantly sidled into place behind the students. Finally, the bell stopped, everyone returned to the building, and classes resumed.

Jesus warned Peter when Peter stated, "You will never wash my feet!" In so many words, Jesus explained to Peter that it was God's plan that he should wash Peter's feet. One would think that after this incident, Peter would have learned his lesson, yet on the night Jesus was betrayed, Peter had said, "Lord, I will never deny you." In this particular instance, Peter's "never" preceded a long, hard night. Saying that we will never do something makes an assumption that we have the power to plan and control our destiny. We do not control our futures; God does.

God chose you and placed you in your community, your school, and your role as teacher. Your place has been ordained since the beginning of time. So, to say, "I will never do such and such" is a prideful statement and an affront to the God who already knows what we will and will not do. I once said, "I will *never* teach in a city school, and I will *never* work in a place where I have to fear for my life every day." Less than six months after uttering those words I found myself learning completely new meanings for words such as drive-by (not a drive-through), rag (not something for waxing your car), tag (not the little paper that tells a price), and piece (not part of something else).

That day we were on the news, having survived the threat of a drive-by shooting. So, I have learned to never say "never" because Jesus rightly warned against it; saying that you will never do something is a dangerous practice. Here's a tip: Make a vow to never say or even think "never." To use it while speaking of our lives and plans offends our God. Additionally, the use of the word in nearly every other situation almost always sets us up to be wrong. Never say "never" again!

PRAYER: I am yours, Lord. Forgive me for thinking that I can control my life. Please do not let me get in the way of the plans you have already made for me. What a relief to know that you are in control and my plans and vows cannot alter your purposes.

21

Class Size

SUGGESTED SCRIPTURE READING: Hebrews 5:1-10

VERSE DU JOUR: *During the days of Jesus' life on earth, he offered up prayers and petitions with loud cries and tears to the one who could save him from death, and he was heard because of his reverent submission.* (Hebrews 5:7)

"Welcome to biology," I say, greeting the tenth over-max student. "Let's just keep packing 'em in," I mutter in disgust. Weeks into the semester I'm still receiving more students—we ran out of desks during week one and now have kids perched on stools all over the room. Instead of two students to a microscope, we have three and four. The overcrowding is not fair to them, not fair to me, and it has definitely compromised our safety. I'm tripping over electrical cords and squeezing between tight rows of desks. How will I possibly teach this crowd? For a brief moment, I recall a time when my classes were capped at twenty-four. Wouldn't it be great if we always taught courses where our student load was limited to a predictable and manageable number? Just think what could be accomplished . . .

Jesus capped his most intense and advanced class at twelve, but he also taught huge lecture classes (oh, about five thousand or so) and spoke for hours to large crowds. Jesus did his best to relate to all even when he lectured to a packed house. On occasion, Jesus taught more people in one sitting than I've taught in a lifetime, yet the total number of people he personally taught would make barely a dent in the world's population. His expectations of what could be done must have been realistic. It was the small group of disciples who were charged with continuing his teachings, and the repercussions of their fervent missionary work set the course of history. Also keep in mind that Jesus frequently asked God for help. It was God who spoke through Jesus when he lectured to the crowds and taught the chosen twelve disciples.

Every time I look at a new class list, I consider tearing my clothes and covering myself in ashes. Each revision lists more and more kids; the last one took two pages. It's highly unlikely that I will ever teach a class that will contain twenty-four students, let alone twelve. But it's also unlikely that I will be crucified for my teaching after a mere three years on the job. It is not too late to ask God to help you with the students crowding into your class-room. God will also speak through you. God's wisdom and words are available to you whether you are teaching a class of forty or a class of twelve.

PRAYER: Lord, speak through me today. Help me to reach all of the students placed in my care, and when I feel my limitations, let me remember to call on you.

22

Your Eyes, My Ears

SUGGESTED SCRIPTURE READING: 2 Corinthians 4:1-18

VERSE DU JOUR: *So we fix our eyes not on what is seen, but on what is unseen. For what is seen is temporary, but what is unseen is eternal.* (2 Corinthians 4:18)

Assigning seating on the first day of a new quarter, I placed Lionel, a big, confident, and well-spoken student right behind Johnnie, a smaller, shy young man who seemed a bit lost. As they sat down, another student warned, "That might not be a great idea, Ms. Drake. Those two are brothers." Not sure what to make of this warning, I glanced at the roster list, noticed that the last names of these two were different, and continued to assign seats.

I had no sooner started class when I noticed that every time I said something, Johnnie and Lionel started talking. When I stopped, they stopped. When I started up again, so did they. Although they were hunched over and whispering, this behavior was distracting. I finally interrupted the lesson to ask, "What is with you two? Can you please be quiet and listen?" Lionel rose, standing next to his desk like an attorney addressing the court.

With a tone of authority and apology, he stated, "I'm helping Johnnie. We're brothers, foster brothers, so we work together." Confused and slightly annoyed, I figured I'd get to the bottom of this after class and decided to keep a wary eye on these two.

Jesus, who had the perspective that resulted from seeing things through the eyes of God, reacted much differently than I do. If I could see through the eyes of God, I might be a different person. I would think differently and would react differently when faced with difficult people and challenging situations. I would know when to act and when to avoid action; I wouldn't worry about things and would be a better person and teacher. If only I could see things and people through the eyes of God. Get this: God promises extraordinary, even divine, insight. In addition, Jesus has offered to serve as my interpreter. Through Jesus, God will direct me and give me the vision for what I am to do.

After school, I thumbed through the student information cards to make my usual "Hi, I'm your kid's teacher" phone calls. I called the number listed for Lionel's mom and got her on the first try. She quickly explained that Lionel, her biological son, is bonding with Johnnie, the foster child the family had recently taken in. "Lionel has taken it upon himself to help Johnnie understand things and, in a way, has become Johnnie's interpreter," she continued. I thought but didn't ask, "What's there to interpret? We all speak English." Then the mom added, "Before Johnnie came to us, his parents took him away with them on a special 'vacation.' They checked into a hotel, locked him in the room, and left him, never to return. The trauma really messed him up; we are hoping to adopt the boy so that he can have a stable home."

As I hung up the phone, I was flooded with grief for Johnnie and admiration for his foster family. Apparently Lionel was interpreting life for Johnnie just as Jesus tries to interpret it for me. Lionel acted as Johnnie's eyes and ears, explaining what I wanted them to do and learn. If I will listen, Jesus is willing to explain what God wants me to do and learn.

PRAYER: Lord, help me to see others through your eyes as I remain open to you.

23

Practice What You Will Become

SUGGESTED SCRIPTURE READING: Luke 8:4-21

VERSE DU JOUR: *He replied, "My mother and brothers are those who hear God's word and put it into practice."* (Luke 8:21)

Why I ever wanted to become a varsity basketball player is anybody's guess. Already active in various school activities and clubs, including playing clarinet in the band, I was busy enough. But I was ready for more. The girls' basketball coach explained that although I had the right spirit, my coordination hadn't quite caught up with my growth. Because I was five seven and severely sight impaired, such a lofty goal would require some serious practice time. I also wanted to be the team's center. I made the final junior varsity team cut but was required to attend regular afternoon practice sessions in addition to special lunchtime practice sessions. While my friends were sucking down chocolate milk and nibbling cookies, I was in the gym shooting foul shots. Eventually I became a varsity basketball player, center position. I use the term *player* loosely, as it denotes that one is off the bench and on the court, but that is another story.

Jesus modeled, and the Bible verifies, that what we practice, we become. If I want to master a skill, I need to do it a lot; in so doing I will become more relaxed and more adept at doing it. If I want to teach like Jesus, I must practice great teaching. Not every practice session will be a successful attempt, but my willingness to take risks and to work hard will lead to greater mastery. If I want to become a solid Christian, I need to practice doing the things that Christians should do. I need to practice thinking about good, pure things. I need to practice prayer and humility. I need to practice using the power of God in my daily wanderings.

I am no longer a high school varsity basketball player, but I can still play a mean clarinet. During high school, I also did a fair amount of clarinet practicing and playing. At least I was decent enough to warrant a seat in the college symphony, or was it their desperation? Nonetheless, I still collect on the effort of my instrumental practice time: Once a year, I play Christmas tunes with the band formed from the other frustrated musicians of my house church. We make a joyful noise—although no one within earshot seems joyful about the clamor but us . . . What greater rewards will we reap when we practice the Christian life, when we put God's word into practice? What should you practice?

PRAYER: Lord, show me what I need to practice today. Please give me the discipline to practice being a model teacher; let me model my teaching after your example.

24
Under God's Wings

SUGGESTED SCRIPTURE READING: Psalm 91

VERSE DU JOUR: *He will cover you with his feathers, and under his wings you will find refuge; his faithfulness will be your shield and rampart.* (Psalm 91:4)

The memo stated, "Any teacher is authorized to search any student suspect of carrying dangerous weapons or unlawful substances." I wondered briefly why this was waiting in my mailbox *this* morning. I had no sooner finish reading the memo when I saw another one informing me that I was scheduled to attend a disciplinary meeting. This newly scheduled conference was with a student who turns out to be a recently released felon—seems this particular boy was angry with me, yet he wanted to remain in my class. I started to feel uneasy. No, strike that—I was scared and wanted to go home NOW.

Do you think that Jesus was secure in his mission and bold with his message simply because of good genetics? Certainly, the lineage of Jesus included bold and powerful men and women of God. But it also included people who were less than perfect in their walk with God. All of Jesus' ancestors were sinners like us, and his lineage even included a prostitute. Whatever his family history, Jesus clearly had an intimate connection with God, who served as his protector and comforter while he was on this earth. Jesus relied on this divine refuge. Prior to his arrest and crucifixion, Jesus said, "But a time is coming, and has come, when you will be scattered, each to his own home. You will leave me all alone. Yet I am not alone, for my Father is with me" (John 16:32). Although Jesus understood the humiliation and agony he was about to endure, Jesus trusted God's plan and presence. Throughout his life, Jesus not only knew that he was accompanied by God but also relied on that resting place. How else could Jesus have ever slept a sound night in his life?

The followers of the Lord are promised protection. King David pictured God protecting him in the same way that a bird protects its offspring. Can you visualize God as a huge, fierce, and mighty bird? You are a straggly little chick. God has you under an all-encompassing wing, enveloping you with feathers. God is your protector, your refuge, fortress, and defender. Nobody else can mess with you. They can and will try; the devil will tempt you, and the world will try to hurt you. But you are under the cover of God's powerful wings, lying in warmth of downy feathers. God's wings protect you and shelter you; evil can neither penetrate those wings nor reach you. When you listen closely, you hear a steady heartbeat. If you are afraid and unable to rest, you can give up your fear and ask for refuge. Will you allow God to shelter you in his wings?

PRAYER: Mighty God, please let me feel the power of your protective wings. I offer up my anxiety and fear to you. Thank you for your protection and rest.

25

On the Move

SUGGESTED SCRIPTURE READING: Luke 9:57-62

VERSE DU JOUR: *Jesus replied, "Foxes have holes and birds of the air have nests, but the Son of Man has no place to lay his head."* (Luke 9:58)

I looked down quickly to take mental note of my drink's location and moved on. I didn't want to confuse my mug of diet iced tea with the acid-filled beaker that jiggled as I pushed the wobbly cart down the hall. Then the wheels hit something, and the jolt caused the books and papers on the bottom level of the cart to slide forward. I dove to catch them and was near tears when I heard the warning bell. Could my job be any more frustrating? I was a new hire without my own classroom, a vagabond wanderer. Everything crucial to my teaching life was crammed on this cart or stacked somewhere in one of the three different classrooms I visited throughout the day. Moving from room to room was such a hassle. Things got lost, equipment disappeared, and pencils rolled away faster than I could sneeze.

Jesus was a traveling teacher, too. He didn't have his own room, his own desk, or even a wobbly cart. The Gospels record his many movements and interactions with the people he met and influenced along his way in an age of difficult and dangerous travel. While pursuing his mission, Jesus did not even have a bed to call his own. He slept on the ground or in the homes of friends and followers. He relied on the kindness and charity of others. He ate what was put before him and had little control over finances, the clothes he wore, or where he would stay.

Jesus depended on God's provision and must've allowed his disciples to manage the minutia that often consumes the rest of us. If Jesus wasn't offered a comfortable bed for the night, he would camp outside and warm himself by a fire. Jesus admonished those who let their riches control them, yet he welcomed the hospitality of generous friends. Jesus was familiar with the wandering lifestyle, but it must have still been tough. Where did he hang his cloak? Was anything about his lifestyle comforting? When Jesus was sick, did he ever yearn for home and a hug?

I take comfort in the fact that, like me, Jesus was one on-the-move teacher. Compared with the situations in which Jesus often found himself, I should have no complaints. It also seems that Jesus' travels and their related hassles allowed him to encounter those who needed his help. Jesus knows what it's like to feel unsettled. He also knows that it is not where you are that counts, but who you are. God can use your frustrating situations for good, allowing them to mold you toward perfection and mastery. Will you let God turn your cart around?

PRAYER: Thank you that you can use my biggest professional challenges to fulfill the greatest of dreams. Please help me push my cart today.

26

Doubt

SUGGESTED SCRIPTURE READING: Jeremiah 29:4-14

VERSE DU JOUR: *"For I know the plans I have for you,"* declares the LORD, *"plans to prosper you and not to harm you, plans to give you hope and a future."* (Jeremiah 29:11)

I find myself flat on the floor, strangely wondering about the proper etiquette related to hallway gunfire. I hear the echoing shots die and watch students stand and brush the dust from their clothing before I'm back up off the floor and standing with the crowd. Several students have simply flattened themselves up against the tile walls. What do the other teachers do when this sort of thing happens?

I'm no sooner hustling off to my next class when a flood of doubt overtakes me. I wonder why I am here, question my sanity, and begin to doubt my career choice. Perhaps I misread God's plan for my life, or maybe I'm not called to this job. Maybe I wasn't supposed to be a teacher. As the dust cleared, I wondered—what am I doing in this God-forsaken school?

If you are like me and occasionally experience doubt, please be assured that you are a normal follower of Jesus. And sometimes, what we read as doubt might be a healthy reaction to a dangerous or sin-riddled environment. Jesus knows that we will sometimes doubt ourselves and doubt our given missions; his disciples had their less than stellar moments. Even Peter, the rock, doubted. When Peter fell into the water that he had intended to walk on, Jesus pulled him out and said, "You of little faith, why did you doubt?" (Matthew 14:31). Jesus promises to help us overcome doubt with God's strength and protection. God has plans for us; they are good, important, and carefully developed plans. God assigned our individual life plans before we were born, even before the earth's formation. Doubt can kill our confidence and ultimately can kill our dreams. We need to fight against the doubt that makes us question ourselves and our God.

I later learned that the gunshots had been a round of firecrackers thrown into the hall. The student who lit and threw them did intend to create havoc and confusion; he was apprehended by day's end. I felt foolish for hitting the floor the way that I did but was glad that I wasn't the only one mistaking firecrackers for gunfire. Students much more street-savvy than I later told me that I had done the right thing. I need to see the challenges that come my way for what they are: challenges that can be overcome. Every little pack of firecrackers is not a warning to desert the cause; God will protect me here, because my school is not God-forsaken. Jesus said, "I have told you these things, so that in me you may have peace. In this world you will have trouble. But take heart! I have overcome the world" (John 16:33).

PRAYER: Let me go boldly with you, wearing the cloak of your blessing and trusting in your plans. I trust you with my future, and now I will trust you with today.

27

Questions

SUGGESTED SCRIPTURE READING: Matthew 22:15-22

VERSES DU JOUR: *"So I say to you: Ask and it will be given to you; seek and you will find; knock and the door will be opened to you. For everyone who asks receives; he who seeks finds; and to him who knocks, the door will be opened."* (Luke 11:9-10)

It's 10:00 a.m., only my second block class, and I'm already sweating in my lightest white lab coat. A contingent from the chorus has just arrived to sing a Valentine love song to Donny, the lanky, well-dressed, and popular new boy who insists on sitting on a lab stool behind the back row of my class. While the five chorus members surround him with song, the intercom interrupts with one more "very important announcement." Carlos wants a pass to the rest room. I see the class narcoleptic nod off as her head hits the hard desktop. How can she sleep in the middle of this cacophony? LaKeisha, the outspoken girl with the newly braided extensions under a trendy pink beret, is waving her arms wildly—apparently she has a question that can't wait. I could swear I just heard a kid bark . . . If this weren't my life, it would be downright amusing!

Jesus knew his subject so well and believed so strongly in his message that he was not flustered by interruptions or intimidated by the questions that might be flung his way. As a matter of fact, Jesus was so adept at fielding questions and at using others' questions as teaching tools, sometimes I've wondered if he had plants in the audience. Jesus' best teaching seems to follow in response to questions. Whether the questions come from within a crowd or from a solitary man standing on a dark garden roof, none are considered interruptions but rather are used as openings for important instruction.

What was so important to LaKeisha that it couldn't wait? She was concerned about my face and wanted to know what was wrong. Unbeknownst to me, my face had changed before her eyes from its usual pasty beige to a fiery red. Earlier that morning, I'd taken a hefty dose of a vitamin called niacin. Niacin, also known as vitamin B3, is touted as a natural cholesterol reducer, but it does have a side effect. When a therapeutic dose is achieved, a dilation of the blood vessels leads to skin redness and increased temperature, somewhat like a hot flash. Rather than just another interruption, LaKeisha's question, combined with my niacin-induced flush, were the perfect lead-ins to the day's topic—reducing cholesterol and risk of cardiovascular disease. Although they may be annoying, questions can be our greatest teaching tools and our strongest allies.

PRAYER: Jesus, please teach me to see questions and interruptions as tools for instruction. Give me wisdom and finesse as I field unanticipated questions. You are the ruler of the tongue and the brain. Help me, Lord.

28

I Believe in God— and in the Impossible!

SUGGESTED SCRIPTURE READING: Matthew 17:14-21

VERSE DU JOUR: *"For nothing is impossible with God."* (Luke 1:37)

"It's impossible! Your students will never understand this stuff, let alone be able to generate a project of this magnitude," my experienced mentor warned. "They won't even do a simple handout for homework, and you think they'll be able to create a pedigree and track a genetic trait using genotypes and phenotypic symbols? *And* you're assigning this a week before Thanksgiving break? H-e-l-l-o."

Two weeks later, my usually narrow eyes opened wide with wonder as Charade unfurled her project. The only place large enough to view the pedigree project, fifteen feet long and three feet wide, was on the laboratory floor. The scroll, showing solid proof of weeks of research and evidence of comprehension, loomed before me. Charade giggled as she saw my reaction—screams of surprise and tears of relief. At least one student got it! She then proceeded to explain how she had traced the genetically determined disease of sickle-cell anemia through the extensive family tree that covered my floor. As I listened and checked the genotypes (which all matched up correctly), the words that I'd heard just a few weeks before echoed through my skull.

Jesus regularly accomplished the impossible. He healed incurable diseases, drove out insufferable demons, described and modeled God's love to the resistant masses, and loved the unlovable. He empowered a motley band of sometimes obtuse learners to do the impossible, too. Jesus explains that it is the presence of God in us that allows the impossible to happen. It is not our doing but God working through us.

"It's a lucky thing you assigned this before Thanksgiving break," Charade continued. "My mom was getting upset about all the long-distance phone calls I was making to track down this information from Grams and the aunties. We had a huge family reunion over Thanksgiving break, and I got all the information I needed then!"

I smiled. I can't take credit for Charade's work and can't credit myself for going ahead with the lesson. It wasn't that I was so full of faith but rather that I was too stubborn and unwilling to change the plans I'd already presented. Knowing all this, God still chose to use me. And he chose to reward me! Most of my students did complete the assignment, and many did it well. Recently, I learned that Charade is now a research scientist in a prestigious lab, working on the genetics of cancer. The next time that your task seems too big, your job too hard, or your position impossible, remember that it is God whom you serve. With God, nothing is impossible.

PRAYER: Lord, please give me your vision, allowing me to see my students' full potential. Please empower me to do the impossible for you.

29

Worthy in All Ways

SUGGESTED SCRIPTURE READING: Psalm 139:1-18

VERSE DU JOUR: *You know when I sit and when I rise; you perceive my thoughts from afar.* (Psalm 139:2)

It was while teaching in an urban high school that I reached the pinnacle of my vulgarity problem, which I blamed on my surroundings. I had no control over my tongue. How was I supposed to listen to all the #**# and never use it myself? My potty mouth was curbed when I was with my students, but when I was with colleagues or friends, my mouth was out of control. My husband was not too crazy about my new linguistic skills; he considered my speech crass and unrefined. Finally, when my toddler daughter's first sentence was, "Oh, sh-t," I decided it was time to make some changes. I was just as guilty of using vulgar words as were the students whose speech in the hallways often prompted me to look them in the eye and say, "Do you kiss your grandma with that mouth?"

"Before a word is on my tongue, you know it completely, O LORD" (Psalm 139:4). O Lord, indeed! Perhaps this is not good. Some of the words that have rolled off my tongue have not been words that I want anyone else to hear, let alone my God! I can hear God whispering the same question that I pose to students I catch using profanity in the hallways: "You kiss your grandma with that mouth?" Nothing that I do or think is done in secret. God knows everything that I'm about to do and everything I'm about to say even before I do or say it! Nothing is hidden from my God. All my worries, all my thoughts, and all my actions, including my words, are known to God.

Maybe the words of Psalm 139 are meant not merely to comfort me but also to hint at what God can do to reform my words and my thoughts. If I know that God knows what I'm going to say before I say it, might I better filter the stuff about to exit my mouth? Maybe if I ask God for guidance and help in this matter,

I can begin to avoid saying things I shouldn't. Perhaps if I ask, God can teach me to choose and direct my words more carefully. As God's emissary, I want a mouth worthy to kiss Grandma. How about you?

PRAYER: Lord, guard my thoughts and my lips as I think and speak. Teach me to think about you and talk as though you are part of me. Let my words be pleasing to you today.

30

Repetition

SUGGESTED SCRIPTURE READING: John 8:1-30

VERSE DU JOUR: *Let the word of Christ dwell in you richly as you teach and admonish one another with all wisdom, and as you sing psalms, hymns and spiritual songs with gratitude in your hearts to God.* (Colossians 3:16)

One semester I had the easiest prep ever; I taught the same introductory biology class five times a day. Sounds like a dream come true, but the teaching sometimes drove me to distraction. I couldn't remember to whom I told what. I was impatient when my students in the fifth period didn't understand a concept the first time around (for them). I felt I had repeated myself thirty times—but not to them . . . Why couldn't they get it?

Reading John's Gospel, I am struck not only by the wisdom and the teaching of Jesus' words but also by their number. How did the author remember all these things that Jesus said, and did he record them verbatim? Perhaps after a long, hot day on the road with Jesus, John spent a few hours writing down the important things that Jesus said that day. Maybe he had a way to write Jesus' words during Jesus' lectures. One explanation for the remarkable similarities between the accounts recorded in the four Gospels is that Jesus repeated some things over and over. Perhaps he decided on the points that he really wanted to make, repeating himself time and again. If Jesus said, "I was sent by the Father" once, he likely said it a million times. Perhaps Jesus knew that constant repetition would eventually yield comprehension and that the disciples and other followers would finally get it.

Did Jesus, a master teacher, force his students to memorize? Did they learn by constantly hearing the same things over and over? Were the disciples better able to remember Jesus' words because they had some kind of heavenly help, or were their minds more able to recall because they were raised in a culture heavily dependent on an oral tradition? We have no clear answers to these questions, but it is appears that Jesus did repeat himself. Those of us who spend our lives repeating ourselves are in great company. Jesus said the same things over and over again. Eventually Jesus' disciples understood. Eventually we will, too. Let's wait patiently for our students to get it so we can bask in the light of their comprehension.

PRAYER: Jesus, please give me patience and strength as I teach. Remind me that repetition is the mother of comprehension. Thank you for never tiring of teaching me.

31

Bold as a Lion

SUGGESTED SCRIPTURE READING: Proverbs 28:1-28

VERSE DU JOUR: *The wicked flee when no one pursues, but the righteous are as bold as a lion.* (Proverbs 28:1, NRSV)

"Anything but student court!" Tyrone wailed, holding the summons as if it were hot coals. "Going there is the worst. I'd rather get suspended or even expelled without going through that!"

The students in our high school hated when their transgressions led them to a court where a panel of peers judged and doled out sentences. I can understand how they feel; I recently went to traffic court to plead for mercy on a speeding ticket. I deserved the ticket—I was definitely going way over the speed limit. I was so scared when I went into that courtroom. The judge was tough, and as I saw her hand down sentences to the people preceding me on the docket, I started to sweat. I knew I was guilty.

When I think of Jesus, I think of him as both gentle and bold. I see him laughing with children right before he rebukes the pious Pharisees. I see him confidently tromping the beaches of Galilee the day after he has been pressed by mobs of humanity. I hear Jesus call Mary gently by name, in the garden, after courageously breaking the chains of death. Jesus lived a bold, exciting, dangerous life and yet was caring and tender in his relationships. He was equally kind to his friends and his enemies. How did he do it? Perhaps his boldness was driven by the perspective and power that was given directly to him by God.

In the end, my courtroom debut worked out pretty well. The judge took away my points and put me on probation. I tried to keep the probation quiet; it wouldn't have gone over well with the neighborhood carpool moms.

Despite the outcome of my court experience, thinking about it still makes me nervous. I wasn't bold in that courtroom, for good reason—I was guilty! I was afraid about standing in front of a local magistrate in a noncriminal traffic court. What would I do if, without Jesus, I had to stand before God's judgment throne? A frightening thought, indeed. But when Jesus switched places with us, he also gave us his righteousness and promised to intercede for us at God's throne. Our mistakes and weaknesses have been given to Jesus. The hearing has already occurred. Forgiven and powerful, we can boldly approach the eternal throne. If we can approach God, we can also boldly approach any challenge or any earthly authority.

PRAYER: Jesus, give me your boldness. Let me stand up for that which is right and holy. Thank you that I can be bold because you cover me.

32

Don't Play It Safe

SUGGESTED SCRIPTURE READING: Matthew 25:14-30

VERSE DU JOUR: *"For everyone who has will be given more, and he will have an abundance. Whoever does not have, even what he has will be taken from him."* (Matthew 25:29)

Wanting to teach about currents and tides in an active way, I planned a nontraditional lab. So, I searched out Beach Boys music, collected every pair of sunglasses and every hat I could find, and even dug out my lifeguard whistle. I decided that my students would act out the motions of the tides and currents to loud music. I was more than a little nervous, especially since my oldies music was not likely to be judged as cool. But seeing paroled, street-wise, tough students running and laughing in old pink sunglasses and purple leis, while learning a foreign concept (we were two thousand miles from the nearest ocean) was my reward. The students talked about it for years later, and although life may catch them in bad circumstances, I doubt that any of them will ever be caught in a rip tide!

It seems that Jesus had trouble with people who played it safe. Didn't he tell the disciples, "Come and follow me"? Jesus didn't tell them to take care of their affairs, say their goodbyes, and meet him in one month's time. He expected them to drop everything and follow him. It bothered Jesus when people were afraid to risk and afraid to try. In the parable of the buried talents, the reply of the master to his faithful yet fiscally conservative servant is, "You wicked, lazy servant" (Matthew 25:26). And notice the explanation of the chastised servant, "Master . . . I was afraid and went out and hid your talent in the ground" (Matthew 25:24-25). Although I doubt that Jesus is making a statement about our financial portfolios, he is making a point about our approach to life and risk.

Today's Bible verse sounds a little unfair, doesn't it? It doesn't seem right to pound down the underdog. But does this parable refer only to literal talents (in this case, money), or does it speak to our treatment of out figurative talents (real-life strengths and gifts)? Perhaps Jesus is commenting on how we are to use our abilities and talents for him. Sometimes well-meaning Christians are guilty of the same sin described in the parable. When we allow fear to prevent us from trying something new, it buries our strengths and gifts, takes away our joy, and can make us a little too conservative. Jesus wants apprentices who are not afraid to risk, who are not afraid to succeed, and who are willing to step outside of their comfort zones. I urge you take one small risk for Jesus today.

PRAYER: Lord, I do not want to live a life that is controlled by fear. Release me from the fear that strangles me and limits me. Give me an attitude of joy, and let me show it to my students. I want to live recklessly for you.

33

Ready and Alert

SUGGESTED SCRIPTURE READING: Ephesians 6:10-18

VERSE DU JOUR: *And pray in the Spirit on all occasions with all kinds of prayers and requests. With this in mind, be alert and always keep on praying for all the saints.* (Ephesians 6:18)

"Boo!" they both growled, as one grabbed my ankle and the other poked me in the waist. Whoever was waiting for me in the deep, dark prep closet said "Boo!"—how clichéd. Still, I was surprised enough to offer up a scream of genuine shock as I literally fell on the floor—perhaps that was the fall that broke my coccyx (tailbone) . . . I was truly surprised that these rapidly developing adolescent boys still had a sense of play that allowed them to engage in mostly harmless mischief. This would be the first of many times that these two freshmen boys surprised me. The silver lining of this unsettling new behavior was that although Buck and Billy were usually late for class, they had to arrive early in order to sneak into the closet and wait for me.

What did Jesus do when he was waiting to be surprised, or when the going got tough and temptation tantalized? He prayed. He took a time-out and prayed. Whether Jesus was sequestered on a mountainside, taking an extended time-out in the desert, or traveling the country with his disciples in tow, he made prayer a top priority. It would be reasonable to assume that Jesus prayed while walking, working, and teaching; the Scriptures tell us that he was in constant communication with God. In Ephesians, we are instructed to pray at all times and to bring all requests to God. We are also warned to remain alert and instructed to always pray for each other.

The boys waited in the darkened closet for me day after day. I came to expect them, but my occasional memory lapses were their reward. I also didn't want to mess up a good thing; after all, they were on time for class every time they stalked me. Once I relaxed and forgot about their little attacks, I was open game again. Similarly, once I break my prayer connection and my spiritual awareness, I am open game to the Evil One. Rather than worrying about what is waiting for me in the dark, I need to be alert and constantly in prayer.

You, too, can pray constantly: for help to make your deadlines, for the students who make up your nightmares, for wisdom to create classroom order, for more sleep, and for whatever else you need. Pray while you are in the middle of your school stress, and pray for a time to get away from it all to pray a little more.

Pray, pray, pray away your day. Easy to say, but for many of us, remembering to pray is the hard part. When we're away from the situations that freak us out, it's easy to say, "I should have prayed." When your hands are doing two different things, your feet are moving, and several students are simultaneously asking questions, you're probably in no mood to pray. But this is the time when you most need to pray.

PRAYER: God, let this be the first of many times that I come to you today. I want to stay alert and in constant communication with you. Let's go together . . .

34

The Eyes of God

SUGGESTED SCRIPTURE READING: 1 Chronicles 29:10-13

VERSE DU JOUR: *For the eyes of the* LORD *search back and forth across the earth, looking for people whose hearts are perfect toward him, so that he can show his great power in helping them.* (2 Chronicles 16:9, TLB)

Jeannie approached me as I was trying to dislodge a slide stuck in the projector. Class had just ended when she whispered in my ear, "I'm not sure if God really is powerful enough to take care of my problems." Then she followed up her statement with the litany of her problems. I stood stunned and in need of the restroom. This weighty dilemma would not be solved in the four-minute class change. We talked then and later, and I found that Jeannie's image of God was limited. Her God was old, white, frail, and somewhat nasty. Her God couldn't wait to find a sinner in need of punishment. This negative image of God, however, is not the God we find presented in Scripture. The God we strive to know is a God driven by love and filled with power and grace. The God who watches over us is a God who doesn't want to hurt us but wants to help us. Better yet, God has the power to help us!

We cannot comprehend the power that could raise Jesus from the dead. Could the power of a hundred atomic bombs accomplish that? We cannot fathom the power that could form the stars of space and fill the vastness of the universe. This is the same power that could strike mighty armies or open the seas. This same power is ours for the taking. In fact, God is searching the face of the earth trying to find someone on whom to bestow this power, someone sorely in need of power, someone who needs his support; perhaps that someone is you. God is searching to find you—not to catch you in an act of sin, not to chastise you for a mistake, but to offer you help. Notice, the text does not say that God will give you a little bit of help. Rather, God's eyes are moving to and from, searching for someone to strongly support. Imagine! We often forget to ask for support and don't expect to get much of it.

I'm sorry to say that other than discussing this single disclosure, I never became a mentor or spiritual advisor to Jeannie. The last I heard about her, she was due to appear before the disciplinary review board. I wonder if Jeannie took my words to heart or, if with more investment, I could have made a positive effect on her walk with God.

Imagine the difference we all could make in the life of a child with a few words of truth and affirmation. But the job ahead is tough, and the day is long; often, getting through the day is challenge enough. How will we find the power to do even more than we are already doing? God promises to give us power and support—all we need to do is ask for it! I encourage you to ask for power and support; then go out into your world believing that God will freely give both to you.

PRAYER: God, I believe that I am in need of some of your power. Fill me with the power of your love, the power of your strength, the power of your protection, and the power of your wisdom as I go into my day. I need a strong dose of your power as I teach today.

35

A Man of Few Words

SUGGESTED SCRIPTURE READING: Luke 24:1-12

VERSE DU JOUR: *Then they remembered his words.* (Luke 24:8)

It's no wonder that teachers are always getting sore throats. Just thinking about the plethora of bacteria and viruses that swarm around us day after day is enough to send even the most cavalier educator into a bubble. You don't even want to know what my biology students grew in agar plates from the samples they took from the classroom light switch, the pencil sharpener, and my desktop. Top off pathogenic exposure with the constant chattering that makes up a typical day, and the mystery is solved.

How many times do you get home from work and wish that you could spend the rest of the evening without saying even one word? I would like to think that my every teacherly utterance is necessary and filled with great knowledge, imparting wisdom to my young charges, but, alas, I fear that is not so. Sometimes I am teaching what I think are amazing facts, and other times I feel as though I am blathering. Often I am still lecturing in an authoritative and overly loud voice during dinner. I am reminded by those who still love me to tone it down. For me, this obnoxious behavior is another one of those occupational hazards.

By contrast, Jesus offered pithy advice. "If any one of you is without sin, let him be the first to throw a stone" (John 8:7). "From everyone who has been given much, much will be demanded" (Luke 12:48). "Blessed are the meek, for they will inherit the earth" (Matthew 5:5). "Take up your mat and go home" (Mark 2:11). "A man building a house . . . laid the foundation on a rock" (Luke 6:48). "Trust in God; trust also in me" (John 14:1). Jesus' words challenged minds and changed the world. His wise and well-chosen words were explosive and dangerous. Jesus knew that his audience could take in only so much. Therefore, he often chose familiar analogies or clever parables to make a point. Jesus ran his narratives through the filter of God's will before ever speaking a word.

If only I could access God's wisdom to speak only carefully chosen and uplifting words. How thrilling it would be if I could think of the right thing to say at the moment it is needed, not three hours later. If only I had the discipline to always think before speaking . . . and if my words could be sparser yet more powerful. If I could speak with authority, like my Lord, what a great teacher I could be! Yet what a blessing it is that my words can be guided by God. If I allow it, God will run my words through divine filters and will direct my speech. Can you make a decision to let your words be meaningful, uplifting, and worth listening to today?

PRAYER: Direct my words. Let me speak as though I am a mouthpiece for you. Give me the wisdom to filter my words through you.

36

Imagine!

SUGGESTED SCRIPTURE READING: 1 Corinthians 2:6-16

VERSE DU JOUR: *However, as it is written: "No eye has seen, no ear has heard, no mind has conceived what God has prepared for those who love him."* (1 Corinthians 2:9)

FloFlo, my sweet great-auntie, was a retired veteran teacher who'd put in more than fifty classroom years. She started her career in a one-room school that was heated by wood she chopped. FloFlo pumped the students' drinking water and shoveled the path to school on chilly winter mornings in northeast Pennsylvania. As a young child, I remember FloFlo getting visits and letters from her past students. In fact, they were still coming to see her when she was in her mid-nineties. Some of her former students had grand-children, yet they were excited to communicate with the lady who had left her mark on their lives. At ninety-six years of age, she had a linen closet filled with gifts from her students. I loved getting into that closet; it was filled with soaps and lotions, expensive antique perfumes from Paris, handmade lace handkerchiefs and linen nap-kins. FloFlo was blessed with the opportunity to look back at a long life of teaching and witness the beauty of God's plan for her life. She was able to witness the difference that she made in the lives of so many thankful students.

During his teaching career, Jesus was confident in the job he was doing and was certain of the importance of his mission. Jesus knew that his life and teaching ministry were an important part of God's plan. He willingly sacrificed for the sake of his call. Recall how Jesus, when facing agony and death, surrendered to God saying, "Not my will, but yours." He was able to sacrifice his will, know-ing that one day he would be restored to his rightful place in heaven. Although he didn't get to see all the benefits of his ministry while still here on earth, Jesus was nonetheless assured of mission success.

As Christian teachers, we need to be aware that we are an impor-tant part of God's plan. God will use us to make a difference in this world. Through his teachers, God will enter a needy and hurting world. Our presence in our schools has been determined by God. God watches over us and over the students with whom we work. The prayers that we offer up for our students and the requests we bring to God on behalf of our schools result in blessings far beyond any imagination. Our diligence and commitment to work for these children and ultimately for the Lord will result in blessings that may never be known until we meet God in heaven. We may not yet have a closet full of little gifts, but the huge gift of God's providence and promise remains. We go nowhere by accident.

PRAYER: Lord, motivate me so that I can wait to see the results of your grand plan. I can't even imagine what you have in mind for me. Let me be satisfied in knowing that I am working for you.

37
Children of God

SUGGESTED SCRIPTURE READING: John 1:10-13

VERSE DU JOUR: *Yet to all who received him, to those who believed in his name, he gave the right to become children of God—children born not of natural descent, nor of human decision or a husband's will, but born of God.* (John 1:12)

I am so sick of hearing, "You're not my mother. I don't have to do what you say." I promise myself that the next time a misbehaving student uses this tired old excuse, I will look him or her in the eye, laugh, and respond, "Thank God for that!" However, my promise doesn't hold. It's not two days before I hear the same lame refrain, and instead of emitting a jolly laugh or a snappy comeback, I feel anger and frustration. I expect my students to follow certain rules of safety and civility. I don't expect them to love me, but is it too much to ask for a little respect?

"When all the people were being baptized, Jesus was baptized too. And as He was praying, heaven was opened and the Holy

Spirit descended on him in bodily form like a dove. And a voice came from heaven: 'You are my Son, whom I love; with you I am well pleased'" (Luke 3:21-22). This proclamation identified Jesus as Messiah and affirmed his position as God's Son.

Even before sending Jesus to earth, God's acts were immeasurable. In John 1, we see that God has made all things, including life and light. God is the light that overcomes darkness, full of grace and truth. In great mercy, God has allowed us to become children of God—not acquaintances or associates of God, not servants or slaves of God. The use of the word *children* not only implies a family relationship but also a type of proud parentage and a set of hopeful expectations. God expects his children to show others his love and to sacrifice for others. We are to reflect God's image as a son resembles his father or as a daughter shows her mother's mannerisms. The way that we work and live should reflect our relationship to God. As God's children, we must not tire of showing our family heritage.

The "you're not my mother" comments seem to be driven by the general acknowledgment that parents should command and earn the respect of their children. I do expect that my students' behavior will reflect the respect and care that I show them. Although I sometimes fall short of communicating it, I hope my students know that I work hard for them and love them. As God's children, our actions, attitudes, and words should reflect the love and acceptance of our heavenly Parent. Today, yours may be the only face that shows the light of God. Your mouth may be the only mouth that speaks the truth, or your eyes the only eyes that see the promise in someone else.

PRAYER: God, help me to reflect your image. Let me act like your child. Give me the strength and maturity to act the way your child should. Let me touch someone else for you today.

38

Queen of Something

SUGGESTED SCRIPTURE READING: 1 Peter 2:4-12

VERSE DU JOUR: *But you are a chosen people, a royal priesthood, a holy nation, a people belonging to God, that you may declare the praises of him who called you out of darkness into his wonderful light.* (1 Peter 2:9)

One Halloween, I dressed my husband, children, and myself as the royal family. Don't ask me which royal family; we don't claim relation to Queen Victoria, and we certainly didn't dress as the Romanovs. We were just the royal family. We each had a crown, a rich velvet cloak, and plenty of flashy faux jewelry. Was it fun! While giving out candy, I made sure that the grubbing minions bowed to the queen.

The next morning, rather than putting away our royal vestments in the attic where they belonged, I allowed my son to place the large, flashy golden crown on my head. I promptly forgot that I had it on. We were running around the house getting ready to leave when the gas meter reader came to the door. When I let her in, she gave me a strange look. I let the look pass. It was too early in the morning to be clear-headed.

For those of us who aspire to royalty and prefer more than a one-night Halloween royal flush, we need to know this: God's children all are part of a royal family. The God of the universe, the Almighty, has embraced us as family. That puts us in the royal lineage. You can't get any higher than that. Since we are accepted in Christ as children of God, we have the responsibility and privilege to think and act like royalty. Yet Jesus teaches us to treat others as better than ourselves. If we are indeed of royal lineage, consider that others are also of royal standing and deserve to be treated as such. God sees all persons as royalty.

But my visiting meter reader must have thought I was off my rocker. The same woman came to read my meter almost three months later. When I came to the door, she quipped, "Sorry. I almost didn't recognize you without your crown."

PRAYER: Thank you, sovereign God, for accepting me into your royal family. Teach me to behave as one of your children and to show others your mercy. Let me treat everyone I meet today as royalty.

39
Comfort Level

SUGGESTED SCRIPTURE READING: Romans 10:1-15

VERSE DU JOUR: *And how can they preach unless they are sent? As it is written, "How beautiful are the feet of those who bring good news!"* (Romans 10:15)

If truth be told, I have a love-hate affair with shoes. My colleagues and students told me that when I took off for maternity leave, they knew that I would return soon, because I had left at least a dozen pair of shoes scattered throughout the department. Most of my shoes were stored below my desk; that way I could surreptitiously sneak a quick shoe change when whatever I had been wearing became uncomfortable. After I moved across the country so that my husband could pursue a medical residency, I received a call from an ex-student. She claimed that she knew I was leaving forever when she saw that all of my shoes were gone.

After spending most of my life wearing shoes that were a size too small, I figured out that I am a much happier and productive person when my feet are comfortable. The best way for my feet to be happy is for me to change shoes regularly and frequently. How much happier are you with your feet in the sand than with your tortured tootsies crammed into shoes that pinch and squeeze?

It's probably safe to say that Jesus never wore pumps, heels, platforms, or cowboy boots. I have nothing against such footwear, as can be evidenced by my collection of shoes, but do you think that sore feet ever affected the quality of his teaching? It is unlikely that Jesus owned any other footwear than sandals, the shoes of the day for regular guys in his part of the world. It also seems as if Jesus, along with others of his day, recognized the importance of podiatric maintenance. He lovingly washed the feet of others, a necessity and a treat after a long day of walking on hot, dusty roads. Maybe Jesus enjoyed running barefoot on the beach in Galilee or wading in the cool sea water.

Please do not misunderstand. I am not advocating that you go to school today and whip off your shoes—believe me when I tell you that it won't be well received. I've tried the unfettered foot teaching gig, and it is neither popular nor appreciated by anyone but you. I do, however, challenge you to consider your current state of physical comfort; how you feel may influence the quality of your teaching. Then, decide what you can do to make yourself more comfortable and more physically fit. Perhaps new inserts in your shoes, a quick healthy snack, or an icy glass of water might help you teach more effectively.

PRAYER: I want nothing to get in the way of being the best teacher that I can. Today, please show me one thing that I can do to change my attitude and comfort level so that I can better serve you.

40

Power to Become

SUGGESTED SCRIPTURE READING: 1 Corinthians 1:20-31

VERSE DU JOUR: *But to those whom God has called, both Jews and Greeks, Christ [is] the power of God and the wisdom of God.* (1 Corinthians 1:24)

The fossils are set out on the cracked, fake slate lab tables. The timeline is positioned on the overhead, and my lecture notes are organized and ready. Everything is in place, but my stomach is churning, and I'm starting to sweat.

Today is the day that I introduce the concept of evolutionary biology. I have to be so careful about how I teach this; I don't want to break the law or initiate a hundred parent complaints, but I also don't want to compromise my faith or my God. I'm more than a little stressed out, although there is a correct way to teach this. I've done it before but wonder if I can pull it off again. I'm starting to doubt myself.

We can't know what went on inside the mind of Jesus, yet his actions betrayed little self-doubt. He was an extremely confident and directed man. Jesus did not apologize for speaking what he knew to be true, nor did he consider himself below others. Jesus never apologized for his social status, the place of his birth, or his family. Likewise, Jesus never spoke against anyone on the basis of on their sex, race, social status, or profession. He chose educated and uneducated men and women to serve as his closest associates. Jesus saw promise in everyone and seemed to view people from a unique perspective. Jesus took sides with the weak, the poor, and the sick. Jesus broke Jewish sabbath laws to heal the sick and assist the helpless, thereby putting himself in the spotlight and in danger with the Jewish leaders.

God sees you for who you are—and for who you are becoming. God does not place value on your alma mater or the amount of money you have. God is not impressed by your resume or worried about your limitations. In this chapter, Paul seems to indicate that those who are able to recognize their limitations and weaknesses are more likely to be used by God. Those who understand that God is righteous and holy are more likely to credit God for the source of their good works. Furthermore, we are told that since God has chosen us, we will have access to divine power and wisdom. I encourage you to ask God for power and wisdom, believing that if you ask, you will receive.

PRAYER: Lord, I will become the person that you allow me to become and will do what you enable me to do. Please take away my self-doubt and replace it with your wisdom and your insight. Thank you for choosing to use me and my imperfections.

41

Attack of the Psychic Vampires

SUGGESTED SCRIPTURE READING: Matthew 11:25-29

VERSE DU JOUR: *"Come to me, all you who are weary and burdened, and I will give you rest."* (Matthew 11:28)

This morning, Melody confided in me that her best friend is pregnant. Did I know what she should do or whom she should call? Then, Dante brought me his sign-out papers. Seems his dad doesn't want him anymore. I have a meeting with the dean of students to follow up on Daneisha's discipline referral. In addition to teaching three classes, this all happens before lunch. Between mothering on the job and trying to keep my head above water, how does one get a life?

Needy children, abused children, hungry children, confused children: they all need instruction, role models, and yes, good teachers. My buddy and teaching colleague Tammi occasionally refers to her students as the psychic vampires. "They got me again!" she'd say at the end of a typically grueling day. Where do we get the reserves when they have sucked us dry?

Jesus knew about fatigue and stress. He knew how the needs of others could become overwhelming and acknowledged the fatigue that comes with fighting the good fight. Jesus likened the Christian life to being in a battle. Yet he spoke of pursuing living water and promised to provide water that would quench overwhelming thirst. Jesus also took time out from a hectic and physically demanding schedule to replenish himself. Jesus rose early but slept well. He fasted yet also took time to feast and drink. Jesus spent forty days in a desert without one shower, yet he allowed perfume to be poured on his feet. The Master allowed others to serve him, yet he washed the feet of his best friends. Jesus did so much in so short a time, and yet he took the time to be alone in solitude, to connect with God, and to enjoy the beauty of nature.

Do you feel as though you are parenting a hundred or more children? Perhaps you feel that way because you are. The job you do is critical to eternity. It is challenging, and it is draining. God alone holds the power to keep you going. He can stop your breath today, or he can sustain your breath until you're 110 years old. Are you willing not only to take care of yourself but also to ask God for help? Jesus promises rest to the weary and rest for our souls. Will you take him up on his offer?

PRAYER: When my burdens gets heavy and the stress makes me weary, Jesus, please strengthen me and lighten my load.

42

Compassion

SUGGESTED SCRIPTURE READING: Matthew 9:32-38

VERSE DU JOUR: *When he saw the crowds, he had compassion on them, because they were harassed and helpless, like sheep without a shepherd.* (Matthew 9:36)

I swept into the dean's office and sat down in an empty chair directly across from James, the student for whom this meeting was scheduled. Yesterday James had yelled wildly at me during class. I had reciprocated his emotional display and then called for this meeting. I went in with all intentions of refusing to work with James any more; I wanted him removed from my class. This muscular teen had been nothing but trouble from the start; his behavior was distracting, his demeanor threatening, and his anger only thinly veiled. In an already challenging and crowded class, I didn't need one more time bomb waiting to explode.

Educators are expected to possess compassion for their students. Jesus modeled an attitude and behaviors based on compassion. In the middle of exhausting and dangerous travels, Jesus felt compassion for individuals and collective masses. He not only felt compassion but also acted in response to this emotion. You have to wonder why Matthew recorded this incident and how he sensed Jesus' compassion. Did Matthew witness tears, or did Jesus later explain how he had felt? No clear answer is given in the text. I'd like to think that if Jesus looked out at the fatigued and jumbled crowd of teachers at the next faculty meeting, he might feel similar compassion. Would seeing a group of us at a faculty meeting move Jesus to tears?

I was somewhat fearful walking into the disciplinary meeting with James and the dean. I wasn't sure what to expect from James and was shocked when he started the meeting with a seemingly heartfelt apology. As I listened, my heart softened, and for the first time I was able to really see James. The young man in front of me suddenly reminded me of my brother. "You are built just like my brother and have some of his other traits, too," I said to James. The meeting then went so well that I forgot my vow to send this boy packing. A moment of God-given compassion eventually led to amazing changes—James's behavior in class improved, as did his academic performance and his grade.

Jesus was a teacher and knows all about our occupational hazards: the constant pressure of performance, the challenges our students present, and the stress the job entails. Jesus understands our situation and offers his compassion and assistance. It's not a trite, "I feel your pain" statement but a real and deep compassion. We, who have experienced Christ's compassion, can share it with others who need it so desperately.

PRAYER: Lord, give me compassion for my students, just as you give compassion to me. Help me through another day.

43

Judgment Call

SUGGESTED SCRIPTURE READING: Luke 6:37-42

VERSE DU JOUR: *"Do not judge, and you will not be judged. Do not condemn, and you will not be condemned. Forgive, and you will be forgiven."* (Luke 6:37)

"What do you think about what's going on outside your green-house? Can you smell it in your room? Lots of kids are smoking weed out there, 'cause it's so close to the official smoking area but still out of the way." Several students had cornered me after class. "You're cool with it, aren't you? They're not hurting anyone . . ."

I wanted my students to trust me, and I wanted to seem like a cool teacher. They knew what I was supposed to do. As a Christian, however, I didn't know how to respond. I know that I'm not supposed to be judgmental; isn't that what Jesus taught? Non-Christians prefer this Scripture to all others. They love to tell us how we should behave. Even Christians, who feel convicted about a sin they continue to indulge, like to quote this verse. These are the words of Jesus, but if I put these words together with his actions, what is the full message that Jesus wants to convey? Does Jesus mean that we can't speak up for good, or that when we're questioned about our beliefs, we must be silent?

Whether speaking to the woman at the well, answering the Pharisees, or conversing with the rich man seeking advice, Jesus is clear about his view on sin. Jesus does not, however, start a relationship by discussing someone else's spiritual shortcomings. He does not voice his feelings about sin or the behavior of others until he is questioned. When the rich man asks the way to heaven, Jesus bluntly comments on the difficulties that accompany wealth. When the woman at the well asks Jesus specific questions related to her lifestyle, he answers her directly. In the temple, Jesus does not question the authority of the Pharisees until they question him. Jesus commands us not to judge, but he shows us how to be direct and truthful when we are questioned. Rather than pointing out the sins of others, Jesus chose to reach the world by showing love through service and by sharing his wisdom through his honesty.

"Actually, I'm not cool with it. Maybe you'd better spread the word so that they stop smoking weed out there. You know that if I smell it or see it, I need to report it," was my unwelcome and unhip reply. But they had asked, and, as a Christian, I had to be honest and direct. In my role as teacher and in the position of supposed authority, I couldn't be cool with it. Will you be able to stand up for what is right, and will you willingly risk looking or sounding judgmental? When someone asks you specifically about your stand on issues of sin or morality, will you speak honestly and boldly, or will you say nothing? Your silence does not demonstrate strength of character or make you more godly. I surely don't want to suffer the judgment that I am afraid to give.

PRAYER: Lord, let me be bold when others question the honor of your name or my beliefs. Help me to be honest and direct but not preach when asked about my life in you.

44

Clear Tape

SUGGESTED SCRIPTURE READING: Philippians 4:4-13

VERSE DU JOUR: *Finally, brothers, whatever is true, whatever is noble, whatever is right, whatever is pure, whatever is lovely, whatever is admirable—if anything is excellent or praiseworthy—think about such things.* (Philippians 4:8)

"We're out of clear tape. How are we supposed to hold these models together?" the students asked as they held up the cut-out pieces that would make up their DNA paper model. "Let's use the masking tape. That'll work if you stick it at the bottom and avoid covering the labels on top," I replied. Not ten minutes later, we were also out of masking tape. In desperation, we switched to staples.

Once the staples were gone, all we had left was saliva and tears. My tears, that is; the science department had still not received our supply order.

It's not as if I ask for a lot. I was trying to do a forty-five-minute lab that requires no more than photocopies, scissors, tape, and a few brain cells. I'd already spent too much of my own money at an office-supply store and was now sorry I hadn't spent even more. Aggravated, I told the students to try to finish the lab without finishing the models.

Paul's letter to the Philippians addresses practical concerns. He tells us how to relax and live a godly life, a life in which we trust God for our everyday needs and for our protection. Although Paul was far from perfect, he had learned from Jesus and was able to share some great advice. Paul had learned to be happy in all situations and knew that if we model our thoughts and actions on those of Jesus, we will be satisfied. Paul's advice to the Philippians boils down to this: Model your life after Jesus, don't worry about anything, pray to God for what you need, be gentle, think about good things, do good things, and deeply love others.

I got home from school, finally put up my pulsing and tired feet, and grabbed the paper. Front-page news included "Teachers' Pay Linked to Poor Performance," an article blasting teachers for society's ills. The article went on to blame teachers for low student test scores, high drop-out rates, violent student behavior. On and on it went. My cortisol levels soared. How dare people write these lies, implying that all teachers are greedy, lazy, and spoiled? Why don't they come to my classroom and try out my job for size? Bet the reporter who wrote these words had plenty of office supplies on his desk . . .

The anger within me grew until I threw the paper down and reached for something better. It was time to forget and forgive, to refocus and relax. Time to think on noble, right, pure, lovely, admirable, excellent, and praiseworthy things. I took a deep breath and turned my thoughts to my hard-working colleagues and students, toward my family and faith. Tomorrow, I would find some clear tape.

PRAYER: Lord, let me ignore the evil lies around me and focus on the truth of your love, acceptance, and provision.

45

A Model of Forgiveness

SUGGESTED SCRIPTURE READING: Ephesians 4:29-32

VERSE DU JOUR: *Be kind and compassionate to one another, forgiving each other, just as in Christ God forgave you.* (Ephesians 4:32)

Why was I staring at a nearly empty cart? The rulers, colored pencils, and Petri dishes were gone! Just that morning, I had put out all the materials that I needed to run my third block biology lab. I had placed the cart in the science prep room and checked it an hour before the lab time. Maybe some student was playing games with me. I'd heard of science departments where teachers sabotaged each other's labs, but that had never happened here. At least it had never happened to me. Frantic, I ran next door to my pal and veteran teacher, who helped me find another stash of rulers and a less prolific but satisfactory cache of colored pencils. I found several mismatched Petri halves sitting near the sink and tossed them onto the cart. The bell had already rung, and the students were waiting. Flustered and frantic, I pushed the cart into the room and somehow pieced together most of the lab activity.

Why does Jesus tell us to forgive? He tells us to forgive seventy times seventy, and if my calculations are correct, that's a lot more times than I feel willing to forgive any one person. Does Jesus tell us to forgive to develop a breed of mindless, senseless, unfeeling followers, or might he advise us to forgive in order to develop healthy, happy, and mentally sound followers? Without forgiveness as part of our lives, we could go insane. How many bitter, unforgiving people do you know who you would classify as mentally sound and healthy? I know a few people who carry with

MORNING MEETINGS WITH JESUS

them wounds and pain from so far back that they are not only miserable but make everyone around them miserable, too.

Our Creator knows our minds and our bodies better than we know ourselves. God would warn us against the very things that would destroy us. Not only does Jesus tell us to forgive others, but also he modeled for us the ultimate in forgiveness. Jesus showed us the possibilities of a forgiving spirit and forgave his enemies even as they tortured and killed him. Jesus also promised to forgive us for all our sins, past, present, and future.

During my block four prep period, I found the missing materials—on a colleague's desk. My incredulous inquiry was countered with, "I needed that stuff, too." I was furious! Later, I recalled times when I had borrowed materials from him. I also recalled the many times this teacher had shared with me his ideas and activities. I needed to give this man the benefit of the doubt and my forgiveness. Ironically, I wasn't able to relax until I granted him forgiveness. Forgiveness releases me from despair, bitterness, and guilt. Forgiveness also delivers me from the insanity of tomorrow. I refuse to be a slave to sin. I *will* forgive.

PRAYER: Lord, forgive my sin, and give me the grace to forgive others who have sinned against me.

46

Sealed and Delivered

SUGGESTED SCRIPTURE READING: John 6:25-33

VERSES DU JOUR: *Now it is God who makes both us and you stand firm in Christ. He anointed us, set his seal of ownership on us, and put his Spirit in our hearts as a deposit, guaranteeing what is to come.* (2 Corinthians 1:21-22)

The students hovered around the cadaver; we were in the hospital morgue, about to start our anatomy lesson. The proctor finally removed the sheet covering "our" body for the evening.

The students gasped from the shock of seeing their first cadaver, yet I noticed that most couldn't keep their eyes off the deceased's forearm. Sometime during this male cadaver's life, he had been tattooed. We witnessed the evidence: a large American eagle sat on a branch, all previous color faded to an indescribable green-ish-gray. The picture was altered by the effects of gravity and time, yet a clearly identifiable tattoo remained. We hypothesized that the man had been in some branch of the armed forces.

When we yield to God's will for our lives, we are tattooed with his seal. I don't remember ever feeling the pricking of the needle and see nothing alarming on my forehead, except for those nagging lines that the students recognize as wrinkles . . . Still, I trust that the mark is there because the Scriptures tell us that a seal that marks us as God's property is placed on our foreheads. God has secured us with his seal of redemption—the seal that marks us as his own, assures our eternal destiny, and serves to protect us against the Enemy. God has delivered us from slavery—the slavery of sin and its consequences. Because God has signed for us, sealed us, and delivered us, we are God's own.

Later, my students referred to "tattoo man." It was almost as if the tattoo owned the body and not the other way around. Spending a night with a cadaver prompts you to think about deep things. That night, as I pondered God's provision and faithfulness to me, I came to a new understanding of the blessings of my life. I had no more say in my place of birth, my family, the natural gifts given me, or the loved ones in my life than I have control of the weather. And I know that when my life here ends, I will stand with God's seal on my head. Just call me tattoo woman.

PRAYER: Thank you for signing me in, sealing me as your own, and delivering me from evil. Please continue to keep me in your thoughts and actions. Don't leave me out of the action but stay with me as you put me in the mix.

47

Be with Me

SUGGESTED SCRIPTURE READINGS: Genesis 2; Psalm 8:1-9

VERSE DU JOUR: *So God created humankind in his own image.* (Genesis 1:27, NRSV)

Sweating bullets on the exercise equipment, I turn to Tammi and relate my school experience regarding bullets of another kind. Tammi, a fellow science teacher, pauses briefly before offering me consolation, advice, and assistance.

I love to be with Tammi! When we are together, we laugh, talk, and open up to each other; our conversations are truly therapeutic. Time seems to fly when we're together, even when we're working out. Unless Tammi is next to me on that equipment, there is no hope of my doing more than thirty minutes. I have been blessed to find a friend like Tammi and know that God uses relationships like ours.

Jesus wants to spend time with us. The Scriptures tell us that God created people so that we could enter a special relationship; our raison d'etre is to be with God. God wants to spend time with us in the same way that God walked in the garden with Adam. Surprisingly, God doesn't withhold friendship until we become better people. God wants to be with us now, just as we are. God made us so that we could be companions, not just so we could do things, however great they may be. God has the power to do anything, anytime, yet wants our company. And the more I pursue God, the more it is likely I will become the kind of person I'm meant to be.

When I spend time with Tammi, I feel accepted and valued. I also take on many characteristics of her persona: I become more outgoing, I giggle more, and my speech eventually reflects her charming lilt. Perhaps if I spend more time with God, as I experience this relationship, I will also become more like God. The formula (Be with God = Be like God) seems a bit too simple, but the Scriptures prescribe it as the way to a satisfying life and true happiness. Rather than becoming caught up with the things that we should be doing or the things that we are doing, maybe we all need to spend a bit more mental energy seeking God. Walking in God's light will be its own reward.

PRAYER: Lord, I seek you and desperately want to walk with you and talk with you. I yearn to learn your ways. I am listening for you and looking forward to taking you with me everywhere I go today.

48

An Advocate for All

SUGGESTED SCRIPTURE READING: Luke 10:38-41

VERSE DU JOUR: *"Martha, Martha,"* the Lord answered, *"you are worried and upset about many things, but only one thing is needed. Mary has chosen what is better, and it will not be taken away from her."* (Luke 10:41)

"Thanks a lot for filling my daughter's mind with all sorts of crazy goals," Sonoma's mother sarcastically quipped over the phone line. "Now she's driving around in *my* sedan and filling the back seat and the trunk with corpses. Dead bodies of humans, mind you," the mother continued. "The stench is horrific!" I wasn't sure how I should respond, and I was a little confused. Then Sonoma's mom broke into a hearty, friendly laugh. "Actually, she's happier than I've ever seen her, and despite the body bags, I can't thank you enough. Your class has opened up a whole other world to her. We've talked about how college and a professional job can be a reality for her. I want her to have a better life than what so many of the girls around here have."

Jesus was one of the first women's rights advocates. Through his actions and teachings, Jesus advocated and demonstrated his respect for women. In a society where women held no executive positions, had no political or economic rights, and were considered barely better than cattle, Jesus listened to and discussed religious issues with his friends, Mary and Martha. The Scriptures tell us that Mary loved to sit at Jesus' feet. Jesus probably spent more time than did any other man debating, discussing, and teasing with these sisters. How refreshing this relationship must have been to these women who were living in first-century Bethany! Can't you imagine the sparkle in his eyes when Jesus got them laughing?

The record of Jesus speaking to the Samaritan woman at the well further demonstrates his nontraditional approach to women. Jesus' actions speak clearly about his beliefs in the worthiness and value of all women. His boldness in breaking social and political taboos says more than any law could. The loyalty and dedication of Jesus' female friends speak volumes about his relationships with them. While many male friends were running scared, the women Jesus loved couldn't stay away from the cross.

The mother I'd been speaking to about the encroaching body bags was the mom of one of my favorite students. Sonoma, a young lady with a sharp wit and a bright mind, had not only scored an A in my advanced biology class but had also secured, at my urging, an intern spot at the county coroner's office. Apparently the experience allowed her to consider further education and a chance for a better life. Like Jesus, I need to continue to make an effort to notice each student, to respect and open each mind to the many possibilities ahead.

PRAYER: Jesus, thank you for all the women who have influenced my life. Please guide me as I work with each student today. Help me to recognize and develop my students' gifts and talents.

49

A Marathon of Thanksgiving

SUGGESTED SCRIPTURE READING: Psalm 77

VERSE DU JOUR: *I will meditate on all your works and consider all your mighty deeds.* (Psalm 77:12)

"Mommy, thank you for the yummy oatmeal you made for me this morning. Thank you for putting two packets in the bowl instead of just one. Thank you for picking out my clothes. Thank you for letting me use the computer. Thank you for packing my lunch for me and for giving me a healthy snack. Thank you for this apple. It's delicious. Thank you for walking me to school . . ."

My young daughter continued this marathon of thank-yous during the course of a day. She thanked me for everything, even things that I consider part of our routine together; anything I did for her was fair game. I'm not sure why she did; perhaps it was a twisted form of amusement or somehow related to the approach of Christmas. To add to the appearance of family lunacy, my son, being younger than his sister and quite the mimic, joined in with his own litany of thanks. The things he thanked me for were even more specific and comprehensive.

You'd think this behavior would've been maddening, but it was the most fun I'd had and the most appreciated I'd felt in weeks. And I was proud not of myself, as I'd only done the things that any decent parent does, but I was proud of my children—proud of their skills of observation and recollection, pleased that they had thankful hearts, and humbled that they had a burden to share their praise. You know what else I felt? I felt a deep desire to do more for them. Somehow, the attention I normally give them didn't seem quite enough. As I tucked my daughter into bed that night, she continued the marathon, even reflecting on things I'd done for her that morning. Then and there, I not only felt a swell of thankfulness in my own heart but also vowed to be a better parent and friend.

When he taught the disciples about prayer, Jesus used the model of the Lord's Prayer. This model prayer includes praise, petition, and thanks. Why do you suppose that Jesus taught us thank God? Did Jesus want to add one more thing to our to-do list? Maybe the concept of praise and thanks is important. Perhaps the same dynamic I experienced with my children applies to our relationship with God. Could God ever tire of hearing our thanks and our praise? I didn't tire of it, and I'm made in God's image.

I spend a good amount of my prayer time asking God for stuff: "Please help me manage my classroom better. Help me with that difficult student. God, I need this lab to work out! Please forgive me for losing my patience. Please protect me in this crazy place . . ." Instead of a constant theme of pathetic pleading, wouldn't God be pleased with having us recognize everything we notice, everything that we can find that God does for us and supplies to us? It is the right thing to do because we want to give God something, not just receive. It's amazing what God does for us every day!

PRAYER: Thank God throughout the day as you notice each gift God freely gives. Put a smile on God's precious face as you give the gift of your thanks and praise.

50

Delayed Gratification

SUGGESTED SCRIPTURE READING: Psalm 40:1-8

VERSE DU JOUR: *I waited patiently for the LORD; he turned to me and heard my cry.* (Psalm 40:1)

I can't believe that I am boarding a city bus, along with fifteen of my brightest and dearest students. I pinch myself to make sure that I'm not dreaming. Fifteen select students and I are on our way to a prestigious medical advances symposium. As we board the bus, I'm surprised to notice that I'm not nervous. I'm not worried about what my students might do to the other passengers and not worried about them hurting me. My only concern is for the students I left behind with a substitute.

Seven years ago, I wouldn't have dared to dream of this day—back then I feared for my life daily and cried myself to sleep each night. That my students would be invited to such a symposium, that I would have students able to understand anything taught at such a symposium, and that I'd be free to go with them to such an event were then beyond my imagination. Yet, here I am, and all that is happening.

Jesus demonstrates the ultimate ability to wait. He came to earth, humbled himself by becoming that which he had helped to create, and then followed his impoverished life with an agonizing and humiliating death. Even as a man, with the needs and weaknesses of a human body, Jesus showed complete control. He was able to wait out a deadly hunger; he refused the devil's temptation and would not turn stone to bread. Jesus was able to persevere amid emotional, spiritual, and physical pain; he did not call the angels to attend to him or jump off the cross. He is now seated at the right hand of God and reigns in heaven. Jesus is fully aware of the hate and sin in this world that he came to save; yet, Jesus is able to wait just a little bit longer.

If I could have been sure about how my teaching life would evolve, perhaps my attitude would have been better from the start. My first year teaching in a challenging setting was depressing and the task ahead of me daunting. I didn't know that at least some of my students could be persuaded to learn and that many of my efforts would eventually be rewarded. I didn't know that I would obtain grants, find wise mentors, and benefit from my trials by fire. I never knew that my investment in these students would have me leading them to a medical symposium or that I would ever find fifteen qualified students to go. Perhaps there are blessings in your teaching future of which you dare not yet dream; maybe it's time to dream—and wait. If you find it difficult to wait, look to the master Teacher—the ultimate model in delayed gratification.

PRAYER: Jesus, show me the good that my work can produce. Please help me as I wait expectantly for the fruits of my labor. I trust you to teach me.

51
When Reality Sets In . . .

SUGGESTED SCRIPTURE READING: Isaiah 51:1-16

VERSE DU JOUR: *But my salvation will last forever, my righteousness will never fail.* (Isaiah 51:6)

Remember those college or graduate-level education classes? You were presented with the basics of teaching a new discipline or a new group of students, or you were trained in a new technique. You had visions of grandeur; you envisioned a clean classroom filled with eager, expectant faces. The fifteen or twenty students entrusted to your care were going to be ready to learn, and you were going to be different from any educator they had yet encountered. If a discipline problem ever were to develop, you would take the time to talk it out with the offender and would quickly resolve the issue while forming understanding and an emotional bond. You were ready to change the world, excited to influence lives and affect the future.

Then you got your first teaching assignment. Instead of fifteen kids per class, there were thirty-five. Your students seemed less than eager to learn, at least as evidenced by their apathetic attendance and derelict behavior. None of your students appeared to care about you or your Herculean teaching efforts. They weren't impressed by the breadth of your knowledge. To them, you were just like every other authority figure, so the discipline issues began. And you couldn't properly manage disciplining four kids at a time, since you were the only one in the classroom. You couldn't legally leave the rest of the students alone, so you never did have those healing and bonding conversations that were supposed to get to the bottom of their problems. Your life seemed to become a day to day game of survival. "One day at a time" became more than a recovery phrase; it was your mantra.

Life was not fair for Jesus either. The realities of sleeping on rock-hard ground and dying on a rough wooden cross were different from ruling the universe. Although he was the only fully righteous man ever to live, Jesus was treated as a criminal. Despite holding authority over the entire universe, Jesus lived a poor man's existence. People gave Jesus little respect, no earthly authority, few possessions, and no mercy. But grace is what Jesus came to bring us, and mercy is what he gives us day after day. God's grace says that we don't get what we *do* deserve—condemnation; instead, we get what we *don't* deserve—forgiveness and eternal life.

Remember that God alone is righteous. Until God's reign on earth becomes a reality, we live and work in an imperfect world. Don't become disheartened by the situations that you cannot change. Instead, concentrate on the situations you can change. I urge you to breathe deeply, get plenty of sleep, and pray for strength. God knows what we face and will be beside us each step of the way.

PRAYER: Lord, give me strength and comfort as I deal with the imperfections of my situation. Please give me insight to your righteousness and your grace. Let me rejoice in the expectation of your perfect kingdom.

52
Protected by Angels

SUGGESTED SCRIPTURE READING: Psalm 91:1-13

VERSE DU JOUR: *For he will command his angels concerning you to guard you in all your ways.* (Psalm 91:11)

"Get out NOW!" I yelled. "We need to talk in the hall." I'd had enough. This new student had come in the middle of the semester, only to disturb the dynamics of an already tenuous class atmosphere. I had just begun to gain nominal control over the street-hardened students of the class, but the new boy was already pulling them back into their old ways.

I exited the classroom and found my offender smirking and leaning lazily against the cement-block wall. I stood on tiptoe so that I could get in his face and let loose a torrent of accusations, instructions, and threats—in short, I read him the riot act. As I continued my rant, a quick shiver ran through me. What was it that I read in those narrowed eyes? Was it typical teenage impudence, haughty ignorance, or something more disturbing? "But," I thought, "this one can't be any different. I can't let him think that I am frightened or weak. He must not think that he's gotten the upper hand or it will be impossible to do my job." So I continued to rant and rave before I heard, "You can't tell me what to do. You're not my mother."

Jesus lived life on the edge. He spoke the truth even when it was not welcomed, ran with a rough crowd, and survived without the luxury of wealth. Jesus was brazen when challenged in religious circles and outspoken on matters regarding ethics and social equity. His message disturbed government and religious authorities. Yet Jesus continued to speak out—he seemed to have no fear for his own safety. Although his words infuriated powerful people, until his time would come, Jesus could not be stopped. In several instances, Jesus mentions God's heavenly angels; perhaps Jesus was capable of maintaining his composure despite living dangerously because he was aware of their presence and protection.

The afternoon after my talk with the new boy, a large man dressed in black filled my classroom doorway. "Mrs. Drake? May I have a word with you?" Alone in my room at the end of another long day, I hesitantly agreed. "I understand that you riled my parolee yesterday. I just want to share some information with you for your own protection. It would be best if you do whatever you can to avoid upsetting this young man. Other than attending school here, he is under house arrest. He is awaiting trial for the attempted murder of his mother. We found him on the run. His mother is barely hanging on; she sustained multiple stab wounds. We hope you keep this information to yourself, as it is confidential. Thank you." Then he was gone.

I felt a little dizzy, a lot stupid, and quite relieved I was not this boy's mother. There was no better time to call on the Lord for the protection of his angels. Sorry that I hadn't followed my gut, and angry that this information had been kept from me, there was not much else to do but pray. My survival—and yours—is testament to God's precious provision. Can you trust God and the angels to watch over you today?

PRAYER: Thank you, Sovereign God, for sending your angels to protect me today.

53
Tea Bags and Theology

SUGGESTED SCRIPTURE READING: Luke 7:36-50

VERSE DU JOUR: *"But wisdom is proved right by all her children."* (Luke 7:35)

My new vanilla hazelnut tea bags have amazing quotes on the little paper part that hangs off the tea-bag string. The latest one, which so haunted me during the night that I had to fish it out of the trash the next morning, contained a winner—a quote credited to Fred Rogers: "When we love a person, we accept him or her exactly as is, the lovely with the unlovely, the strong with the fearful, the true mixed in with the façade, and of course, the only way we can do it is by accepting ourselves that way." So the man who taught children to button their cardigans and tie their shoes had not only a gentle soul but also a deep understanding of theology.

Jesus lived a life of love; he fully accepted others and himself. Jesus overlooks the personality defect that makes me blurt out hurtful or bizarre statements when I am nervous. He thinks my thick thighs are cool, and my poor eyesight is of no concern. He sees my annoying habits and my personality quirks as things that make me special. Jesus accepts and loves me for who I am now. In addition, Jesus sees every one of his creations in the same light. The sinful woman who cries on his feet, Jesus sees as generous and loving. The man wildly shaking the branches of a tree while calling out to him through the crowd, Jesus sees as a potential friend. He even sees the man who would later betray him as a worthy disciple. The arrogance that I see in others, Jesus sees as the manifestation of underlying shyness. The pushiness that annoys me in others, he sees as a mask of inferiority. The rudeness that irks me to no end, he sees as the disguise of ignorance. Jesus hates my sin but loves me no matter what! He shows me mercy and grace every day of my life.

The part of Mr. Rogers's quote that so struck me was the part about accepting the true with the façade. I've heard dozens of times that if you love someone, you need to accept the good, the bad, and the ugly, blah blah blah . . . To accept someone else as he or she is can difficult enough. But to accept myself as I am, including pretenses, weaknesses, and insecurities, is even harder. And yet that is what Jesus does for me.

Perhaps, if I am to be like Jesus, I need to accept and love myself as I strive to accept and love others. Do you have a student who you need to see in a different light; is there someone who needs your acceptance and praise?

PRAYER: Jesus, help me to see beyond the outward appearance and the outward behaviors in others. Let me see them as you see them. Let me give someone else the benefit of a doubt, just as you constantly do for me! Please help me to love myself so that I can love others.

54

With the Spirit

SUGGESTED SCRIPTURE READING: Acts 1:1-11

VERSE DU JOUR: *"But you will receive power when the Holy Spirit comes on you; and you will be my witnesses in Jerusalem, and in all Judea and Samaria, and to the ends of the earth."* (Acts 1:8)

Although we had just finished a two-week unit on measurement, my freshman earth science class was filled with students who acted as though they'd never before seen a ruler. When the lab instructions required measurements in centimeters, they became agitated and confused. This behavior, combined with no fewer than seven interruptions since the start of class, a morning transportation fiasco, a minor yet distracting wardrobe malfunction, and an obvious case of nerves, seemed to spell certain calamity for my first teacher observation at Midway High School. I was so rattled by the time we started the lab prep that I forgot to do the little things that I usually perform with nary a thought: I forgot to write the lesson objectives on the board, forgot to turn off the ceiling light near the overhead projector, and failed to complete the required attendance report. "So much for an extended contract," I thought. "Perhaps next year I'll move on to greener pastures. The results of this observation are certain to be disastrous."

Jesus taught and modeled the importance of depending on a higher source for our daily needs. He also promised his followers the indwelling of a higher source of power, the presence of a Holy Spirit that gives direction and wisdom. Without the Spirit, you can do ordinary things—you can react reasonably with reasonable people. You can work hard and do a good enough job. Problems begin when the conditions that surround you or the people with whom you must work are not reasonable, when everything starts to fall apart, and nothing seems to work. Because all of us will encounter extraordinary or unreasonable situations, Christian teachers need more than a good degree and experience. To make a real difference and to do a landmark job for God's kingdom, we need the power of this indwelling Holy Spirit.

"Did you realize that those kids don't know the difference between an inch and a centimeter?" my administrator asked on his way out. After I explained the work we'd already done on the topic, he sighed and said, "You have a different kind of student than I had when I was in the classroom." And he left it at that.

Weeks later, I learned that although my observation wasn't perfect, it was infused with compliments and kudos for my ability and willingness to work with a challenged, remedial population. At that point I knew that the Spirit had guided my observer's perceptions and his pen. Why do I often forget to trust my most valuable and available resource? With the Spirit of God we can reach the unreceptive, collaborate with the uncooperative, and find reason even in the most unreasonable of circumstances. We cannot expect to do any of this alone but must rely upon the Spirit's supernatural power. Will you ask the Spirit to guide you and supply your needs today?

PRAYER: Dear God, I call on your power and your wisdom today.

55

Gratitude Training

SUGGESTED SCRIPTURE READING: Psalm 100

VERSE DU JOUR: *Enter his gates with thanksgiving and his courts with praise; give thanks to him and praise his name.* (Psalm 100:4)

The humidity and stifling heat fog my glasses as I enter the pool area. I've come to assuage a nagging curiosity; my student assistant is part of the swim team and seems inspired by the activity. I'm wondering what it's all about. Once my glasses clear, I see what I can of the swim team; water is churning behind the sleek, hard bodies that own this place.

I've promised Jordan that I will come to her next meet but realize that even in a practice session, these student athletes display great tenacity, endurance, persistence, and skill. These intense daily practices allow the athletes to hone their skills; efficient strokes and fast times do not come easily. Only through repetition of a given physical task does the action become second nature to the athlete. The muscles learn the action, and the repeated practice makes the skill an important part of the athlete's repertoire. A record-setting time is not a fluke but a reward for persistence and training.

Later, I ponder the lesson of the swimmers as I think about my desire to become a more thankful person. I want to have the thankful attitude of Jesus. Jesus taught the disciples the importance of a thankful heart; he did this by following the Old Testament model. I want the psychological and spiritual benefits of a thankful heart and figure that if I develop a natural sense of constant gratitude, I will be a more positive and less critical person. Maybe my mood would be better and I would have more fun. But, sad to say, true gratitude is often an afterthought rather than an inherent part of my persona. How do I manage to integrate a spirit of thanksgiving into who I am, and how do I make it second nature?

We might be able to become more thankful people if we imitated those student swimmers by using repetition and practice. If athletes, students, artists, and musicians can practice and repeat skills until those skills become second nature, perhaps a behavior of thankfulness can also be learned through repetition. Eventually the attitude of thankfulness will follow the practiced behavior and will become part of us. One good way to start on the road toward a thankful heart is to start each day reading or reciting Psalm 100, shown in our prayer below. Why not try it out today?

PRAYER:
Shout for joy to the LORD, all the earth.
Worship the LORD with gladness;
come before him with joyful songs.
Know that the LORD is God.
It is he who made us, and we are his;
we are his people, the sheep of his pasture.

Enter his gates with thanksgiving
and his courts with praise;
give thanks to him and praise his name.
For the LORD is good and his love endures forever;
his faithfulness continues through all generations. (Psalm 100)

56

Affirmation

SUGGESTED SCRIPTURE READING: Proverbs 25:9-15

VERSE DU JOUR: *A word aptly spoken is like apples of gold in settings of silver.* (Proverbs 25:11)

I soon learned that the letters O-D-Y-S-S-E-Y spelled trouble. During my first year teaching in a new high school, I was given the dubious honor of being assigned to the Odyssey program, a pilot program for at-risk and challenged students. When I first met the group, I was intimidated and more than a little frightened—a more motley group you couldn't have imagined. And that was just the teachers!

Joking aside, the Odyssey class was a combination of twenty kids who had been identified as the most likely to drop out of school for reasons related to long-term discipline issues, psychological illness, abuse concerns, attention deficits, and learning problems. It didn't take too long into our first class together to learn that they disliked all teachers. Not only did I experience this generic dislike, but also the Odyssey girls reserved a special loathing for me. As time tends to do, even with the Odyssey group still in my charge, four years passed quickly. The day before Christmas break, several of the original Odyssey girls approached my desk with white envelopes. Inside those envelopes were notes and cards, holiday wishes, and many kind words of affirmation.

Jesus was a master of affirmation. He didn't use empty flattery but spoke the truth and pointed out to others their strengths. Jesus helped others see their value and, no doubt, left a wake of love in his path. Think how Peter felt when Jesus explained that he would be called Peter because he was a rock. Imagine Peter's new self-image and the thoughts that ran through his head: "The Master gave me this new name because he thinks that I am a rock! He thinks I'm a solid kind of guy!" Jesus affirmed the righteousness of Mary when she poured out expensive perfume on his feet. He defended her action to the judgmental men who argued that she was wasting money. The Scriptures also include the statement: "Jesus loved Martha and her sister and Lazarus. Yet when he heard that Lazarus was sick, he stayed where he was two more days." The writer wouldn't have known of Jesus' feelings unless Jesus made his feelings obvious.

The messages from those Odyssey girls got me through many a tough time. When I wanted to give up teaching, I would look at those letters and quickly feel a change of heart. Their affirming words confirmed my direction and renewed my vision. Likewise, our words of affirmation can spread light and love to others. How many children look for love in all the wrong places simply because they crave affirmation? It takes courage to express our feelings to others, and it is risky business. But the rewards that follow affirming words may be worth the risk. Are you willing to affirm at least one student?

PRAYER: Let me share your love, Jesus, by sincerely affirming someone today.

57

Life in the Fast Lane

SUGGESTED SCRIPTURE READING: John 8:54-9:12

VERSE DU JOUR: *He replied, "The man they call Jesus made some mud and put it on my eyes. He told me to go to Siloam and wash. So I went and washed, and then I could see."* (John 9:11)

"I don't have time for this," I mutter as I walk yet another required form down to the office. The tart taste in my mouth reminds me that I've already made a mistake: I had dumped my powdered ice tea mix into the Erlenmeyer flask and the ascorbic acid into my tea cup. The tartness that greeted my taste buds alerted me to the nontoxic switch that would've wrecked today's lab exercise . . .

I live so much of my life in a hurry. At home, my morning more resembles a frantic race than a focused ritual. And the insane pace doesn't stop once I get to school. Instead, the pace quickens; there is always so much to do. I strive to check off my to-do list before the day winds down—I even started writing my to-do list with fruit-scented markers, just to make the process more interesting. I know that a good amount of the time, I look like a lunatic and probably sound like one, too.

The Scriptures describe for us a Jesus who is very unlike me. He was a calm, unhurried, and in-control kind of guy, who despite having a busy schedule and important responsibilities exuded an amazing coolness. Jesus had plenty of reasons to be hurried and frantic: loads of people to teach, a bunch of prophecies to fulfill, a crowd on his tail, disciples to feed, and a hectic travel schedule. Jesus didn't have a minute to waste, but look at his reaction to stress. In the Gospel of John, Jesus has just ticked off a bunch of Jewish leaders. They pick up stones and start to throw the stones at him, not exactly a warm and fuzzy reaction to his preaching. Jesus slips away from the temple grounds and his tormentors. As Jesus is retreating, he sees a blind man. His disciples begin to ask theological questions regarding the blind man's condition. Jesus doesn't blow off their questions by saying, "Hey, guys, I'm a little busy here. Did you notice that we're on the run here from a bunch of rock-wielding zealots?" Instead, Jesus patiently answers their questions and stops to heal the blind man. And he heals with creativity and panache, mixing his own saliva with dirt to make mud and smearing it on the blind man's eyes. This method was a bit more time-consuming than Jesus simply saying, "Be healed, blind man," yet it addressed other issues. Jesus gave his time and his touch to complete a miraculous healing, and there remained no doubt as to the Lord's healing touch.

Can you imagine Jesus ever muttering, "I don't have time for this"? I doubt that at day's end Jesus calculated his miles per hour and distance traveled, lamenting the time wasted on a silly blind man. More likely, the event was the highlight of his day. What will be your highlight today?

PRAYER: Let me slow down and leave my hurries and my worries to you.

58

Lost and Found

SUGGESTED SCRIPTURE READING: Matthew 18:10-14

VERSE DU JOUR: *"For the Son of Man came to seek and save what was lost."* (Luke 19:10)

Did you ever lose something that you couldn't seem to find, no matter how long or hard you looked? It might be a misplaced lesson plan, a book that you loaned out that was never returned, jewelry, car keys, your driver's license, or your bank card. My current loss involves a wallet. My entire life seems to be housed in the wallet that is gone, gone, gone! I've searched every junk drawer, my car, my desk, every purse I own, and even the bottoms of dark, messy closets. To replace and report everything in that wallet will cost me at least a day, an expense I can't afford. Hopeful that some miscreant isn't charging a Corvette and fuel to my various credit and gas cards, I am fatigued from my search and sick with worry.

Jesus came to save the wandering and find the lost. He did not come to earth to catch us in our sins or to punish us. Instead, the Scriptures portray Jesus' visit to earth as a rescue mission to save his friends. Jesus' words describe this mission: "For the Son of Man came to seek and save what was lost." In Matthew 9:12-13, we read, "It is not the healthy who need a doctor, but the sick. But go and learn what this means: 'I desire mercy, not sacrifice.' For I have not come to call the righteous, but sinners." Jesus taught using parables of the lost sheep, the lost coin, and the lost son. His use of these stories demonstrates an understanding of loss. Jesus knows what it is like to lose something precious; he continually feels the painful loss of every single soul ignoring his voice.

My husband just called from Washington, D.C., to tell me that he has my wallet. Somehow it ended up in his car; what a relief! Something precious to me has been found, and my heart is filled with relief and rejoicing.

If I get so excited about a retrieved wallet, imagine the relief and joy God experiences when a lost soul returns to the fold. You may not know when a student becomes redeemed or be aware of your role in their decision. But you can be assured that such news leads all of heaven to great rejoicing. You can help lead the lost to God—to return even one of those Jesus came to save. Today, can you love someone into the kingdom?

PRAYER: Let me show your love to the lost and gently lead them back to you.

59
Rich Attitude

SUGGESTED SCRIPTURE READING: 1 Timothy 6:6-12

VERSE DU JOUR: *Do you want to be truly rich? You already are if you are happy and good.* (1 Timothy 6:6, TLB)

While I was growing up, my mom was a teacher and my dad was a graduate student. During that relatively lean time, they both had me convinced that I was one of the richest kids around. Imagine my surprise when I discovered that we were far from upper class! I still vividly remember the morning that my mom asked God to supply some protein for our evening meal. She appeared strangely unsurprised when a bird flew from the roadside, making a kamikaze dive into the windshield of our old Studebaker. Mom stopped the car and regally picked the quail off our windshield. She came back into the car with the quail and a curious smile. "Here's the meat we asked for," she laughed. My mom defeathered and cooked the tiny yet tasty bird. She presented our pheasant under a glass dome that was usually reserved for the butter stick. The helpings per person were small that night, but we didn't suffer any for it, and I knew God had heard us and that we were very blessed.

One of the songs I heard constantly throughout my childhood (Dad had a guitar and a fine voice) communicated the attitude that permeated our household. The song ended with the line, "Other folks may think I'm poor, but I know that's not so, for when I count my blessings, I'm the richest man I know."

Our happiness can so often be dictated by the attitude that we choose to adopt. The Scriptures remind us that happiness and goodness are the ultimate riches. Why do I get depressed about finances or the material possessions I think I deserve, when in reality I have so much?

What a gift my dad gave me by singing that song! My dad still occasionally sings that song, and you can still hear such gratitude in his voice. Dad can't believe how much God has given him. The Lord has made us the richest in all of his creation. Let's enjoy his goodness. Will you choose an attitude of gratitude?

PRAYER: Today I choose to enjoy the fullness of your goodness. Thank you, thank you, Lord above!

60
Students of the Hour

SUGGESTED SCRIPTURE READING: Philippians 2:5-18

VERSE DU JOUR: *Do everything without complaining or arguing.* (Philippians 2:14)

Blood was splattered and smeared in all directions on the floor, on overturned chairs, and on desktops. It wasn't until I could take my focus from the blood that I noticed a large group of boys surrounding Carson and another crowd holding back David in the hallway. The male students of my fifth-hour class, which had not yet officially begun, had miraculously and maturely separated the two who were the source of this mess.

Before I could get to a phone to call for clean-up assistance, I saw Jerome, a nearly seven-foot-tall student, hunched over cleaning up an area of splattered blood. "Stop! You can't clean that,"

I yelled, shocking Jerome and the others who had joined him to help. "I won't risk you contracting AIDS or something else. I'll call for a janitor to bring solvent."

In Paul's letter to the Corinthians, we are told to emulate the attitude of Christ. We are told to aspire to obedience, humility, and a positive nature. Paul goes on to say that if we are like Christ, blameless and pure, we will abstain from complaining and arguing. We might interpret Paul's teachings to mean that Christians should not complain or argue against God or against other people.

Sometimes our surroundings are such that we feel compelled to complain; perhaps we even feel justified in our whining. "This place is out of control. I can't stand the students, the administration . . . I deserve better" have been thoughts that I am embarrassed to confess have entered my thoughts and prayers. How dare I! And still I claim that I want to be like Jesus?

What was so striking about the bloodbath was not so much the bloody mess, which I later learned was the consequence of a well-directed punch that broke David's nose. More striking was the reaction of my students. They had been helpful and proactive, first separating the fighting boys instead of cheering the fighters and then attempting to clean up for me. They had been supportive and sympathetic; one particularly sweet young woman kept looking at me with concern and shaking her head in disbelief. They had been cooperative, taking the scheduled test despite the bloody surroundings and the consequent overwhelming fumes from the cleaning solvent. And not one of them complained or argued with me about anything. Instead, every remaining student was more accommodating than I'd ever witnessed. It was almost as if the event had somehow drawn us closer together; as if we, teacher and students, were on the same team. The students had risen above the conditions in which they'd been placed, and other than the two fighters, the students of hour five made me enormously proud. Can you, too, rise above the conditions in which you are placed; can you make Jesus proud?

PRAYER: Lord, let me be grateful when my students rise above my expectations. Let me live blamelessly for you.

Winter Term

Over the Midyear Hump

61

Knowing the Creator

SUGGESTED SCRIPTURE READING: John 1:1-11

VERSE DU JOUR: *Through him all things were made; without him nothing was made that has been made.* (John 1:3)

"How exactly was the universe created?" Eduardo abruptly asks. "Where did the first human cell come from?" Keisha inquires.

As a teacher of science, there are so many things that I would like to understand. Sometimes I don't know the answers to questions students pose and offer extra credit to any student who can find the answer first. Yet, many times a student's question has to be honestly answered with "Nobody knows yet," or "Scientists are still working on that one."

The biblical account of creation credits God with formation of everything. Both Genesis 1 and the words of John's Gospel explain that Jesus was the God of creation. Can you imagine that the God who designed all living things on earth purposely became one of those creations? Jesus left the glory of heaven and entered a world filled with evil. Jesus came to earth so that he could show us what God is like. Jesus' direct encounter with humanity was not all pleasant, and he was misunderstood by even the people who should have understood him. Yet Jesus' mission was a success. He conquered death and sin. And now Jesus intercedes with God on our behalf.

Imagine your first visit to the throne of God. The light is so bright that you can barely open your eyes; the throne itself so immense that you can see only a small part of it at one time. Your new eyes finally adjust, and you spot a human figure; it's the Master, Jesus. He looks down at you and smiles, saying, "Welcome. We have a lot to talk about." Then it hits you. "I know God! I know the Creator and Ruler of the universe, the One who made the heavens and the earth, the One who designed my eyes and ears. This is my friend, Jesus. And he knows me."

Jesus, the Creator, will answer the unanswerable questions your students asked. He will be willing and able to teach on any topic for eternity. Take heart; you don't have to have all the answers all the time. There is One who does, and we can know him.

PRAYER: Jesus, let me remember that some day I will see you, and you will be my forever teacher. O Lord, please start early and teach me now.

62

Foolish Interruptions

SUGGESTED SCRIPTURE READING: Luke 8:22-25

VERSE DU JOUR: *"Be still, and know that I am God; I will be exalted among the nations, I will be exalted in the earth."* (Psalm 46:10)

The "professor" tore into my classroom. In less than ten seconds, he had my class enthralled. Clad in a purple, feathered hat, a long, white lab coat, and heavy, black-plastic-framed glasses, he carried on about spontaneous generation. His thick Italian accent was almost laughable, and when viewed together, his nose, glasses, and furry eyebrows gave him a comic look. The students watched with wide eyes and listened to every word from this stranger. At least this was one interruption from which my students might actually learn something.

Sometimes even annoying interruptions can be used for good. Jesus was a skillful teacher who used what others meant as distractions to reach his audience. Jesus also modeled the importance of allowing ourselves to be interrupted by people. In the parable of the good Samaritan, Jesus reminded us that people matter more than our schedules or our convenience. But when things or surroundings posed a risk to his task of reaching others, Jesus had a low tolerance and a high activity level.

Consider the one recorded instance in which Jesus was intolerant of interruption. Take a moment to picture it: Jesus was exhausted and needed some rest. He trusted his friends to take care of the sailing. But soon after Jesus lay down, the sea and the wind threatened to sink the boat. His friends, frantic with fear, wake him and ask for help. Rather than being angry with his circumstances or the guys who woke him, Jesus took action. He stilled the raging forces of nature, told his buddies to relax, and then went back to sleep. In stopping the storm, Jesus not only demonstrated his power over creation but also took action against foolish interruptions.

The professor who interrupted my class that day was none other than Professor Drakeroni—just me, dressed up and carrying on. When the professor left and I returned, most of my students were onto me but nonetheless appreciated my nontraditional approach. Rather than fighting the seemingly endless array of daily interruptions, I purposely became one. And blessedly, it worked.

I have never had the ability to stop a thunderstorm, and sometimes I can't even calm the storm of craziness in my own classroom, but there are some situations where I can influence change. The friend in need of help, the student who needs extra attention, or the colleague who wants to meet at lunch might be opportunities in the form of interruptions. God knows how tough interruptions can be. We can either use them or lose them. Can you trust God to help you recognize the foolish interruptions from those that are God-guided?

PRAYER: You are God, and I am not. Teach me what I can and cannot change and help me to use all that looks bad for good.

63

By Design

SUGGESTED READING: Luke 2:21-24, 39-40

VERSE DU JOUR: *And the child grew and became strong; he was filled with wisdom, and the grace of God was upon him.* (Luke 2:40)

I had been with the vice principal, interviewing for the science teaching job; it seemed that we had finished the formal interview, yet we had been chatting for another twenty minutes or so when the principal peeked in. When my interviewer noticed the presence of his superior, he decided to introduce me: "Sir, this is Ms. Drake. She has a degree in biology *and* a degree in psychology." He then nonchalantly mentioned, "Your psych experience might come in handy here." At that point, perhaps I should've run quickly away and never looked back.

The parents of Jesus raised him carefully. In addition to feeding, clothing, teaching, and protecting the child, they completed for him all requirements of the Jewish law. They had Jesus circumcised on the proper day, took him to the temple to be consecrated, and offered the prescribed sacrifice. They knew Jesus was the promised Messiah, yet they did not feel he was above God's law. Today's Scripture passage mentions that after Mary and Joseph had done everything required by God's law, they returned home, and the child "grew and became strong." The passage does not explain how long it took for the child to become strong, nor does it indicate if his strength was purely intellectual or if it included physical strength. The Scriptures do mention that Jesus trained with Joseph as a carpenter's apprentice and document numerous instances of Jesus traveling long distances in the premodern world. These details support the idea that Jesus had grown strong in mind and body. He wouldn't back down when challenged on issues of righteousness, and he fearlessly defended the weak, the unpopular, and the needy. There was no time or situation wasted in preparing Jesus for his mission.

Can you identify ways your travels, relationships, education, or experiences might have prepared you for the role in which you serve? I know that my interviewer was right; my psychological training and clinical experience did come in handy in my new position. Some of it was downright necessary. God has designed us and directed our lives in a way that has uniquely prepared each of us to fulfill our destinies.

Mary and Joseph spent a good portion of their lives preparing, strengthening, protecting, and teaching Jesus so that he could go on to save the world. Your classroom contains children born with unique missions and purposes for their lives. How many of them can you influence positively? You can use your unique training and preparation to help make your students strong and fit so that they, too, might complete the missions for which they've been designed.

PRAYER: Thank you for preparing me for this job. Help me pass my training and preparation to my students. Let me see you in my students today.

64
No Committee Needed: Every Knee Will Bow!

SUGGESTED SCRIPTURE READING: Psalm 86

VERSE DU JOUR: *For you are great and do marvelous deeds; you alone are God.* (Psalm 86:10)

Today I met with our high school vice principal to address the issue of classroom interruptions. Multiple and continuous interruptions during class time had become such an annoyance to so many teachers that it was time to go to a higher power. Apparently I didn't go high enough. When I asked him if anyone else was concerned about this issue, he looked at me quizzically and without hesitation said, "Do you really think that classroom interruptions are a problem? We need to form a committee to work on this." Fearing that I might be appointed committee chairperson (all we need is another committee!), I quickly excused myself, mumbling something about getting back to him soon.

While on this earth, Jesus, the one to whom all those knees will bow, studied the Scriptures. He knew the Old Testament, including the Psalms. But despite his biblical knowledge and his divinity, Jesus was surrounded by arrogance, deceit, selfish ambition, rude comments, barbaric behavior, and personal insults. He saw firsthand the consequences wrought by a sin-filled world. The pain that Jesus witnessed in others saddened him. Don't you think that Jesus used King David's passages to encourage himself? Jesus might have looked to this very passage from the Psalms when he was grieved by this world and in need of refocusing.

The world and its imperfections weigh on us. You have your own concerns, but you are burdened by the problems of your students, too. Many people are so arrogant and self-absorbed that they think they need no one else. But wise Christian teachers know they are essentially helpless and needy; they know that they must rely on a force stronger than themselves. The knowledge of God's bountiful love and the ability to call on the Lord are huge privileges. We serve a mighty, honorable, great, and fearsome God. Someday soon, every knee will bow to our God, and everyone will confess that Jesus is Lord. No committees will be needed as there will be no question about which direction to kneel.

Prayer:
    Teach me your way, O LORD,
        and I will walk in your truth;
    give me an undivided heart,
        that I may fear your name. (Psalm 86:11)

65

Bread of Life

SUGGESTED SCRIPTURE READING: John 6:25-40

VERSE DU JOUR: *Then Jesus declared, "I am the bread of life. He who comes to me will never go hungry, and he who believes in me will never be thirsty."* (John 6:35)

"The stupid rat ate my lunch!" I wailed on the phone to my mother. And "rat" was not a figure of speech but a rodent—a large, well-fed, indigenous beast. In a hurry that morning, I'd thoughtlessly dropped my lunch on the floor under my desk. I had forgotten about putting it there until the lunch hour, that is, twenty-five minutes. When the allotted time to consume our mid-morning lunch arrived, I found a tattered brown paper bag, a half-eaten sandwich, and a lonely apple core. Only my diet cola remained undisturbed. The nerve of that beast! It had to be Rat—who or what else would leave those remains behind? "A human thief would have taken the soda," I reasoned. Perhaps Rat was smarter than people. Since I had planned on brown bagging, I had no money. I borrowed some cash and hustled to the cafeteria for a replacement lunch.

No one understands the needs of the human body better than does Jesus. As Creator, he designed our bodies to require food. In human form, he deprived himself of sustenance, and as Messiah, Jesus miraculously multiplied it. Jesus so intimately understands our need for food and our preoccupation with it that he used the analogy of bread to explain himself. "I am the bread of life. He who comes to me will never go hungry, and he who believes in me will never be thirsty," Jesus said after the miraculous feeding of five thousand people. Jesus recognized that these seekers were impressed by his way with food.

We know this because Jesus says, "I tell you the truth, you are looking for me, not because you saw miraculous signs, but because you ate the loaves and had your fill" (John 6:26). Yet, Jesus honored these men, offering them a taste of the bread of life. Jesus extends to us that same offer. Although my body repeatedly hungers for food, I'm thankful that Jesus has delivered some of that bread to my soul, the bread of life from a Savior who satisfies.

"You shouldn't have let him out of his cage, Susan," Mom advised between my sobs of self-pity. "He wasn't in a cage, Mom. He's a house rat who runs wild," I cried. Any human who knows me quickly learns that it is a bad idea to interfere with my feedings; a meal skipped spells disaster for those caught in my hungry path. But Rat didn't know that and must have been shocked when he made his usual fifth-period appearance. Screeching loudly, I chased him. The students sat shocked as I gave chase and laughed hysterically when Rat ran freakishly fast into his escape hole. Years later, Mom confessed that she suspected that I'd made up the story to gain a little sympathy. She should've known better; when it comes to food, I never fool around.

PRAYER: Thank you for filling my soul, for supplying my physical and my spiritual needs. Help me guard those blessings from the "rats" in my life.

66

Riley's View of Time

SUGGESTED SCRIPTURE READING: Job 38

VERSE DU JOUR: *"Where were you when I laid the earth's foundation? Tell me, if you understand."* (Job 38:4)

I stop briefly to tie my daughter's shoe. It's not quite Thanksgiving, and the mall is already decorated with lights and Christmas trees. What a backdrop in which to discuss the ever-looming question of Santa's existence. I want neither to lie to my trusting daughter nor to prematurely steal the joy of childhood Christmas, so I divert the question she's asked me back to her. I say, "Do *you* think

Santa is real?" When she responds in the affirmative, I challenge her belief by asking, "Why do you think Santa is real?" She answers confidently, saying, "You know how on Christmas morning, kids wake up and they have all kinds of presents that Santa brought? Well, the parents put their kids to bed the night before, and after the kids fall asleep the parents couldn't possibly have enough time to go to all the stores to get that many presents. And besides, the parents can't leave their kids alone at home during the night. They're not supposed to do that."

Although Jesus for a time lived under its human constraints, he always had God's perspective of time. God's view of time and its continuum is so different from our view. Hebrews 1:1-2 verifies Jesus' divinity: "In the past God spoke to our forefathers through the prophets at many times and in various ways, but in these last days he has spoken to us by his Son, whom he appointed heir of all things, and through whom he made the universe." Later, in Hebrews 13:8, we read that "Jesus Christ is the same yesterday and today and forever." As God, Jesus lives outside the rules of time. His perspectives on time and death are so far removed from mine that I struggle to comprehend his power and viewpoint. Jesus sees the past, the present, and the future all at one time, but my perspective is limited

What a unique way to look at this dilemma. It never occurred to my five-year-old that I might have been buying presents before Christmas Eve and storing them away in the attic or that her parents might have planned ahead. I was almost ready to explain these things when I was hit with the simplicity of her answers and her faith.

Like a child, I can't possibly comprehend the power, planning, and time frame that God sees. He's been stashing presents up in the attic, and I am unaware. God never has to leave me at night, or any other time, for that matter, to take care of business. The parent-child relationship I have with God is so similar to the parent-child relationship I have with my children, yet on a higher and eternal level. Can you stand amazed at the wonder of God's all-knowing and timeless power, looking forward to the plans and the gifts that are being stored up for you?

PRAYER: My time feels so limited, and it goes by so quickly. Let me rest in the knowledge that you control time; it does not control you. Please help me properly manage time as I wait for you.

67
Chosen Ones

SUGGESTED SCRIPTURE READING: Jeremiah 1:1-10

VERSE DU JOUR: *"Before I formed you in the womb I knew you, before you were born I set you apart; I appointed you as a prophet to the nations."* (Jeremiah 1:5)

Every time I introduce a controversial topic, I'm nervous. I don't want to offend my students, don't want to be accused of sounding overtly religious, and don't want to lead anyone astray. Oh, and I'd like to keep my job. So, I said a quick prayer before beginning the astronomy lesson entitled "Origins of the Universe." I carefully introduced the topic, explaining that I was about to teach a number of different theories that might explain a huge scientific puzzle. We also had to cover the concept of a theory before we could continue the lecture, which progressively morphed into a heated discussion. Who knew that freshmen had so many opinions and questions about the universe?

Jesus, through the indwelling of God's Spirit, had great wisdom and God's words to guide him through his life and ministry. We think of Jesus as so very different from us and often feel our service must pale in comparison with his. I knew I needed to guard and carefully measure my words that day; I surely needed God's help. But God promises us the same tools given to Jesus. God promises us the indwelling of the Holy Spirit. God also promises to put the words into our mouths if only we will believe and work. Some Bible translations replace the word *knew* with "chosen" in today's verse: "You have been chosen." My paraphrase of this verse reads: "Before I formed you in the womb, I chose you. Before you were born, I set you apart. I appointed you as a teacher to the many."

I'd given out a worksheet that day. The tenth question asked students to list some questions they might have about the universe. At the bottom of one young man's paper were the following words: "A question for you, Mrs. Drake—Do you believe in Jesus and God, and do you believe that Jesus is the only God?" I penned, "See me on this one."

Through a hand-out, José had opened a line of communication and had given me an invitation to share my faith. This sort of thing happens more than anyone might expect. On those days when you want to climb back into bed and forget about the hassles of teaching, consider the Josés who need you. Remember, you have been appointed by God to do this job; you were chosen before for this mission and will remain one of God's chosen long after your death. God not only chose you once but also continues to choose you. Day after long day, mistake after mistake, victory after victory, lesson after lesson, God continues to choose you to work and witness for the kingdom.

PRAYER: I am going out today to do your work and mine. Please touch my mouth and, as you promised, give me your words.

68
Taking the Bullet

SUGGESTED SCRIPTURE READING: Romans 5:1-11

VERSE DU JOUR: *But God demonstrates his own love for us in this: While we were still sinners, Christ died for us.* (Romans 5:8)

"I know you say you love her, but would you take a bullet for her?" the fifteen-year-old male student candidly asked his friend. A good question! After eavesdropping on this novel approach to defining true love, I began to think about my relationships. There aren't too many people, save for perhaps my children, for whom I would willingly take a bullet. But isn't this approach a good test of true love? If you truly love someone, you would willingly offer that person your protection and ultimate sacrifice, even without being asked to do so? I've heard it said that a good person will help you when asked but only a true friend will help without being asked. Asking someone to die for you becomes quite another ball of wax.

Yet that is exactly what Jesus has done for us. Before we even thought to ask for help, Jesus took the bullet for us. The explanation for this unreasonable sacrifice? God's love, pure and simple. In Romans, the apostle Paul says, "Very rarely will anyone die for a righteous man, though for a good man someone might possibly dare to die" (Romans 5:7). This observation is no exaggeration. How many people have sacrificed their lives for a good person or even a holy person? God's grace and love are not tied to our worthiness; the gift of salvation is not linked to our goodness, our righteousness, or even our sin quotient. Instead, God demonstrates his love through outrageous gifts of sacrifice.

I didn't hear the response offered to the question about love that day. But imagine that a positive response might lead to required action. Can you picture the scene: A young man dives, without hesitation, in front of a gun's fire to protect his lover. As he falls to the ground, she is safe but confused; the attacker flees as she falls to her knees. It isn't until she hears the rasp of his last breath and sees the blood pooling on the sidewalk that she suddenly understands the depth of her friend's love.

Jesus has already taken the bullet for you. He breathed his last breath with thoughts of you. He spilled the blood that covers you in righteousness, and his great love conquered even death. You have already been purchased with a love greater than the power of all the bullets in the world. Can you go about your day basking in the deep love of your Savior as you look for someone with whom to share it?

PRAYER: I'm so unworthy. Thank you for your deep love and your sacrifice. Let me share the love you have shown me with someone else today.

69

Bless the Children

SUGGESTED SCRIPTURE READING: Matthew 18:1-6

VERSE DU JOUR: *"And whoever welcomes a little child like this in my name welcomes me."* (Matthew 18:5)

The mucous covered my arms. There were blotches of chewed and spitty animal-cracker mush stuck to the front of my dress. I'd had my hair clipped up off my shoulders, since it had long ago become wet with drool. I'm sure my eyes had a wild and glassy look. I was ready to get out of there but must have looked a scary sight when my friend met me at the door of the one-year-olds' class.

It had been my turn to watch the children while my classmates went to Bible study class. How could there be fourteen children in one room with ten or so crying at the same time? Why did the mucous of a child who is not my own disgust me? The past five minutes seemed like the longest in my life. I needed ibuprofen. I wondered if my dress would shrink in *very* hot water. I asked myself, "Where are these mothers anyway, and which baby smells so funky? How could any child cry for two solid hours?"

Jesus uses children not only to illustrate faith but also to demonstrate pure love. He promises that little children are his representatives. In Matthew 18:6, Jesus emphasizes that it is these little ones who are so important. So, it must be very young children who are special in God's eyes. In the biblical account, there is no record of Jesus shying away from child spit and no record of him washing up to his elbows with soapy warm water after the encounter with the children on his lap. But his command to receive the children and lead them in the right direction is clear.

I now feel great thankfulness to those teachers who have spent any time watching my kids and am grateful for the preschool and grade-school teachers who watched and mentored me. Those many selfless teachers who lovingly work with little children show the pure compassion and acceptance of their God. They overcome

mucous, tears, and bacteria to emerge as Jesus' blessed servan
Jesus will honor them all in the world to come. Not only are they
dealing with those whom Jesus loves, but also they are working
for and with Jesus. Whether you are teaching God's small ones or
his bigger ones, take heart; you are working for the One who has
already overcome.

PRAYER: Thank you for loving me as if I were a little child. Help
me to love your children as Jesus loves them.

70
Good Company

SUGGESTED SCRIPTURE READING: Isaiah 53

VERSE DU JOUR: *He was despised and rejected by others, a man
of suffering and acquainted with infirmity; and as one from
whom others hide their faces he was despised, and we held him
of no account.* (Isaiah 53:3, NRSV)

Today at lunch, the science department unofficially debated the
hat issue. Our administrators have decided to ban hats in the
building, yet the students are fighting for their right to express
themselves. The teachers are also split on the issue. Some have
more pressing concerns, while others strongly oppose hats; they
argue that gangs use hats to identify their members, so the presence of a hat might trigger violence or compromise safety. "And
why," they point out, "when we are supposed to be preparing our
young charges for the real world, should we allow behavior that
would not be welcomed in the workplace?"

Our intraoffice debate lost some steam when our informed
and esteemed colleague, Lonnie, quoted a newly released statis-
tic: "Two to three years following graduation, fifty-one percent
of our student population were working at minimum wage jobs
or not working at all." Do you sometimes feel like you are bang-

ing your head against the wall? Are you trying to teach kids who reject your attempts to better their lives through education? Are you feeling unappreciated, maybe even ridiculed or despised? Take heart. You are in good company. Jesus experienced similar responses from the majority of the people he encountered. He had a motley crew of disciples who dropped everything to follow him and a few seekers who took his teachings to heart. But if you examine the grim statistics of Jesus' ministry, you might wonder how he so dramatically changed the world. What percentage of students obeyed his commands? How many spoke in his defense when he was sentenced to die compared with the number enthusiastically calling for his crucifixion? In general, people didn't want to hear his message and were reluctant to believe him. Jesus' life was an offering of love; the rejection he experienced must have been overwhelming.

So, take heart if your students don't want to hear about your subject matter, if they don't get it and don't care. You might be tired of fighting a battle against ignorance that your students don't even see. Jesus also taught people who didn't get it. The inhabitants of his town should have been his biggest fans, but they scoffed at him, and the crowds that sought his miracles were quick to turn on Jesus. The Creator of all was systematically rejected by those he came to free. May it help us to know that we are in good company with Jesus when we feel our efforts are in vain. And may we also know that with him, we can overcome every day (John 16:33).

PRAYER: Jesus, thank you for understanding my frustration. Please show me the few who hear my words and my teaching. Do not let me forget that by changing just one life, I can change the world.

71

Wanting Wisdom

SUGGESTED SCRIPTURE READING: 1 Kings 4:29-34

VERSE DU JOUR: *If any of you is lacking in wisdom, ask God, who gives to all generously and ungrudgingly, and it will be given to you.* (James 1:5, NRSV)

Kant once said, "Science is organized knowledge, and wisdom is organized life." I've been trying half of my life to get the science portion of that statement tackled, but the wisdom part looks like it will take a few more lifetimes. Oh, how I could use a little organization in my life and in my teaching.

Every year my mother would ask my younger brother, Georgie, "What do you want for Christmas?" And every year, from the time he was four or five years old, he would respond, "Wisdom. I want wisdom." Clearly, the Sunday-school flannel-graph story of King Solomon had made a lasting impression on Georgie. He'd learned that if you have wisdom, you have it all. Now, thirty or so years later, George still answers that question with the same response. It's become a family joke, but if you have to ask for something, asking for wisdom is a great idea. You don't have to take it back, it's never the wrong color, and it always fits.

When Jesus encountered people who asked him directly for godly things, he rarely refused them. Thomas asked Jesus to remove his doubt. It was a done deal. Peter asked to walk on water. Done! The centurion asked Jesus to heal his servant boy, and it was done before the man got home. Jesus indulged the desires of those who were seeking righteousness and healing and those who were truly searching after God's heart. We are to keep asking God for wisdom, and we are told in the Bible that if we need wisdom, we will get it.

The risk we take in asking for wisdom is that, in order to develop wisdom, we might be thrown into a situation requiring it. My mother always warned us to be careful what we prayed for because we might get it. We learned never to pray for patience, because you were sure to be put into a situation soon that would require its development.

Wanting wisdom is a good goal for teachers, despite the risk. I know that there is nothing I could use more than a good dose of godly wisdom (except wisdom *and* a good, long nap). When Solomon asked for wisdom, he got it and a whole lot more; he became a great teacher, too. God wants to give us wisdom, yet we are told to take the first step in acquiring wisdom. Like Solomon, we have to ask for wisdom. God instructs us to make this one request. Not only that, but God promises to grant the request if we only ask. Are you up to it? Will you ask for wisdom from the Creator of the ages?

PRAYER: God, please give me wisdom today. I know I am going to need it! I thank you ahead of time, because I know that you honor your promises.

72

A Cheerful Giver

SUGGESTED SCRIPTURE READING: 2 Corinthians 9:6-15

VERSE DU JOUR: *Each of you must give as you have made up your mind, not reluctantly or under compulsion, for God loves a cheerful giver.* (2 Corinthians 9:7, NRSV)

Rudy was intelligent, with a quick wit and the appearance of a thug. He couldn't be bothered with anything that might waste his time, and he marched to the beat of a different drummer. Maybe that's why I liked him.

"Did I ever tell Rudy that I love strawberries?" I wondered as I admired the beautiful Christmas wreath that my at-risk group, the Odyssey class, had presented to me the last day before winter break. It was a gorgeous thing; made entirely of hard candies, all strawberry flavored, each one carefully tied individually with string to the wreath frame.

As I packed the wreath into the back of my car, I noticed my colleague, who was also part of the Odyssey teaching team, packing up her vehicle. "Did you notice how excited Rudy was to give you that wreath?" she called. "He spent hours tying those candies on for you—and he insisted that the wreath he was making would go to you. He was so happy making that thing; one night he was working on it until after dark. He just wouldn't give up."

While on this dusty old earth, Jesus willingly and sacrificially gave of himself. He did it without grumbling and without second thoughts. He gave up his heavenly throne, his unquestioned authority, and the hope of physical comforts and earthly wealth. Jesus then gave tirelessly of himself, down to shedding tears in compassion for those he loved. Jesus generously gave people his time, energy, and love; he willingly performed the tedious jobs and the front-page miracle cures. In short, Jesus was a cheerful giver, and he wants us to be cheerful givers, too. It is not just the giving of our money; it is the giving of our time, talents, and lives that pleases God.

The precious wreath was comprised of more than it appeared. It was made of candy but also of time. When I thought back to the look on Rudy's face as he presented that wreath, I can't say that I'd ever seen him look happier. He was so excited about giving me that wreath that while creating it, he was willing to endure that which he loathed—tedium. He hated to be bored, yet he sat for hours tying tiny strings in knots.

The gifts of our time, our talents, and our intellects are precious offerings to God when we give them cheerfully and without reluctance. Let us not tire of giving ourselves for others. God honors the cheerful giver. God will take our money but doesn't need it. God will take our lives but doesn't need those either. However, God can use our time, our talents, and our intellects for good. And our spirits will rejoice when we please our Lord.

PRAYER: God, I have given you my life. Take my time, my talents, and my intellect, and use them for your glory. I want to please you and make you smile today.

73
God with Skin

SUGGESTED SCRIPTURE READING: John 14:5-11

VERSE DU JOUR: *"Believe me when I say that I am in the Father and the Father is in me; or at least believe on the evidence of the miracles themselves."* (John 14:11)

"God cares about you and will protect you. God will never leave you and will always be by your side, no matter where you are," I reminded Kimmy. "He has an army of angels protecting you even now. Please don't doubt," I pleaded to this sophomore believer who had already experienced a frightening and unnerving day. She had endured verbal harassment en route to school and a stabbing incident between two boys from rival gangs that occurred in her band classroom. She was fearful for her safety, didn't know how she would make it through the day, and by only ten in the morning had sought me out for consolation.

"I am the way and the truth and the life. . . . If you really knew me, you would know my Father as well," Jesus taught (John 14:6-7). By these words, Jesus proclaimed himself to be one with God. If Jesus is God, you must wonder why he would spend so much time, energy, and pain on experiencing what it is to be human. God willing went to a grungy manger, in a dusty country, during a volatile time. He chose a teen for a mother and lived an itinerant life of poverty and service. God came to earth to die a painful and humiliating death. This resume does not include activities worthy of any ruler, let alone the King of the universe! Perhaps God knew that we are too limited to grasp the concepts of divine power, love, and kingdom unless we have a human teacher to whom we can relate. Jesus was that teacher—the way by which we can experience God with skin.

"I need a hug," Kimmy sniffled, her eyes wide as saucers. Knowing that physical contact with students is forbidden, yet unable to deny this pathetic request, I complied. A tight bear hug and a few back pats later, I heard the rest of the story. Kimmy's anxiety was worsening, and she came to me before heading home. "Do you believe God's promises? Do you think that God cares enough about you to protect you?" I asked. "Yes, I do believe, but right now I need comfort from a warm body, someone with skin," she replied.

God has sent us, as Christian teachers, into the world as ambassadors. We now are the representatives of God's kingdom. Just as our students sometimes need someone with skin, we also need a God to whom we can relate. How amazing that God sent us Jesus in the flesh, a real incarnation of the holy One.

PRAYER: Thank you, God, for coming to me in a way that I can understand. Thanks for coming clothed in human skin. Please go with me as I go out into a hurting world.

74
God and Santa Claus

SUGGESTED SCRIPTURE READING: Matthew 7:9-11

VERSE DU JOUR: *"Do not be like them, for your Father knows what you need before you ask him."* (Matthew 6:8)

A trip to a wholesale store in the second week of December was not the smartest move I'd made this week. I'd spent way too much money and was worn out by dragging all my purchases into the house from the car. So, I was hardly receptive to my five-year-old son's reaction when I showed him a present that I'd bought for a friend's upcoming December birthday. Looking at the Bionicles complete book set, Wolfie immediately burst into tears. "That's what *I* want for Christmas!" he cried. "That's the problem with Santa. He always gives me good things that I end up liking later, but he never gives me the stuff I ask for and the stuff I really want."

Jesus taught us, in so many words, that God is not Santa Claus. He tells us that God hears our prayers and requests, but it is not God's priority to grant our every wish. Instead, God gives us what is good for us. Jesus told us that God is a wise parent who knows what we need. And God knows what we want even better than we ourselves know.

God is not a Scrooge, holding back blessings from us, but has carefully planned a way to protect us, to provide for us, and to accomplish a good work in us. Yet, our reaction to our God's generosity often is not too different from Wolfie's response. We wonder why we don't get exactly what we asked for. We wonder why God doesn't give us the stuff we really want. We become angry when we don't like what God has given us or where God has placed us. How long will it take us to appreciate God's good gifts: the circumstances of our lives, the family dramas that surround us, and the material provisions we enjoy? Is it possible that, unbeknownst to us, God has given us what we need *and* want?

Suppressing my desire to argue with Wolfie about Santa's faults, I hugged him and mentally filed away an easy and inexpensive route to guarantee Wolfie's Christmas morning happiness. Instead of an expensive bicycle, skis, or a NASA-encrypted telescope, a fifteen-dollar book set was a no-brainer!

I was glad that my son had confided in me but did warn him about speaking ill of Santa so close to Christmas. The next time you are not happy about what God has given you, why not consider trusting and thanking God? Your wise, all-knowing heavenly Parent does have your best interest at heart.

PRAYER: Thank you, Lord God, for knowing me better than I know myself. Thank you for your many blessings and gifts. Thank you most of all for sending the gift of Jesus, who is my redeemer, teacher, and friend.

75

Let Angels Prostrate Fall

SUGGESTED SCRIPTURE READING: Revelation 4:1-11

VERSE DU JOUR: *"You are worthy, our Lord and God, to receive glory and honor and power, for you created all things, and by your will they were created and have their being."* (Revelation 4:11)

"You pray how many times a day?" the incredulous students asked Ahmad. "And do you really get down on your face? How do you know when to do it? Where's your mat? How come you don't wear a towel on your head?" I was as curious as the questioners were, so I carefully listened to the new boy's response.

Have you ever been so overwhelmed by someone or something that you felt the need to lay prostrate? I'm not talking about a medical need but the awakening of understanding that someone or something is so much greater than you that the safest thing to do and the right thing to do is to get down as low as you can.

Those who have met the Lord God Almighty tend to report the irresistible urge to get their faces to the ground. The prophets of old knew that their earthly bodies were no more able to handle a direct view of the presence of God than they would be able to hold up to God's glory. Remember the story of Moses. When God spoke to him from the burning bush, God's voice instructed Moses to remove his shoes, as he was standing on holy ground. In other cited instances of God appearing to mortals, we do not read instructions such as, "Get down on your knees! Don't look at me," or "Hit the floor, worship me!" Instead, those in tune with God know what to do. They can't help but worship God.

Ahmad explained that when Muslims pray facing Mecca, they "get down" as an act of worship. I never did witness Ahmad's style of worship but am aware that various sects of the Christian church are also prone to such practices. Imagine how it will feel when we are all in the presence of our God and can't help but fall down to

orship, along with the angels, the music, the bright light, the
ilory. Why not listen to some worship music or recite the prayer
below and get down on the floor and worship your God?

PRAYER:

Holy, holy, holy
is the Lord God Almighty,
who was, and is, and is to come. (Revelation 4:8)

76

What Jesus Wants Us to See

SUGGESTED SCRIPTURE READING: John 9:1-5

VERSE DU JOUR: *As he went along, he saw a man blind from
birth.* (John 9:1)

The morning was dark when I dressed, and I was so rushed to get
to school for my first observation of the year that I didn't notice
that I had on one black shoe and one blue one. Not only were the
shoes from pairs of different colors, but they were also of different heel heights (and still I didn't notice!). Just as I was about to
start the lesson, I noticed my error and slipped on the extra pair
of shoes stashed under my classroom desk.

Jesus probably doesn't care whether we notice the color of our
shoes, but what does he want us to notice? Perhaps he wants us
to see what he sees; he wants us to notice people and respond to
their needs. Notice that as Jesus and his disciples were hiking the
countryside, the disciples walked past a blind man. It was Jesus
who called attention to the blind beggar at the side of the road.
Jesus did not avert his eyes from the uncomfortable sight, as most
people probably did, or pick up the pace in order to pass more
quickly. Notice also that the Scripture does not say that Jesus saw
a blind beggar, which the blind man almost certainly was, but that
Jesus saw a blind *man*. The text goes on to say that Jesus saw a
blind man who was blind from birth. Who else walking by that

man would have known that he had been blind since birth, and who else but Jesus would have cared?

The blind man must have caught the attention of Jesus' disciples, too, since they posed a question for Jesus regarding this man's situation. They asked Jesus why the man was blind. Jesus not only explained that the blindness has nothing to do with sin or punishment but also showed the disciples how to focus on the value of the man rather than his circumstances.

Since Jesus trained and modeled to his disciples the importance of noticing and acknowledging the needs of people, this behavior must be important. Jesus wants his emissaries to be aware of and responsive to others around them. Since I tend toward being oblivious and sometimes can't even keep track of the shoes on my feet, I might need some divine assistance on this expectation. Who is in your classroom; who needs to be seen by you?

PRAYER: Open my eyes, Lord, so that I might see what and whom you want me to see today. Help me to see those who cross my path as you would have me see them.

77
Things of This World

SUGGESTED SCRIPTURE READING: Matthew 24:32-44

VERSE DU JOUR: *"Heaven and earth will pass away, but my words will never pass away."* (Matthew 24:35)

"I've waited too long in line for this to happen now," I thought with fury in my heart. "This piece of junk copy machine had better unjam quickly. Class starts in twenty minutes, and I've been here since 6:45 a.m. First the toner cartridge runs out, then the copier overheats, and now there's a paper jam of proportions beyond imagination . . ."

Resentful that I fritter away so much of my life doing this, I felt an insane urge to do something drastic. Before I knew it, I'd grabbed the emergency hatchet from the glass case on the wall, the one they keep by the fire extinguisher with the sign that says Emergency Use Only. "This is an emergency," I thought as I lunged toward the copier with destruction my only intent. I felt arms tugging me back and heard shouts from behind that couldn't stop me now: "Don't do it! It's the only one we have! Stop, they'll make you pay!" "It's time to take this thing down," I growled as the hatchet came down time and time again.

Jesus says that heaven and earth will pass away. I guess that means that the things of this world will disappear, too. And I'll be happy to see some things go, thank you very much: my grade book up in smoke; the in-box gone, gone, gone; the copier shattered and falling into a gaping hole. I know I should be happy to have access to technology that makes my life and the lives of my students easier. I should be thrilled that I live in the age of technology and that the school budget includes ten thousand dollars for copier rental. I *am* thankful for the blessings given to me through this school. But I'm still happy to know that the things that cause so much frustration here on this tired earth will go down along with everything else. When Jesus returns, all of our things will be useless, old, tired, and most likely destroyed. Yet Jesus and his words will endure. When Jesus comes to take me home, I won't need this old copier.

Paper trays cracked, and chunks of plastic flew through the air. Sweat beaded on my forehead and trickled into my eyes, stinging for a moment and then waking me . . . from my dream, a fantasy sequence. What have I become? I harbor frustration with an inanimate object so intense that it leads to this? Weary and shaken, I get up to wipe my face and remember the words of my Lord: "Come to me, all you who are weary and burdened, and I will give you rest" (Matthew 11:28). "Heaven and earth will pass away, but my words will never pass away" (Matthew 24:35). Tomorrow will be another day—for me and for the copy machine.

PRAYER: Jesus, help me remember that the things that make me crazy today will someday be non-issues. Thank you for your mercy and your enduring words.

78

Angels and Lice

SUGGESTED SCRIPTURE READING: Romans 8:28-39

VERSE DU JOUR: *And we know that in all things God works for the good of those who love him, who have been called according to his purpose.* (Romans 8:28)

In *The Hiding Place,* Corrie ten Boom, a survivor of World War II concentration camps, describes the horrors of life as a prisoner. Her stories of capture, pain, and great grief are true. Also amazingly true are her stories of miracles and forgiveness. In one of her last speeches before her death in 1983, Corrie recounted the day she was waiting in line to be searched at the entrance to Ravensbruck. Knowing that if she were searched, the New Testament Bible she had hidden under her clothing would be confiscated and lost to her, she pleaded with God to surround her with angels, so as to block her from the view of the Nazi guards.

As Corrie approached the head of the line, the woman ahead of her was searched, as was the woman behind her, yet she passed through without giving up the book that would later give hope and life to many contained in those deadly walls. Corrie could only conclude that the guards couldn't see her, and she was convinced that God did use angels to protect her and her precious Bible.

The God who made the universe and hung the planets in space can do anything. Compared with setting the forces of gravity and centripetal force in motion, using people and creations for good is likely no big challenge. Why should we then think that we are not good enough to be used by God? Jesus taught that God can use all things toward perfect purposes, even things and situations that look bad. We are told to be thankful in all situations and know that God is in control. Despite our weaknesses and failures, if we are willing, we will be used by God.

While she was interned in Ravensbruck, Corrie was forced to sleep in a room with about seven hundred other women. The room was intended to hold only two hundred, so as time went on, the squalid conditions gave rise to many unpleasantries, one of which was lice (a condition to which many elementary teachers can relate). The room was filled with lice; virtually all the prisoners of barracks 8 had lice, and because of this infestation the prison guards refused to enter the barracks. So it was that the women prisoners of barracks 8 also had free access to Corrie ten Boom's smuggled Bible. In Corrie's difficult situation, God was able to use angels and lice!

PRAYER: Lord, I believe that if you can use lice, you can use me. Let me be a vehicle for your goodwill today.

79

Jesus Added to Your Class List Today!

SUGGESTED SCRIPTURE READING: Colossians 3:22-25

VERSE DU JOUR: *Whatever your task, put yourselves into it, as done for the Lord and not for your masters.* (Colossians 3:23, NRSV)

During several high school and college summers, I worked as a lifeguard. The job had great perks, such as continuous exposure to sun and water, but it did include mopping floors, emptying ash trays, and cleaning rest rooms. I suppose it was good training for my future teaching career. At school, I do more dishes and scrub down more areas covered with other people's bodily fluids than I do at home! Back then, I didn't like scrubbing the toilets any more than I enjoy cleaning dissection pans and test tubes now, but my mom told me to scrub those toilets as if I were doing it for Jesus. The toilets may not have looked a whole lot better, but my attitude about the task changed. When I imagined that Jesus was with me, it made more sense to do it right, and the job seemed to be of greater importance.

Jesus taught Paul how to be happy in all circumstances. Paul seems to be explaining to us the importance of giving every job your all. The satisfaction of a job well done might be adequate consolation for the work that you do. How much greater satisfaction will you experience if you know that your good work has been done for the Lord? At the time Paul wrote these words, he may have appeared to be rotting in prison, yet he was writing letters that would become part of the greatest publication of all time. He probably had no idea that this letter and others would become part of the Bible. Even so, he took his own advice and worked at his letters with all his heart.

How could Paul have known the importance of the notes he was sending off to his friends? Likewise, how can we know the significance of every little task we perform? We can't, so we need to do our best all the time.

Paul wrote from his dark prison cell. The man who had met Jesus was shackled in a stinky hole in the ground, but he was having a blast! Paul realized that even while he was imprisoned, he could serve God. His writings to the early believers speak of joy and exhortations to serve God by serving others.

Can you see Jesus in your students? Can you teach them as if you are teaching Jesus? Picture Jesus coming into your classroom to hear the lecture, do the lab, or sit in one of those wobbly desks. Can you see a little bit of Jesus in your students?

PRAYER: Jesus, it is you whom I serve. Let me see you in my students today.

80

Treasure

SUGGESTED SCRIPTURE READING: Matthew 6:19-21

VERSE DU JOUR: *"For where your treasure is, there your heart will be also."* (Matthew 6:21)

"You're a rich white woman. What're you doin' here?" Shaniqua blurted during what was an otherwise relatively quiet microscope lab class. "Why do you say that?" I asked. "Well, you always wear nice suits, and you have a watch to match every outfit. Look at the one you're wearing now. It's a Rolex!"

I had to laugh. I thought everybody knew my watches were fakes and my suits used. Wanting to exude a professional appearance, I took time to dress professionally; usually that meant wearing a suit and heels, matching accessories, and a long white lab coat. I am convinced that dressing the part correlates to more professional behavior on my part and on the part of my students. Unable to afford designer clothes or jewelry, I learned to alter used men's suits that I found at the local Goodwill store and was quick to share my clever trick with others. I also loved wearing knock-off watches that I acquired on trips home to the East Coast. While another student explained these details to Shaniqua, I continued my lab-table rounds.

Jesus did not say, "Where your heart is, your treasure will be." He said it the other way around. Jesus' carefully ordered words indicate that the accumulation of treasure comes first and your heart follows. Jesus did not place his priorities on material goods, education, or a respected position within the community. He owned no buildings, had no formal education and no degrees, erected no buildings, and didn't have a traditional job. Jesus traveled by foot, lived by accepting gifts from others, and most likely ate fish during a good portion of his time here on earth. His priorities were not centered on or in this world, and therefore neither were his treasures. Jesus was not encumbered by accoutrements that could have pulled him away from his mission. Nowhere in the

Bible are there accounts of Jesus whining about his lack of material goods or complaining about his lot in life. Instead, Jesus takes the time to teach us that the things we collect and treasure will determine the direction of our hearts and lives.

Happy that Shaniqua had been enlightened but sorry that maybe I had pushed the envelope a bit in wearing *that* watch, we both left class laughing. I even offered to pick up a "Rolex" for her the next time I headed home. How easy is it to get down on ourselves for not making the salary we deserve, for not obtaining the respect within the community that we think we should have, and for not pursuing the material possessions that we could acquire by working in another profession. How hard it sometimes is to keep all of these issues in the perspective of Jesus. We don't need to make a lot of money, but we do need to be resourceful and avoid worshipping the things we have. Instead of allowing material treasures or our lack or them to control us, we should look to Jesus. If we look to him each day, it will be easier to acquire a healthy and heavenly perspective.

PRAYER: Lord, keep me focused on what matters in life. Help me collect treasures that will last for eternity.

81

Hard to Love

SUGGESTED SCRIPTURE READING: John 13:31-35

VERSE DU JOUR: *"And so I am giving a new commandment to you now—love each other just as much as I love you."* (John 13:34, TLB)

Damien entered my class three weeks into the semester with a lame excuse for his belated registration, something to do with vacation at a mountain retreat. My class was over capacity six students ago, so I was in no mood to enthusiastically welcome the boy who spelled trouble from the get-go. Damien had bushy red hair pulled into a ponytail and a habit of closing his eyes mid-sentence. He scratched himself constantly, seemed to leave a wake of trouble in his path, and displayed a haughty, rebellious attitude.

On his second day, I found Damien squeezing the oxygen hose that ran into my fish tank. When I asked him to stop, he became defensive and denied any wrongdoing. I threw him out of class, and we had loud words out in the hall. This interaction led to a meeting between Damien, the dean of students, our police officer, and me.

Jesus commands that we love each other. And he significantly raises the bar by challenging us to love each other as much as he loves us. The command is part of a Scripture in which it appears that Jesus is commanding believers to love each other, but he might also mean for us to love everyone.

What could be more attractive to nonbelievers than to experience God's love through us? Jesus knew that our connectedness to each other motivates us to love and serve each other. Jesus considered love so important that the topic was his most recurrent teaching theme; he continued teaching about love all the way up the hill to Calvary. Jesus did not merely suggest that we should try to be connected with and love others; he used this idea as the focus for a new commandment.

The meeting with Damien went well; our dean was masterful. We discussed the issue of my authority in the classroom and Damien's problems with authority. When the dean asked Damien why he'd been incarcerated at a facility reserved for felons, Damien nonchalantly replied, "I committed a few assaults and grand theft autos." "With a gun?" the dean asked. "With a gun," Damien replied. I agreed to start over with Damien, and he agreed to respect my authority. As I left, I thought, "How will I be able to love this kid? He makes my skin crawl."

The police officer stopped me as I left the office. "See if you can figure out if Damien is on drugs. All that eye closing and itching is a signal of drug use. We'd appreciate any information you could give us. Be careful, okay?" I knew I was in for the challenge of a lifetime—I'd just committed to continuing my work with this boy, had a police assignment, and had to find a way to love Damien. Do you also have a student who is hard to love?

PRAYER: Please help me to find something to love in every one of my students. Without you, I can't love some of my students. Please put your love in me.

<h1 style="text-align:center">82</h1>

Look Ahead

SUGGESTED SCRIPTURE READING: Revelation 21:1-4

VERSE DU JOUR: *"He will wipe every tear from their eyes. There will be no more death or mourning or crying or pain, for the old order of things has passed away."* (Revelation 21:4)

At lunchtime, the science teachers overheard a few tidbits on the walkie-talkie that one of our colleagues carries for safety. It was not exactly appetizing news; a body had been found not far from our school. Apparently the unidentified body was discovered by a man walking his dog. The man alerted the police, and the police then alerted the school administrators. We were not all meant to hear of this discovery but were not about to ignore the news that crackled over the radio that day. The bell rang, and off we went to our classes feeling a bit anxious.

Imagine just for a few moments what lies beyond this uncertain and unpredictable life. Instead of unsettling realities and challenging work, think of what awaits each and every one of us who are called to God's kingdom. God promises to wipe away every tear. No worries will remain: no concerns about what to eat, what to wear, how to navigate traffic, or survive health problems.

When pain and death are out of the picture, everything gets a whole lot easier, don't you think? And Jesus will be there to understand everything and to comfort us—to enjoy our worship and to throw the biggest party ever! The Scripture teaches that tears, pain, sickness, and even death are temporary. Someday, we will leave this tired world and all of its hassles behind. Our old worries will fade from view, and the only trace of past troubles will be how they have molded and refined us.

Classes finally ended, and we were called to an emergency staff meeting, where I was met by the sober and shocked faces of my colleagues. A school counselor broke the news: "Wendel Werner's body was found near the school today. He committed suicide—shot himself in the head last night."

I bit my lip but couldn't stop the tears that flowed for the boy who'd been in two of my classes. He had been a bright boy who listened to Christian rock music and had become a disciplined student and an ROTC member. Wendel had been a favorite student of mine; he was honest and respectful but seemed to have few friends. I never knew that he was so unhappy, so desperate. Why didn't I notice? I felt anguish and a sense of stupidity. For weeks after, I'd be doing something unrelated to school and suddenly think, "Wendel's dead, and there's nothing that I can do about it!"

As time passed, I learned to focus on the students I could help and on the promise of a brighter tomorrow. The tragedy also served as a painful reminder to be more aware of the students around me. I did not want to overlook another desperate soul again. Take heart, there is a much better place and we hold special reservations!

PRAYER: Lord, thanks for creating a heaven where you will welcome me. Please help me remember that the heartaches of this world are temporary. Let me use them to become the person you want me to be.

83

Best Friends

SUGGESTED SCRIPTURE READING: Matthew 26:36-46

VERSE DU JOUR: *Some friends play at friendship but a true friend sticks closer than one's nearest kin.* (Proverbs 18:24, NRSV)

The space used as the science office was tiny, yet it contained five full-sized teacher desks, two filing cabinets, a storage cabinet, a telephone, and shelves and shelves of books. Also inside might be anywhere from none to ten teachers, visiting students, and various live or deceased members of the animal kingdom. Cletus the Fetus, the jerky-like dried remains of a once-dissected fetal pig turned department mascot, hung from a piece of twine wrapped around an exposed nail. Near Cletus, a framed print depicting human vivisection completed the peculiar ambience. It was in this space that I was introduced to the new hire.

Sometimes friends do come from the most unexpected places. While being chased by the paparazzi, Jesus found a friend up in a tree (Zacchaeus). He found some stinky, rough fishermen by the docks who became his best friends and companions. Another time, Jesus was on top of a friend's roof, trying to relax and savor the stillness when an unexpected stranger dropped by to ask a few questions. That stranger, Nicodemus, became one of Jesus' most loyal friends.

While Jesus experienced the joys of human friendship, he also experienced its disappointment. Jesus learned that even the best of friends do not always "stick closer than a brother." Imagine the disappointment Jesus must have felt with his best friends in the Garden of Gethsemane. Jesus had known that some awful things quickly approached—he'd asked his friends to sit with him to pray. The Master needed their prayers and company, yet they fell asleep!

The new hire I met in that closet-like space known as the science office became one of my nearest and dearest friends. More than ten years after our introduction, Tammi and I refer to each other as sister-friends. I marvel at the blessings she has brought to my life and still can't believe where I found her. On a rooftop, in a tree, at the docks, or in a science lair—it doesn't matter where you find them; friends are precious.

I'm thankful that although God values our friendship with him, he also blesses us with human friends. True friends are a blessing because true friends support and serve each other. True friendships mimic the relationship that God wants to have with us. God promises to never leave or fail us but warns us that our human friends may do so. Could it be that the friend who sticks closer than a relative is none other than God?

PRAYER: Thank you for the friendships that you have given me. Teach me to not be too surprised when my friends let me down. Please help me learn to be a good friend. Teach me to support and serve my friends. Thank you for being my unfailing God and my unswerving friend who sticks closer than my kin.

84
Don't Break the Sugar Bowl!

SUGGESTED SCRIPTURE READING: Matthew 7:7-27

VERSE DU JOUR: *"Enter through the narrow gate. For wide is the gate and broad is the road that leads to destruction, and many enter through it."* (Matthew 7:13)

"The monkey's in the court. The monkey wants to speak. No talking, no laughing, no showing your teeth." Those are the opening lines of the monkey game, a game similar to "Don't Break the Sugar Bowl," a game that we used to play with my great-aunt FloFlo. I now realize that my sweet auntie asked to play this game when she wanted me to quiet down or sleep. The game went like this: Whoever spoke, giggled, or made any audible noise (other than breathing) broke the sugar bowl and lost the game. Even if I had no intention of doing anything but going to sleep, as soon as the game started, it was nearly impossible to stay quiet.

Somehow, when you declare a behavior forbidden, it suddenly becomes more attractive than ever and almost irresistible. Even if the restriction on the behavior is self-imposed, the attraction remains—I will not eat that cupcake. I will *not* eat that cupcake. I will not *eat that cupcake* . . .

Ever notice that the same thing happens when you give students a negative command? If you say, even in jest, "Whatever you do, don't slip with the scalpel and slice open your finger," this is the first thing they'll do. One small suggestion, and soon the blood will be flowing. If you hadn't said anything about it, nothing would've happened. I want to consider teaching in the positive; I don't want to give my students any *more* bad ideas.

Jesus must've known about this phenomenon. A survey of his teachings reveals that Jesus almost always tells his followers what they should do as opposed to focusing on what they mustn't do. Jesus dwells on the actions and attitudes that he desires in his followers, and he teaches along these positive lines: "So in everything, do to others what you would have them do to you" (Matthew 7:12). "Knock and the door will be opened to you" (Luke 11:9). "Enter through the narrow gate" (Matthew 7:13). "He who has ears, let him hear" (Matthew 11:15). "Watch out for false prophets" (Matthew 7:15). "Love your enemies and pray for those who persecute you" (Matthew 5:44).

Jesus gives his students ideas on how to act and tends to avoid the negative alternatives. The few times when Jesus uses negatives instruction, he is usually issuing important warnings or using contrasts to strengthen the allure of his positive ideas. I challenge you to check out the red writing in the Gospels. See if you don't agree that Jesus focuses on a positive didactic style; his teachings focus on how to act and think.

Like Jesus, we must carefully chose our words and plan our instructional design. We need to be thoughtful and positive with our teaching words. Why not try to focus on the "should dos" today instead of exposing your students to the "don't do" alternatives?

While you're testing this positive approach, remember that not only our words teach; our actions model more than words could ever say.

PRAYER: Lord, guide my words. Let me give positive and helpful instruction to my students. Let my words and actions reflect a positive attitude. Please speak through me today.

85

Like a Rocket

SUGGESTED SCRIPTURE READING: Matthew 24:36-44

VERSE DU JOUR: *"And he will send his angels with a loud trumpet call, and they will gather his elect from the four winds, from one end of the heavens to the other."* (Matthew 24:31)

My children have been up all night coughing and vomiting. The fight I had with my husband is still heavy on my mind. There is much to do today, and my eyelids feel as if they are littered with sand. Feeling tired and frumpy, I think my life looks bleak. I feel bleak. And I have yet to deal with my *other* children—the 130 or so souls entrusted to my care . . .

When the kitchen phone rings, trying to cheer myself with a spike of twisted humor, I answer "Drake's Vomitorium, Susan speaking." No one's laughing on the other end; I hear the click of quick retreat. As I hurriedly change a stinky diaper, my two-year-old son, who is obsessed with space and rockets, says, "Don't worry, Mommy. When Jesus comes back, we gonna shoot up like a rocket!"

Isn't this an example of the attitude that inspired Jesus to say that the kingdom of God belongs to children and those who can humble themselves to be like little children? Children have no problem with the concept of flying up in the sky like a rocket, and it isn't something they fear, either, but an event for which, they expectantly wait—no fear, no doubt, no worry.

Isn't it time for all Christians to realize that this life and its concerns are simply temporal? The things of this life, our worries, and our overwhelming responsibilities will pass beyond our grasp in the "flash of an eye" when we meet Jesus. Will we leave behind our clothes, shoes, and dental fillings? Will we fly until we meet Jesus? Will there still be an ozone layer? No matter—when Jesus calls us home, we probably won't care about the details but will be happy to leave the world and its hassles behind.

Jesus indicates that on that day, the angels will "herd us" up into the heavens. He also warns that we are to watch and prepare for his return. Despite our imperfections and human frailties, God desires that we prepare ourselves and others for the coming of his kingdom—unbelievable!

Perhaps our work here will be more manageable and acceptable if we remember its temporal nature. Except for matters concerning the soul, all that now dominates our time will eventually pass away and count for nothing. Material concerns will be irrelevant, and grade books will disappear. Problems will vanish, as will diapers and vomit. Our bodies will be changed, requiring little or no sleep, and our accommodations will be seriously upgraded. The return of Christ is near. Are you ready to fly up like a rocket?

PRAYER: Lord, remind me that my worries, concerns, and fears are temporal matters. Help me live today as if I might shoot up like a rocket at any time. Let me keep my concerns and worries in the perspective of your eternal plans.

86

Heavenly Messengers

SUGGESTED SCRIPTURE READING: Hebrews 13:1-15

VERSE DU JOUR: *Do not forget to entertain strangers, for by so doing, some people have entertained angels without knowing it.* (Hebrews 13:2)

We had just a few moments while the kids were playing in the basement. It was a chance to chat with a precious friend. Our conversation led to a discussion of our children's teachers. Although I should have known better, I began to whine about my daughter's teacher, Ms. Clarkson. "I can't believe that with everything else going on, she picks on Riley. This woman is a little harsh. I'm not too crazy about her . . ."

No sooner are the judgmental words out of my mouth than I hear Riley coming up the steps. She proudly hands me her latest artistic creation. Bright and sparkly, the mini-banner reads, "I Love You, Ms. Clarkson!" It is adorned with glitter flowers and will need several hours to dry. As I put the banner up to dry, I am simultaneously shamed and chastised. I feel the embarrassment of my behavior. How dare I talk and act like the unappreciative, critical parents who drive *me* nuts?

The Bible warns us that God uses messengers who look a lot like regular people. Sometimes God's messengers are people, but other times they are heavenly beings disguised as human. Jesus is God, and he surely looked like a man. Jacob wrestled with an angel that looked like a man. I believe that God's messengers are not always in the form of an angel or an ethereal being covered in light. Our children, our spouses, our students, our friends, or our acquaintances may be the messengers chosen by God to protect us or to teach us. A simple statement made by an unexpected messenger may weigh heavier on our hearts than the judgment of any jury.

And why is it that just when we think that a situation is really bad, children can see the flip side? My daughter had already forgotten that she was not allowed to do something in class that another student was allowed to do. She had quickly forgotten the action of her teacher that so offended me. She saw only the hard work and the caring that Ms. Clarkson had given her. And it was Riley's insight that sent a message to my heart.

I can only hope that my students are as magnanimous and forgiving as my little "angel." We would do well to heed those around us who have been given the role of heavenly messengers. Their message may be of hope and support or a reminder of responsibility. We must keep our minds and our eyes open to hear the messages that God sends to us wherever they come from.

PRAYER: Who are you sending to me today? Here I am, ready to recognize your messengers, Lord.

87

Use Me!

SUGGESTED SCRIPTURE READING: John 21:4-17

VERSE DU JOUR: *Jesus replied, "Love the Lord your God with all your heart and with all your soul and with all your mind."* (Matthew 22:37)

I'm typing another letter of recommendation for Marcus. But I don't mind; in fact, I'm thrilled to do just about anything for this boy, my ex-student. This is the boy who laughed at my jokes, even the lame ones. It's not surprising that I developed affection for the very student who followed me around, carrying armloads of my papers and books, worrying that I was overworked. He would act as if it were sheer joy to help me staple stacks of handouts in the copy room.

Marcus was always a diligent and bright student, but more important, he was polite and unpretentious. I'll never forget the time he noticed an error in my lecture and instead of calling me on it in front of the entire class, patiently waited until all students had filed out of the classroom to humbly correct me.

Biblical accounts tell of men and women who were mightily used by God—these were mere mortals who sought after God, worshipped God, and were willing to let God use them. If you doubt this, check out the Old Testament stories of Daniel, Moses, Rahab, and Ruth. We can also look at the New Testament accounts of Jesus selecting his disciples. We are unsure of the exact selection criteria, but we do know that several disciples were men who Jesus had previously met and with whom he had spent time. Did Jesus choose them because he thought they were particularly strong, especially religious, or that they would add wealth to the cause? Perhaps Jesus chose them because he sensed their admiration for him and knew that they enjoyed being with him—that they enjoyed Jesus' company and loved eating fire-roasted fresh fish breakfasts on the beach with their Lord.

Marcus's respect and affection for me were undeniable. It was, therefore, easy to like him in return. I was eager to accept his assistance and wanted to do extra work for him. Contrast the warm and fuzzy feelings we have for Marcus-like students with the feelings we have for the students who show us their loathing. Isn't it harder to work with the students who have made it clear that they don't want to be with us or that they truly dislike us? With God's help we can learn to care about these kids, too—but it doesn't come naturally. Although God won't love us any more or less, might God be more willing to work with us if we express our praise?

PRAYER: I want to show you my love through my adoration and obedience. Please feel free to use me. Thanks for loving me.

88

Refueling

SUGGESTED SCRIPTURE READING: Mark 6:30-31

VERSE DU JOUR: *"Come to me, all you who are weary and burdened, and I will give you rest."* (Matthew 11:28)

"Just how chronic is this chronic fatigue thing supposed to be?" I nervously asked my doctor after receiving his unwelcome diagnosis. It was only three months into the school year, and I had already used five sick days, more than I'd used in the past three years combined. The rumor around school was that I had already died; a few students were surprised to see me stagger into the science office. Just walking to the bathroom from my bed was exhausting. "You can go to work, but you need to rest while you're there," suggested my internist. "Find a time to sneak away for naps, perhaps between classes," he added. I might have been fatigued, but I wasn't brain dead. Naps at school? between classes? four-minute naps? Any teacher, chronically fatigued or not, would have mustered the energy to laugh at that doctor's order.

Jesus recognized that food and rest were not merely pleasures to be savored but necessities to be pursued. In addition to the spiritual hunger that Jesus saw in the crowds, he saw the fatigue and hunger of the body. Notice that prior to the miracle of feeding the crowd of five thousand, Jesus recognized the physical needs of his own followers. He did not say to the disciples, "Hey, I know everyone is tired and hungry, but let's just tough it out a little longer. These people crowding around us are so spiritually needy that we must ignore our own discomforts and tend to them." No, he says something very different: "Come with me by yourselves to a quiet place and get some rest." Jesus, being our Creator, recognized better than anyone else the limitations of the human body. He knew that his friends needed nourishment and rest. He knew that if the disciples were not cared for, they would be physically unable to effectively help others. Jesus was direct in telling his friends to stop and refuel.

My fatigue was either misdiagnosed or miraculously cured. Extra rest and nutrition combined with the prayers of many friends might have done the trick. I know that Jesus the master Teacher is also Jesus the great Physician. This great Physician recognizes that the soul and the body must be continually nourished. If Jesus were to visit you today, would he say, "Take care of yourself so that you can take care of my flock"? Why not take Jesus' words to heart as you take the time to rest and refuel?

PRAYER: Lord, fill me with your Holy Spirit and teach me to care for myself so that I can be ready to help others.

89

Time Passes

SUGGESTED SCRIPTURE READING: Psalm 31:15-24

VERSE DU JOUR: *My times are in your hands; deliver me from my enemies and from those who pursue me.* (Psalm 31:15)

Hoping to diminish the annoying clock-watching behavior of my students, I copied the idea of an esteemed colleague. Thinking her sign and its message were incredibly clever, I'd commissioned my artistic assistant to print and decorate a copy and even had it laminated. "How long will it take my students to notice it? Will they understand the tongue-in-cheek challenge?" I wondered as I taped the sign at the front of the room below the classroom clock. In bold letters it said, "Time will pass. Will you?"

When we pass through the golden gates into heaven, no sign will be needed. When Jesus meets us and gives rewards to all who have loved and served him, the mood will be upbeat. Simply being with Jesus will make us reflect his glory. We won't be distracted by any clocks, worrying about the time or thinking about moving on to the next location. Those who lived in obscurity here on earth will suddenly be recognized. Those who formerly lived as slaves (don't you sometimes feel like one?) will live in freedom.

The poor will be rich, the blind will see, and the lame will run with wild abandon.

It didn't take long for the students to notice the new sign, and they understood the message. Several students told me that when they read the message, they were reminded to get back to work and that the sign was helpful. Others were insulted by the sign and told me, straight out, that it was obnoxious. "If you want to be a winner and pass this class," I responded, "it would be best to get your eyes off the clock and onto your work—don't you think?"

Unlike the kingdom of heaven, my class was filled with some who would pass and some who would not. This sign was one more tool that I used to increase the odds for student success. None of my students is less valuable than another, but some perform better than others. The stark realities of life on earth and in my classroom contrast sharply with the kingdom of heaven, where everyone is rewarded and everyone wins. We don't all look like winners, and we might not feel like winners. But we can take comfort in God's word and assurance—our heavenly existence will be different from our earthly lives. Time will pass, and so will we.

PRAYER: Lord, let me serve you cheerfully today as I look forward to a new reality. Thank you for the rewards that you are preparing for me.

90

A Name for Every Face

SUGGESTED SCRIPTURE READING: John 10:11-18

VERSE DU JOUR: *"I am the good shepherd. I know my sheep and my sheep know me—just as the Father knows me and I know the Father."* (John 10:14)

Years ago I went to the centennial celebration of the Brooklyn Bridge, where I was part of the largest crowd of people I'd ever seen. Millions of people covered the bridge and its surrounds while spectacular fireworks exploded in the night sky. To witness such a throng of humanity and to be part of it was thrilling; I'll never forget that experience, and yet it was also a frightening thing to see. How could I be significant if there are so many others? How could I be special and loved by God?

But when my God looked on that same scene, the throng became millions of individuals, millions of friends, all with faces and names, all with a special place to fill within the kingdom. The Maker of the cosmos, the moon and stars, the Creator of every living and nonliving thing, used creative energies to make each one of us different and special. God designed our every cell, has numbered our hairs, knows our every gesture, and can read our every subtle nuance.

God knows us better than any human lover could and still loves us more than we can comprehend. And God sees us as beings of beauty—even when we're a tad overweight or sporting postadolescent acne. When God looked down on that crowd, the beauty of each individual in that crowd appeared. God saw the creation as a divine reflection. God knows each child and calls each one by name.

As a second semester begins, another list of names awaits—even more names to learn before the year is finished! It is helpful to remember that once we learn those names, we'll reap the bounty of our efforts. Years after teaching certain students, their names still evoke deep emotions. Rolan constantly played with the class-pet rat, and his name will make me laugh. Patience will always remind me of my quest for that virtue (she irked me to no end), and the memory of Serina, the sweet daughter of a local minister, will never cease to make me smile. I know the importance of learning each student's name and look forward to the reward of knowing them all. Today the task feels overwhelming, yet I know that with the Lord's example and power, I will eventually have a name for every face.

PRAYER: Please give me the patience and the brain power to learn the names of each one of my students. Let me learn more about each one so that I can be a more effective teacher for you.

Spring Term

Countdown to Summer Vacation

91

Water into Wine

SUGGESTED READING: John 2:1-11

VERSE DU JOUR: *[The master of the banquet] said, "Everyone brings out the choice wine first and then the cheaper wine after the guests have had too much to drink; but you have saved the best till now."* (John 2:10)

The classroom smells like a brewery, and paper cups are lined up for sampling our recently fermented ginger-ale alcohol; this is the last day of a practical laboratory study focused on anaerobic respiration. As students gulp the questionable liquid, I remind them not to drink too much. But I'm not too worried. The alcohol that we produced using ginger root, boiled water, yeast, and plenty of sugar is vile.

Years ago, Jesus and his mother were guests at a wedding feast. First-century weddings, like modern versions, were occasions of celebration and feasting. Guests expected a good party where they would be wined and dined. When the wine ran out at this particular reception, it was not a life-or-death situation but was a lapse that could cause great embarrassment to the hosts of the wedding feast. In addition, such a shortage would have put a damper on the party, a celebration of love.

Mary didn't order Jesus to help but simply said, "They have no more wine." How do moms know how to do that? Can't you see the pleading in her face—the look that said, "Oh, please, can't you do something to help?" Though Jesus indicated to his mother that he was not yet ready to perform miracles, he turns water into wine, which quickly throws his ministry into action and him into the spotlight.

To tease me, students started staggering and slurring their speech. Every group offered me a sample of their special brew. Any one of their samples would clean your sinuses.

Unlike our amateur laboratory experimentation, Jesus turned ordinary water into some very fine wine. He did not mess around making the likes of the rotgut that we produced in our biology lab. His wine was most likely the best that the wedding guests had ever tasted. In making that wine, Jesus demonstrated his compassion for others, his respect for marriage and love, his commitment to excellence, and his appreciation of a good time. Can you show respect for these same things?

PRAYER: Let me show a genuine love for others and joy for the life I have in you, Jesus.

92

Honor All You Meet

SUGGESTED SCRIPTURE READING: 1 Peter 2:9-17

VERSE DU JOUR: *Show proper respect for everyone: Love the brotherhood of believers, fear God; honor the king.* (1 Peter 2:17)

I was still dressed in my teacher clothes when I rushed into the medical school poster session. A neatly dressed man with intense eyes and an easy smile enthusiastically shook my hand and introduced himself as the janitor of this particular medical school building. I complimented him on the building's cleanliness and told him that he was doing a great job. He asked me what I thought of the poster that stood in front of us; this one was my husband's poster, so I told the janitor that the science on this one was brilliant. The elite crowd milled around us as we exchanged stories and pleasantries. Before our conversation was cut short by announcements and a presentation of the poster session winners, he casually mentioned that most people don't usually bother to chat with the janitor.

It is possible to honor God by honoring and showing respect to all persons. Throughout his life, we see Jesus demonstrate this outlook. Jesus had a knack for making individuals of any race, religion, class, or occupation feel welcome and special. Jesus would tell you that the student with the leather clothing, fixed sneer, and jail time is just as worthy of respect as the clean-cut, smiling, high achiever. Although the Scriptures teach us to show respect for all, it is not always easy to ignore our prejudices, our feelings of uncertainty, and our anger when dealing with others. How can I show respect for the teacher who sabotages my laboratory experiment? How is it possible to show respect to the students who never seem to listen to me? I want to show respect only to those who show me respect; however, Jesus tells us that the way that we honor God is to show respect for everyone.

As I left the session that night, my husband asked if I was planning to enter medical school. "Why do you ask?" I laughed. "Well, you spent plenty of time talking to the chairman of the department of medicine," he replied. After explaining that I'd been having a nice conversation with the building janitor, it was my husband who laughed. "That was NOT a janitor who had your ear. That was the chairman of medicine! He's been known to play around with people, just to see how they treat him. He was having fun with you." Thankful that I was friendly with the "janitor," I vowed to always be kind and attentive in my dealings with anyone from my school's custodial staff.

PRAYER: God, let me honor you today by honoring everyone I meet. Help me to remember that I honor you by respecting others and by showing to them your love.

93
Chosen and Loved

SUGGESTED SCRIPTURE READING: John 15:15-16

VERSE DU JOUR: *"You did not choose me, but I choose you and appointed you to go and bear fruit—fruit that will last. Then the Father will give you whatever you ask in my name."* (John 15:16)

Embarrassed and dejected, she stood biting her lip, shoulders slumped, looking down at her feet. The short, slightly plump girl with the bad skin was not known for her beauty or her brilliance. It was no surprise that she was the last pick for lab groups. One look at her and I vowed that I would never again allow the students to pick their own groups. I knew exactly how that dear child felt. I guess that's because the hurt of being the last kid picked is seared into my memory. I was once the clumsy and plump kid with the thick glasses who rarely hit the baseball; clearly not the number one draft pick. Although that was long ago, the memory of such strong emotional pain remains clear.

News alert: Jesus picked me and you from a huge applicant pool. We were first draft picks on the Jesus team! Jesus not only chose us for the job he wants us to do but also chose us as his children and his friends. Imagine, we were chosen as friends and co-workers of God somewhere between five and ten billion years ago (give or take a few billion or more). This might seem unfathomable as you sit there covered in papers, wondering how you will ever finish the grading, the planning, and the filling out of the forms.

Deadlines loom. You're tired and hungry and haven't taken time to care for yourself in several days, or maybe even weeks. Perhaps you feel like a slave, a servant, with little else to do but work. Before you despair, get a glimpse of how God sees you. Our status is heavenly. We cannot take credit for following God or for accepting our Lord. It was God who chose us and appointed us for the most important tasks in the universe. Remember that you are chosen and loved.

PRAYER: Thank you, Lord, for choosing me to do your work and to be your friend. Thanks for being with me and for always hearing me.

141

94
What Would Jesus Do?

SUGGESTED SCRIPTURE READING: Luke 6:39-49

VERSE DU JOUR: *"A student is not above his teacher, but everyone who is fully trained will be like his teacher."* (Luke 6:40)

The yelping outside was getting louder and becoming a distraction. I was trying to get some papers graded before heading home for the evening and was hunkered alone in the cramped back office. Hesitantly opening the heavy fire door that led into the smoking plaza, I saw a most unsettling sight. Two bulky boys dressed in black leather jackets and torn jeans adorned with dark, heavy chains were holding someone high up against the dirty dumpster. They were pummeling their unfortunate prisoner. The attackers were barking insults while punching the dazed boy, whom I quickly recognized as Adam, one of my students. Adam must have noticed me, too, because in between gasps and grunts, he frantically called my name. Although Adam's body had filled out and he had gotten taller than when he'd been in my freshman science class, he was no match for these two.

There had been times when I wanted to pummel Adam, too, but I surely didn't want to stand around and watch someone else do it. Not knowing what else to do, I charged the attackers, shrieking at the top of my lungs. I had no intention of touching them, let alone hitting them, but I knew I had to do something. No doubt shocked by my wild banshee approach, the attackers stood back stunned. The distraction I created gave Adam just enough time to fall from the dumpster edge unnoticed as I yelled, "Run Adam, run!"

To whom do you think Jesus was speaking when he said, "A student is not above his teacher, but everyone who is fully trained will be like his teacher"? Students might think Jesus is speaking to them, perhaps warning them to keep their subjugated place in the educational hierarchy. Or maybe Jesus is giving hope to the students who are impatient to learn lessons and skills that seem formidably difficult. It is possible that in this passage, Jesus is speaking directly to those of us who are teachers, pointing out (and perhaps warning us) that students often learn by imitation. Is he reminding us to be aware that our actions and our words teach their own lessons?

By experience, Jesus fully understands the difficulties of being a teacher. He knows how it feels to constantly be watched, with each action carefully observed and critiqued. Perhaps in this Scripture, Jesus means to offer the beleaguered teacher words of hope. I surely needed a few words of hope after news of my wild rescue spread. Plenty of students, and even some teachers, were none too pleased with my effort, and they let me know about it. We need to remember that because we are teachers, our every action is watched, assessed, and judged. God will help us deal with that pressure and will give us the wisdom to act as we should.

PRAYER: Lord God, please help me deal with the pressure of having people watch me. Help me, as your apprentice, to be more like you.

95

Despite Doubt

SUGGESTED SCRIPTURE READING: Matthew 21:18-22

VERSE DU JOUR: *Jesus replied, "I tell you the truth, if you have faith and do not doubt, not only can you do what was done to the fig tree, but also you can say to this mountain, 'Go, throw yourself into the sea,' and it will be done."* (Matthew 21:21)

It's almost six o'clock on Friday night. Instead of kicking back, banishing school from my thoughts, I've just finished a rushed supper and am due back at school in thirty minutes. Tonight I'm taking a group of my students to a local morgue. I know that my students are excited to culminate their anatomy/physiology unit with this hands-on experience. I'm excited too—this is the first trip I have ever scheduled in a working morgue.

I have purposely scheduled our session on a Friday night, hoping that the after-school timing might self-select the right group of students. As I change into morgue clothing (something washable), waves of doubt suddenly wash over me: What if the students behave improperly? What if the chaperoning parents think that this activity is morbidly inappropriate? What if my students pass out from the smell or shock? What if I faint? And I've had more than one parent ask why I scheduled our descent through the doors of death on Friday the thirteenth.

Jesus constantly spoke out against doubt. He told his disciples that if only they could overcome doubt, they could accomplish great things. Jesus knew the human condition—that doubt is our natural emotion. Jesus was also familiar with God's servant, Moses. Despite living a life plagued by doubt, Moses is now considered a great man of God and biblical hero. The concerns around which our doubt centers might be different than those of Moses, but the dangers of doubt are the same. When we allow doubt to keep us from doing our best work and God's will, we become ineffective, fearful, and sometimes even paralyzed. It appears that doubt is a natural condition that must overcome before we can reach our full potential. The story of Moses teaches us that, with God's help and assurance, even a natural doubter can serve God's purposes and accomplish great good.

Blessedly, my doubt didn't paralyze me on that night. The trip was not only a smashing success but also the first of many morgue adventures. And none of us passed out that night. Gloved and masked, we stood elbow to elbow around the male cadaver. Strangely, it was the exploration of the deceased body and the handling of dead organs that made our studies seem to come alive. Eventually, I used future morgue trips as incentive for academic performance; the greater a student's academic improvement, the greater his or her chance of attending the next trip.

We may doubt our effectiveness, our abilities, our calling, and even our God. Despite our doubts, God's power and ability will always be with us. Strategically placed, uniquely prepared, and always accompanied by the great I AM, you have been sent to do great things. Can you ask God to use you, despite your doubts?

PRAYER: Lord, you say you will go with me. Banish my doubts, and allow me to trust you.

96

Too Much Change!

SUGGESTED SCRIPTURE READING: 1 John 4:7-21

VERSE DU JOUR: *"I have loved you with an everlasting love. I have drawn you with loving-kindness."* (Jeremiah 31:3)

It's only a few months into the school year, and the administrators are calling for more change. Not only will my class list change when we start the new semester in a few weeks, but my class assignments will change, too. The teachers have been told that we will be moving from a regular schedule to a block schedule and that we need to follow a new set of curriculum guidelines. Our standard educational approach must change to an outcome-based education, or OBE, modality. Scratch that, this morning a memo informed us that we will no longer switch to OBE but to performance-based education (PBE), and we should prepare to use new performance-based assessments. Oh, and evidence of those new assessments will soon be required.

This is too much! I finally think I've learned how do to my job well, and my job changes. One day the kids love me, and the next day they hate me. One day I am happy with my work, and the next day I think I am dumb as a doorknob for doing this.

Thank God that God doesn't change! There is at least one constant in my life. God will not change or grow tired of me. God won't withdraw redemption or forgiveness from me; God will never leave me or reject me. God won't change the plans for me. Most important, God will always love me.

On a personal level, change can be disorienting and painful. The friendships that I thought were solid are rocked by change. I move away geographically from a best friend and move away emotionally from another. I look up an old college professor and find out that while I have been off living my life, he has died. The people around me often fail me, and I, no doubt, fail them.

My responsibilities continue to increase, and my resources appear to decrease. Is that a whole section of gray hair I see? When there is too much change and too little time to adapt, I need to look to the Creator of time. I will always be God's child. I will always have a place in God's kingdom, and God will always welcome me there. God will always be happy to hear my prayers and will consistently answer them. I remain thankful that my God never changes.

PRAYER: Thank you for your everlasting love. Thank you for always accepting me with your deep and unchanging love. I will always be your child and your servant.

97

Serving Jesus

SUGGESTED READING: Ephesians 6:5-9

VERSES DU JOUR: *Render service with enthusiasm, as to the Lord and not to men and women, knowing that whatever good we do, we will receive again the same from the Lord, whether we are slaves or free.* (Ephesians 6:7-8, NRSV)

The third block class is assembling. One sugared-up student slides across the floor into his seat, and his buddy gives him a thumbs up. Several students wait outside the door, savoring every last second of freedom. I look down to check the attendance list when hands push a sign-in sheet within my view. Before looking up to see the face that goes with the hands, I spot the new student's name. It's Jesus. I don't even notice his last name, but think I see a young man in a rough tunic and ratty sandals—not exactly trendy clothes, but what do I know? He has broad shoulders, clear eyes, and a rough, unshaven face.

Flustered, I welcome the new student and ask him to take the only available seat: row two, desk five. So, it looks like today I am going to teach Jesus.

The apostle Paul explains how we can personally serve Jesus; he tells us how to turn our work into service done personally for our Lord. He goes so far as to say that even the work that slaves are forced to do, if done in the right attitude, counts as service done for God. It doesn't matter if you are washing lepers in Calcutta, digging a ditch in prison, or teaching math at Midway High, you can be working for your Master. Perhaps you are directing a freshman science class or grading three hundred papers. If you are working wholeheartedly and dedicating your work to God, then you are doing holy work. This message is continued in Colossians 3:23-24, where we read, "Whatever you do, work at it with all your heart, as working for the Lord, not for men, since you know that you will receive an inheritance from the Lord as a reward." Even if you don't physically see Jesus, he is there, and you can serve him today.

I blink my eyes and focus on the occupant of row two, seat five. I now see the disheveled, dark-haired boy with sagging jeans and big white sneakers. This is more like the Jesus I was expecting today. Was my mind playing tricks on me before, or was I seeing something that is usually hidden from view? The Bible tells us that there is an unseen world hidden from our view. To make a difference in that world and in the one we can see, we are told to emulate Jesus as we work for the glory of our God. Rather than just plodding through our days, why not combine business with pleasure and dedicate the work that we have to do to Jesus?

What you do today will count, so I challenge you to teach as if Jesus is not only in the room with you but also as if Jesus is one of your students; as if it is Jesus raising his hand, turning in his paper, or asking for help with the assignment. May every biblical name you encounter (Tom, Paul, Pete, Ruth, Matt, Mary, Noah, Jonah, and Jesus) remind you whom you serve.

PRAYER: Lord, let me see you in my classroom. Help me to work hard and do my best, because it is for you that I go to school today.

98

Love and Laughter

SUGGESTED SCRIPTURE READING: Colossians 3:1-14

VERSE DU JOUR: *And over all these virtues put on love, which binds them all together in perfect unity.* (Colossians 3:14)

Urine fell from the sky like rain. Well, it didn't exactly fall from the sky, but rather from the classroom ceiling. It splattered all over us and all over the students' lab notebooks. The notebooks were speckled and swollen until the end of the semester, reminders that the teacher's instructions to balance the centrifuge should have been heeded—at least when spinning student urine samples for what became the infamous physiology urine lab! Fortunately, urine is a benign bodily fluid, considered to be generally sterile and not harmful. Even that knowledge did not stop the screams of surprise and the howls of laughter as we peeled off our lab coats and discussed what went wrong.

Love and laughter . . . Don't they go together? Do you picture Jesus as a sour-faced stoic, or is your Jesus a laughing Jesus, a Jesus with a twinkle in his eye? Can you envision a Jesus with an unnaturally good sense of humor? Picture him having a good, deep laugh while watching his disciples as they battled the nets, barely able to pull in the miraculous late-night catch. And Jesus had to be fun to be around, or else who would want to be with him? Even informal study of human nature reveals that people just do not like to hang out with those who are boring, scowling, or overly serious.

Furthermore, negative people rarely form a large fan base. Following this logic we can surmise that Jesus was not boring or overly serious. Scripture indicates that Jesus had a fairly filled social schedule and was in great demand.

I know that God loves me and accepts me. I am secure in myself because I am forgiven me and believe God has prepared a place for me in heaven. The Holy Spirit fills my being, and God has promised me protection and provision. God will give me wisdom and the perspective that was given to Jesus. With such security and acceptance, I can take risks and can allow myself to relax and enjoy the people God has placed around me. I can have fun whether bathed in the showers of blessing or dodging urine rain. By the way, students from the urine-rain class never failed to balance a centrifuge in my laboratory ever again! Today I challenge you to find something funny and really laugh.

PRAYER: Help me to study your ways now, so that I relax and laugh.

99

Parenting 101

SUGGESTED SCRIPTURE READINGS: Matthew 1:18-24; 2:13-23

VERSE DU JOUR: *"The virgin will be with child and will give birth to a son, and they will call him Immanuel"—which means, "God with us."* (Matthew 1:23)

A few chuckles and questions about my true age surfaced before I started the lesson on meiosis and reproduction. "What is wrong with you, Ms. Drake? You don't have any kids of your own yet? I already have three, and I'm only sixteen," Tina blurted in those hectic minutes before the start of class. "You must be as old as my grandma—what are you waiting for?" she continued.

I was taken aback. I had never thought about my students' sexual and social status quite this way before. The reality is that one million teens in the United States will become pregnant over the next year and more than half of teen mothers are seventeen years or younger when they first become pregnant. Less than one third of teens who have babies before the age of eighteen finish high school. My students, however, appeared unfazed, and soon there was a buzzing conversation between several girls: How old is your baby? Does the dad of your toddler help out? Let me see your baby's picture.

Jesus knew about teen pregnancy. His mother had almost certainly been a teenager at the time Jesus was born. Jesus started his life in a barn, and although he was born in Bethlehem, the family quickly relocated to Egypt but then moved back to Palestine before he was five years old. Jesus may have endured the taunts of the classmates who had heard the tales of his origins. Despite these humble circumstances, Jesus lived and grew to fulfill his destiny as Savior to the world.

I was about thirty years old and happy to pursue a career while directing my parenting skills toward my students. My retort of "I don't have any kids because I have a hundred and thirty of you" didn't satisfy the curious class that day. In fact, it never occurred to me how close I was to a different world until Tina's questioning opened my eyes. Here I was surrounded by young men and women, older than their years, and in situations more complicated than I could imagine. Like Jesus, we need to respect and encourage them. The next time you're angry that a student hasn't completed an assignment, why not remind yourself that the student, in addition to being in your class, might also be in a difficult or unstable family situation? The student might crave the attention of an absent parent or might be a mom or dad. We can represent "God with us" to them.

PRAYER: Jesus, please bless all the young women and men who need your support and guidance in their lives.

100
No Substitute

SUGGESTED SCRIPTURE READING: 1 Samuel 2:1-10

VERSE DU JOUR: *"There is no one holy like the LORD; there is no one besides you; there is no Rock like our God."* (1 Samuel 2:2)

There is no substitute for roses on Valentine's Day—sorry, daisies don't cut it. Dare you contend that margarine can easily replace butter? And lolling in the baby pool does not count as aerobic exercise. Listening to a CD of a symphony orchestra cannot replace the experience of hearing and seeing the concert in person. Sometimes we do have to use substitutes to cover our classes when we are ill. Even then, we usually pay a price. The aftermath of such situations is often overwhelming. The pre-prep time is tedious, and the hassle of the whole experience makes us wonder why we didn't drag our sorry, sick selves into class anyway . . .

In many instances, replacing a substitute for the real thing leaves us feeling disappointed. Something is amiss, lacking—not quite right. Apparently, to God, there is no substitute for our praise and our company. Bible scholars have gone so far as to suggest that we were put on this earth so that we could worship God. Jesus suggests that our main focus on earth should be to praise God.

One of the greatest theological mysteries is this: Why does God care so much about humankind and expend precious thought and energy to bother with us? God doesn't need us, and the human race has a pretty bad track record when it comes to companionship. We are often unfaithful and unkind to each other and are even worse when it comes to God. We have been doubtful, unfaithful, and willing to remain ignorant of God's ways. We are blemished by any number of different sins and often make foolish choices that lead us to evil. If God is an all-powerful and all-knowing being who is holy and sinless, why choose to be with us? God is the Creator of all and the ruler of the universe and beyond, yet God wants our company. Why didn't God create beings more dependable and amiable than us?

God wants to communicate with us and hear our praise. God wants to see our lives demonstrate grace as our thanks. Perhaps there is no substitute for what God yearns to see and hear: the orchestra of his people loving and serving each other in Jesus' name. Likewise, there is no substitute for God's presence in our lives. We cannot buy enough toys or play enough games to satisfy the part of us that is wired to be with our Maker.

If we ignore our need for God, something will always seem amiss, lacking, not quite right. We cannot substitute family, job, loved ones, or material possessions for God. It doesn't matter how talented, attractive, or good we are. There will never be a substitute for God. Will you worship and praise almighty God today?

PRAYER: Thank you for your patience with me. I know I was put on this earth so that I can praise and serve you. Please go with me.

101
Engage!

SUGGESTED SCRIPTURE READINGS: 1 Corinthians 7:12-15; Luke 8:16-18

VERSE DU JOUR: *"My prayer is not that you take them out of the world but that you protect them from the evil one."* (John 17:15)

"Robert Hooke, while living in a monastery, examined the bark of a cork tree under the microscope; he saw tiny chambers that resemble his monastic room, or cell, and so that is what he called these tiny structures, which eventually are defined as the basic units of structure for all living things." I pause for a moment in my lecture, briefly thinking how nice it would be to visit a monastery right now. How peaceful it would be—one desk, one peg for my robe, and one tiny bed, prayers required in the morning, a simple breakfast, a mug of stout ale every evening . . .

"So, what happens next?" I hear as an attentive student interrupts my reverie. Oops, time to get back to my classroom and my job of engaging the real world.

Throughout the centuries, monastic orders have played important roles in serving humankind, and I do not discount their good works. Yet monasteries and convents are not the norm for God's children. Jesus teaches that we are to live lives separated from the world by our actions and our love, not by geography or social structure. He prayed that we, his disciples, might be protected from the evil one and proclaimed that we are salt and the light to the world. How can we be those things if we are sequestered?

God promises to watch over those who believe and bless them. God also will bless the places and people with whom we interact. Your classroom, the athletic field where you coach, the table where you tutor children, your entire school: all are blessed with God's presence simply because you are there. God is with your students when you are with them; God hears your prayers for your students, and because of your prayers, they will be blessed. Your prayers may save a child from suicide, drug addiction, or a life of violence. Your smile may change an attitude or save a life. Your presence and prayers may prod the angels to protect your students from some great danger. You can make a positive impact wherever you go today; it's time to engage!

PRAYER: Thank you for your protection and for recognizing my work. Let me remember that I am where I am because of you and that you are watching me and protecting those with whom I work.

102

Spit Out

SUGGESTED SCRIPTURE READING: Matthew 12:25-32

VERSE DU JOUR: *"He who is not with me is against me, and he who does not gather with me scatters."* (Matthew 12:30)

The stench of the ginger-brew wafting through the classroom turns my stomach. I should have had a more than a scant piece of toast and tea for breakfast this morning. It's the final day of our ginger-ale lab, and I've promised the students that I will sample each group's "brew." I have already managed to swallow (very small) sips of samples from groups one and two. The third group offers me their concoction. Are my eyes rolling to the back of my head, or does it just feel that way? This stuff is awful— vile, bitter, horrible! I want to finish the job and just swallow, but can't control the reflex that takes over. I run to the nearest sink and spew the vile cider into the open sink and down the front of my shirt.

Throughout his entire life, Jesus demonstrated a passion for God, for us, and for his mission. In his every act, Jesus showed how to live a life of enthusiasm, engagement, and unfettered fervor. Jesus showed an attitude of wholehearted devotion in the way he washed feet, welcomed children to his lap, loaded the disciples' nets with fish, and produced fine vintage wine. The wine Jesus made for the wedding feast was the best the partygoers had ever tasted; it was not mediocre and did not leave the bitter aftertaste of a halfhearted attempt. Jesus pronounced that if you are not distinctly fighting for him, then you are fighting against him. In the kingdom of heaven, there is no room for neutrality and no time for indifference. Jesus had no tolerance for double-minded faith or for halfhearted followers; his teaching on this issue was clear. Jesus taught that lukewarm followers—Christians who bring neither the thirst-quenching refreshment of cold water nor the healing benefits of a hot spring—these are not true disciples at all and that they would be "spit out" (see Revelation 3:15-16).

Never again would I promise to consume every group's ginger ale. "Maybe I'll try one or two" became my pre-lab mantra. I never forgot how that concoction triggered my reflex to *get it out!* Just thinking about drinking the foul product of the anaerobic laboratory makes me want to gag. I sure don't want to give Jesus an uncommitted heart or halfhearted service. I don't want to trigger his gag reflex or induce him to spit me out! Don't you also want your heart and your deeds to be totally committed to him?

PRAYER: Lord, I choose this day to be on your side. Please help me to show the clarity of my choice to others.

103

Abramesque

Suggested Scripture Readings: Genesis 12:1-8; 17:9-27

VERSE DU JOUR: *"I will bless those who bless you, and whoever curses you I will curse; and all peoples on earth will be blessed through you."* (Genesis 12:3)

Oops—I forgot to call Tina's mom about the field trip, and I'm definitely planning on putting off the call to Micah's guardian. Every time I call him about a disciplinary issue, I have to hear a litany of excuses and accusations. I'll eventually have to make these new calls, though. Oh, and I never got around to helping Sennah with her project yesterday. I don't feel like calling my friend to apologize for my rude behavior yesterday, either. I'm too busy, anyway. Just look at this pile of papers I have to finish grading.

Abram, one of a few monotheists in a pantheistic and violent society, was chosen by God to be the father of a great nation. God appears to Abram and tells him to take his wife and leave everything he knows to go to a new land. God doesn't even tell him where he will be going but immediately offers to Abram a promise of greatness. At seventy-five years of age, Abram picks up and goes. The Genesis account implies neither questions nor hesitation on Abram's part. At ninety nine years of age, Abram is revisited by God. God reaffirms the promise of building a nation through Abram. God also renames Abram and his wife before commanding the newly named Abraham to circumcise himself and all males who are part of his household. The shocker here is that Abraham not only complies with this request but does so immediately. We are told that on the same day that Abraham was given this directive, he carries it out. I think I would have found a few ways to stall on that one! But we don't hear excuses or stall tactics from Abraham; he's a can-do kind of guy. Without hesitation, Abraham does what God orders.

How many of our sins are not sins of action but sins of omission or procrastination? Sin can result from not doing what God tells us to do or by not obeying immediately. We run the risk of forgetting to do the right thing when we put off doing something that God has placed in our hearts. We run the risk of never finding time to do the things that are eternally important. Although Abraham made some grievous mistakes during his life, God still honored him. Perhaps God honored Abraham and made him the father of many nations because God admired his open ear and prompt obedience. Are you stalling on something you should be doing, or are you Abramesque?

PRAYER: Is there something I should be doing that I am not? Forgive me, Lord, and give me the strength and willingness to do what you have told me to do.

104
Power of Words

SUGGESTED SCRIPTURE READING: James 3:1-11

VERSES DU JOUR: *The mind of the wise make their speech judicious, and adds persuasiveness to their lips. Pleasant words are like a honeycomb, sweetness to the soul and health to the body.* (Proverbs 16:23-24, NRSV)

I must confess that one Valentine's Day, a student broke my heart. Literally. And then, he handed it to me.

Leo was a popular, attractive, and personable young man, a student in my fifth-period class. Although bright and eager to please, he was sometimes careless. Leo hesitantly approached me with tears welling in his eyes. "I am *so* sorry. I didn't mean to do this. I'll do anything to make it up to you." He held out my broken heart; the porcelain pharmaceutical model was cracked straight through. He was trying to squeeze the pieces together.

How many times had I told the class to use these carefully? I went to some trouble to obtain a full set of these models that I hoped my students could use for years to come. Now I was down one, and that would mean one less lab group equipped with this cool anatomical tool. I was disappointed and more than a little vexed. What should I say?

Jesus used words to teach, but he also used words to comfort, affirm, and build the confidence of his followers: I love you. I will never leave you or forsake you. You are more important than the flowers and the birds. Jesus had all the right words and said the right things at the right time. His words were not those of empty flattery but were spoken in truth. Jesus' words of encouragement and affirmation are meant for all of us. How amazing is that? Although Jesus had a great way with words, the Scriptures warn us of the tongue's power. James speaks of the tongue as "full of deadly poison," and in the Psalms we see the tongue described as a way of plotting destruction. It is said to be like a razor. Throughout the Scriptures we are warned that the power of words can be used for evil or for good. Words can build people up or break them down; they can begin wars or build bridges. A teacher's words can help heal a broken heart, restore confidence, or save a life. Words are power, and we yield that power.

"I forgive you, Leo," were not words that came easily. "I bet we can glue it back together somehow . . ." What else could I do? I could barely look into his dark, repentant eyes. Words endlessly exit our lips; day after day, on and on we go. But how much are we masters of our words and how much are they masters of us? As competent teachers and effective believers, we must learn to control our tongues and the words we say. It's so easy to let the wrong words fly when we feel wronged or upset. But mere words cause hatred and death or healing and love.

Can you use your words to spread Jesus' love, to extol the good in others, or to offer them hope? You can verbally support a staff member, a spouse, a student, a parent, a secretary, or a friend. Your words can reflect the One whom you serve.

PRAYER: Lord, please help me control my words. Let me lift up at least one person with affirming words today. Let me use my words for your cause.

105

Power in the Real World

SUGGESTED SCRIPTURE READING: 1 Corinthians 1:22-30

VERSE DU JOUR: *But to those whom God has called, both Jews and Greeks, Christ [is] the power of God and the wisdom of God.* (1 Corinthians 1:24)

I woke from a sweat-inducing nightmare. My class had gone wild, students were dancing on lab table tops, and everyone ignored me. Over the din of their screams and coarse laughter, they couldn't have heard me anyway. It was *Lord of the Flies* takes biology. Whew . . . glad it was just a dream. But then it hit me. I had to get up now and go back to the real world, a world that isn't far from the nightmare I just left behind. And in my real world, I have no power or control over anything. I scurry around day after day, trying to control my surroundings and my life, but any control I think I have is only an illusion. This concept feels depressing yet also strangely freeing.

If you are a child of God and are trying to follow God's plan for your life, then the control issue is of no concern, because it is out of your hands. No matter how bad or good things might look, God already has control. Additionally, through Jesus, we hold power beyond compare.

God is in you, with you, for you. God promises to give you power and wisdom. This is the same God on whom Jesus leaned for his power and understanding. The same God supplied Jesus with the will to serve others and the abilities that would result in a world forever changed. The power of God allowed Jesus to perform miracles, to teach to the multitudes, and to possess great intellectual and emotional strength. God has promised this same power to us through Jesus.

My day in the real world turned out to be a bit more normal than the teaching day I'd left behind in that dream. Thank the Lord. There was the incident in the cafeteria when a student stabbed himself, and in the words of a nearby witness, "The blood was spurting everywhere! The bleeding kid just sat there laughing."

Sometimes the system that surrounds teaching, the seeming lack of response to your efforts, the demands of your workload, or any number of teaching-related issues can make you feel powerless. To feel out of control or powerless is a bad thing, but we must avoid the trap of thinking we have complete control. We will lose all hope, however, if we forget the power that we do have; God promises us access to the same power on which Jesus relied. Oh, let us not forget God's promises and power!

PRAYER: Thank you for being in control. Thank you for the power of Christ in me. Let me use it wisely today.

106

Ends of the World

SUGGESTED SCRIPTURE READING: 2 Corinthians 12:1-6

VERSE DU JOUR: *"And be sure of this—that I am with you always, even to the end of the world."* (Matthew 28:20, TLB)

It was in the middle of class when a knock interrupted her literature lecture. The teacher looked at the wide-eyed girl standing in her doorway. "How can I help you?" she brusquely asked.

"I need to speak to my friend, LaToya," the girl said nervously.

"May I ask what it is that is so important that you would interrupt my class?" the teacher inquired.

The flustered girl responded, "I need my friend to help me read the instructions and results of my pregnancy test. I can't do it myself, and she helped me last time."

Hearing my colleague recount this exchange, I suddenly think, "Where am I? This girl is just one of perhaps many in this school who not only can't read but also thinks she is pregnant again.

How can this happen? What can I do?" Then I remember: "I am with you always, even to the end of the world."

While on earth, Jesus shared himself. Jesus also carefully surrounded himself with people who could benefit from his presence. Over a life of indulgence, he purposely chose a life of poverty, inconvenience, and discomfort. Jesus knew that life was a temporary condition, that he would one day return to his home in paradise, the same place where Jesus promises to save us a spot. But we can do more than long for the future. Jesus also promised that we can benefit from his presence and that he will bring us a bit of paradise now!

Is your whole being crying out for a break from a place that seems like the end of the world? Do you need a touch of sun on a lush tropical isle or the promise of a smile from a good friend? Maybe you'd settle for a bit of normalcy—a balanced administration, a secure classroom, or stable students. Perhaps the environment in which you work makes you feel as if you've been assigned to a mission on one of the most remote and bizarre ends of the world. Take heart—you are in the best of company. Jesus has promised his presence and guidance. The God who loves, cherishes, and appreciated you has chosen to be with you wherever you are. God goes ahead of you, beside you, and after you. God goes anywhere and has seen it all! Paradise is not where you are but who you are with; you're with Jesus, and he is the BEST.

PRAYER: Lord, please bring a bit of your presence and your paradise to my world. I invite you and beg you to go with me today!

107

The Whole Package

SUGGESTED SCRIPTURE READING: Philippians 3:7-10

VERSE DU JOUR: *I want to know Christ and the power of his resurrection and the fellowship of sharing in his sufferings.* (Philippians 3:10)

"Mrs. Drake gave the whole class the finger! Can you believe her?" the students howled with delight to anyone who would listen, including parents and administrators. What they failed to mention is that the finger was accidentally isolated while lecturing and attempting to enumerate several points: point one (index finger used and waved around a bit), point two, (middle finger used and pointed around a bit, but it wasn't like *that*).

Don't you love it when the news media, or your students, for that matter, take something that you've said or done out of context, and by doing so, the original message becomes so twisted as to be completely wrong? How many of us, however, are guilty of doing the same thing when it comes to biblical concepts?

In Philippians, Paul, self-described servant of Christ, discusses his desire to know Jesus better. Are your desires similar? I know that as the description of Paul's quest unfolds, my reactions become increasingly less and less enthusiastic. Here's how I react:

I want to know Christ—Yeah! My arm is enthusiastically pumping the air.

I want to know the power of his resurrection—I'm still happily pumping the air.

I want the fellowship of sharing in his sufferings—My arm stops pumping. I'm feeling less sure.

I want to be like him in death—Oh, I definitely don't think so! I'm feeling queasy.

Having worked and studied with Jesus, Paul understood the necessity of joyfully and contentedly sharing all the circumstances of discipleship. Paul's enthusiasm for Christ was not dependent on his personal circumstances but on his relationship with his Lord. Paul's lack of selectivity in this matter was key to his great effectiveness as a leader and in his unworldly sense of contentment. Paul refused to take his spiritual learning or the words of Jesus out of context. He heard and preached the hard words along with the easy words.

Students and teachers all had a good laugh over my finger episode. Because my students knew me, they also knew that I would never knowingly and willingly flip them all the bird. They gladly endured the error that was part of the whole package of the lesson, and at least they all woke up for a few minutes. If we gladly endure the whole package of our experience with Christ, we are offered unworldly contentment, a peace that does not rely on our circumstances or our comfort but on our connectedness to the God of the universe.

PRAYER: Jesus, I am in for the long haul. I will follow your plan and continue on the journey you have set before me. Please show me your spirit of peace and let me feel content in the place you have put me. Thank you for your friendship, protection, and peace.

108
The Mocking Gym

SUGGESTED SCRIPTURE READING: Psalm 82:1-8

VERSE DU JOUR: *Rescue the weak and needy; deliver them from the hand of the wicked.* (Psalm 82:4)

Finally—away from school and into the gym, my time to unwind! Walking toward the locker room, I spotted two trainers who were looking out of their glassy office. They were staring and laughing. Following their eyes, I saw the object of their amusement and derision—a somewhat obese young woman doing squat jumps.

My first inclination was to ignore the whole scene, but a part of me said, "Good for her! That's why she's here." Another part of me became angry with those trainers who were busy using a gym client for their amusement and to boost their egos. I occasionally witness this kind of nastiness in school and have developed ways to minimize it in my classroom, but I was shocked to witness this behavior from adults in a business.

Jesus clearly demonstrates how we should treat others. It was with love and respect that he spoke to the sick, the ungainly, the lame, and the leper. Jesus treated everyone with equal doses of dignity and grace. He gave the same attention and energies to the old and the young, the rich and the poor, the beauties and the repellent, the Pharisees and the prostitutes. He was able to see beyond outward appearances. Jesus valued all people as the precious and beloved children of God. Why should I do any less?

Now I know what I should have done, and what I have vowed to do next time—and there will undoubtedly be a similar next time. I have vowed to do something, even if doing that something makes me uncomfortable. I should have marched into the little glass office and gotten the names of those trainers. Then, as a paying gym member, I should have lodged a formal complaint with the manager of the facility, with a follow-up to the district manager. Whether in the classroom or in the gym, defending the less fortunate or the ridiculed requires willingness to interrupt my day as well as self-assurance and bravery. Whether I walk by and ignore the slight against another fellow human or whether I join in on the abuse, I am wrong. Such actions not only potentially harm someone else but also anger our God.

PRAYER: Lord, let me be a voice for the less fortunate today.

109

The Direct Route

SUGGESTED SCRIPTURE READING: Matthew 5:33-37

VERSE DU JOUR: *"Simply let your 'Yes' be 'Yes' and your 'No,' 'No'; anything beyond this comes from the evil one."* (Matthew 5:37)

Despite years of practice, my downhill ski technique was going nowhere, or perhaps I should say it was going all the wrong places and going there way too fast. The habit of making large traverses across steep slopes was not improving my form, nor was it assisting in getting me safely down. When I came to an intimidating steep slope, my response was to go across it from one side to another. The amount of altitude lost in each traverse was minimal but enough to get me flying faster and faster until I would finally careen out of control, over the edge of the slope and into the woods. I often found myself buried in a pile of powder or enjoying a freezing facial. It took me years before I heeded the advice of others: "Point your skis straight down the hill, look directly down, and go!"

Jesus was not a man to make wide traverses in his dealings with anyone. He was always straight to the point. He chose to tell the truth and to do the right thing no matter what the cost. He was obedient to God, immediately and completely. He spent little time on idle pleasantries. To the woman at the well, he said, "Everyone who drinks of this water will be thirsty again, but those who drink the water that I give them will never be thirsty. The water I give him will become in them a spring of water gushing up to eternal life" (John 4:13-14, NRSV). To Nicodemus he said, "I tell you the truth, no one can see the kingdom of God unless he is born again" (John 3:3). When clearing the temple, he pronounced, "Get these out of here! How dare you turn my Father's house into a market!" (John 2:16). Before healing the lame man at the well of Bethesda, Jesus asked, "Do you want to get well?" (John 5:6). And when calling his disciples, Jesus uttered a simple, direct statement, "Follow me, and I will make you fish for people" (Matthew 4:19, NRSV).

How many times it seems so much easier to avoid dangerous or difficult situations. I give a safe but vague answer to a colleague instead of the truth about why I go to church on Sunday. I choose to stay home instead of going in to do that extra lab prep on Saturday. I neglect to call that unsupportive parent who questioned me at our last conference. I decide to ignore foul language instead of reprimanding the offenders. I can choose many indirect, yet dangerous paths. Instead, let's face our challenges head-on and complete the tasks we have been given. God will help us as we look ahead and go!

PRAYER: Lord, help me to face my challenges and rely on you to help me make it through my day.

110

Why?

SUGGESTED SCRIPTURE READING: Job 38:1-41

VERSE DU JOUR: *"Have you ever given orders to the morning, or shown the dawn its place, that it might take the earth by the edges and shake the wicked out of it?"* (Job 38:12)

Why are science teachers so hyped up about cells?
Cells are what make up all living things.

Why cells, and what do you mean, make up?
Cells are the basic unit of structure and function. They're like building blocks. And they contain DNA.

Why is DNA such a big deal?
Well, DNA contains all the information needed to build your body; your tissues, organs, and systems wouldn't exist without the information from the DNA.

Why are you making us learn all this stuff?
We want you to be knowledgeable, intelligent, and healthy humans.

"Why" questions are important, but an overabundance of them can make even the sanest educator crazy as a loon. No wonder so many parents resort to, "That's the way God made it, honey."

Jesus allowed people to question him. He asked plenty of questions, too. Jesus used questions to provoke thought and discussion. And although Jesus welcomed questions from true seekers, he was suspicious of and hesitant to answer directly those questions that were meant to trick him. But in the record of Job, we learn that there is a limit to the questions that God will tolerate. When we question God's ways or God's wisdom, we walk an extremely thin and tenuous line.

Sometimes I'm no better than my students or my children. It's a wonder God can be so patient with me when I start with my litany of questions. When I had to leave my dream teaching job and the beauty of my home for the unknown wilds of Baltimore, I had plenty of "why" questions. God, why Baltimore? Why now? I went on and on.

Imagine how tired God must be of our questioning. Of course, if we never ask God for direction or a bit of insight, we must be suffering a deplorable lack of curiosity. What God made clear to Job, a man who suffered much, was that Job had no right to question God's motives. In time, God will answer our questions. Our task is to worship and follow God despite our questions.

PRAYER: God, I do not know all the reasons why you have placed me here. Please reveal to me what I need to know, and help me to trust you to take care of the unknowns. You are my God, and I acknowledge your wisdom and power in my life.

111

Upside Down

SUGGESTED SCRIPTURE READING: Romans 12:9-21

VERSE DU JOUR: *Do not be overcome by evil, but overcome evil with good.* (Romans 12:21)

The workmen have been here for three days, and the atmosphere is starting to feel strained. They are in the middle of a project that I hope is completed soon, so I am leaving them alone. The whine of an occasional drill and incessantly banging hammers are a small price to pay for renovation and rewiring. The only real problem is that the students are still trying to complete their lab assignments without stepping on these guys.

When the project started, the presence of outsiders in our room was a novelty; I'm not sure if the students thought these guys would serve as additional entertainment. (They already have me; what more do they need?) But now, a week in, no one is happy about the situation, including the workmen, with their heads under the lab tables while thirty-three students not so gingerly step around their unprotected bodies.

Jesus regularly embraced positive change. He challenged social, religious, and moral standards of his day and encouraged his followers to do the same. Jesus was different from any other teacher of his day, religious or otherwise. He taught that good can and will overcome evil.

As teachers, we are in position to change so much, if only we are willing and prepared. Before we can expect to enact positive change in the world around us, however, we need to change ourselves—we need to be rewired. Our attitudes, hearts, behaviors, and words need to be directed by Jesus. Jesus came to this little planet in order to turn it upside down. If we are truly his followers, he expects us to do the same.

As a boy of eight, Martin Luther King Jr. learned about segregation. After his mother introduced the sad truths of the racism prevalent during his time, Martin looked up at his momma and said, "I'm gonna turn this world upside down!" How prophetic . . . Don't you think that Jesus was beaming over that response?

There is plenty of turning and changing to be done. Jesus wants us to change us as we work to change the world. God will prepare, protect, inspire, and strengthen us as we fight inequity and injustice. How comforting that God never changes but allows us to change. What can you work to change today?

PRAYER: Help me use my position as teacher to turn my world upside down. Please help me to change _____. Lord, change me so that I become more like you every day!

112

Call Me Crazy

SUGGESTED SCRIPTURE READING: 1 John 3:11-24

VERSE DU JOUR: *Dear children, let us not love with words or tongue but with actions and in truth.* (1 John 3:18)

"New Promise for Public Education!" the headlines screamed. The local paper's article echoed the newest press release from the state department of education: Don't fret, citizens; the quality of public education will improve as new teachers replace older, less flexible veterans. Thanks for that vote of confidence, I thought. Nonetheless, school started as usual, with those inflexible veterans stretched further than anyone outside the system could imagine.

That morning, I heard a commotion in the classroom next door, where my new friend and veteran educator, Laura, was teaching English. It sounded as if she were having a very bad day. I soon learned that Laura's students had been defacing and ripping the posters with which she had lovingly decorated an otherwise hideous room. Although she had spent her own money to purchase these colorful cover-ups, several students vandalized them in front of her. Another student brazenly pulled down the classroom clock, yanking it from the wall and disconnecting its wires. When Laura tried to stop the destruction, approaching those who were the obvious vandals and ordering them to stop, one student screamed back. "You have no right to accuse me," the boy shouted as he stood holding the clock in his hands.

Later, when I found Laura in the hall outside her room, I gave her a quick hug and tried to comfort her with words that no doubt sounded trite and strained. "It's crazy sometimes," I said.

"We're the crazy ones," she answered.

How many first-century citizens considered Jesus to be average, normal, or even sane? How many of his activities might have led Jesus to be placed in the category of "crazy man" or "out of his mind"? He claimed divinity, offered forgiveness of sins, and wandered the countryside. Yet, in retrospect, we easily acknowledge that Jesus' life consisted of a continuous string of good works reflecting the perfect will of God. Although many people in his day must have labeled Jesus as crazy, we know that he was saner than anyone since.

"No wonder Laura looks unhappy and nervous," I thought as I turned to go.

"Wait a minute, Susan," Laura said as her eyes filled. "How *will* education improve?" she asked. "Who in their right mind would want to go back into that room with the expectation of teaching those students?" I had just started my new job here, committed to teaching the same students, and even taught in the room right next to this dear lady. For a moment, I didn't feel so bright myself. Was Laura questioning my sanity as well as her own? Who in their right mind, indeed! As God's children, we need the mind of God, a mentality that allows us to enter where others fear to tread. Can you commit to following God's will even if your reality seems crazy?

PRAYER: Let me be crazy only for you. Thank you for leading me and accompanying me wherever I go.

113

Language They Can Understand

SUGGESTED SCRIPTURE READING: 1 Corinthians 14:1-12

VERSE DU JOUR: *So it is with you. Unless you speak intelligible words with your tongue, how will anyone know what you are saying?* (1 Corinthians 14:9)

The morning he was scheduled to visit my classroom as our guest scientist/guest speaker, my husband, Chuck, awoke complaining of a stomachache. When he then tried to cancel, I hauled him out of bed and explained how much the students were looking forward to his visit. Chuck was then a doctoral student in immunology, and I thought he could communicate to my students the rigors of academic science and benefits of higher education. And I wanted Chuck to experience what I do each day.

Despite his nervousness, Chuck did make it into the classroom. But I must admit that before Chuck began his talk, I was suddenly nervous myself. "What if he can't relate to my students? What if he speaks so far above them that he loses them?" My husband is calm, cool, and an experienced public speaker; he is rarely flustered either in front of a crowd or solo. But as he lectured, I noticed sweat beading on his brow.

Jesus was a master of lesson adaptation. He could speak in a way that people understood. He tailored his parables, metaphors, and instructional devices to his crowd. When speaking to an agrarian group, he used examples drawing on farming and shepherding, topics with which his audience was familiar. With the fishermen, he used fishing analogies. When speaking to temple scholars, Jesus drew from the rabbinical texts. Jesus was careful to not speak above or below his audience.

The Scriptures tell us that we, too, are to strive for understanding; we want to understand God's Word, and we want others to understand us. Perhaps today's Scripture not only speaks to the issue of tongues. Perhaps it is a challenge to us—a statement on the importance of effective communication. We waste time and words when our students can't understand us.

I had no reason to fear; despite his obvious nervousness, Chuck successfully adjusted his presentation to the crowd. Afterwards, my students asked pertinent questions about his work and appeared to comprehend Chuck's answers. Overall I would rate his presentation and its reception as excellent. When the first class filed out, Chuck collapsed into a student desk. "Buck up, good man. You have four minutes until the next group arrives," I cheerfully advised. Chuck did make it through the morning, and I must confess that, at least for awhile, he referred to my profession with a bit more respect.

Thinking back to my first days of teaching, or even to the start of each new class, I am reminded of how Chuck felt that day. Adapting our lessons so that we reach our students takes effort and practice. However, if we want to teach like Jesus, we must adjust our teaching to our audience. As we get to know our students and the worlds in which they live, we will be more likely to use language that they understand.

PRAYER: Lord, let me speak in words that my students can understand. Show me how I can reach them as I serve you today.

114
Road Kill

SUGGESTED SCRIPTURE READING: James 1:12-18

VERSE DU JOUR: *Every good and perfect gift comes from above, coming down from the Father of the heavenly lights, who does not change like shifting shadows.* (James 1:17)

It was almost time for class to start when I noticed Jim waiting at the front of the room. He was clearly excited about something; his face was flushed, and he was bouncing on the balls of his feet.

"I can't wait to give you this! I've been waiting since last night. YOU ARE GONNA LOVE THIS!" Jim bellowed. Then he revealed the box he'd been hiding behind his back.

"Good start—no holes poked into the top of the cardboard box and no noticeable movement," I thought, tentatively reaching for the gift. "When I saw this last night, I just had to stop and get it for you. I asked my stepdad to stop as soon as I saw it. I kept after him until he finally turned the car around and let me out to get it. He had to go back pretty far, too," Jim explained. Visions of semiprecious gems sparkling from a downtown jewelry store window filled my head.

James, the brother of Jesus, must've been quite a guy. James admits that he is a servant and under the lordship of Jesus. Can you imagine admitting that you are a willing servant, subject to the control of any one of your siblings? James even refers to his brother as "our glorious Lord" and goes on to spend the remainder of his life spreading news of his brother's divinity. James also tells us that it is God, hence Jesus, who gives every good and perfect gift.

We are surrounded by God's gifts: the abundance of food that tempts us to overeat, the clothes that jam our closets, and nature's ever-present beauty. It's easy to be thankful for the things God gives us that we like: a step up on the salary scale, the occasionally well-behaved and appreciative student, or an unexpected snow day. Yet, James implies that some of God's gifts that do not appeal to us are meant to mold and test us toward perfection. As children of God, we are advised to even see trials as gifts meant to work for our good.

I took a deep breath while visions of wonderful possibilities danced in my head. Perhaps Jim's box contained a homemade craft, cookies, or even a new pair of Nikes. Instead, as I gently lifted the box top and peeked inside, I spied a snake-like tail stuffed next to the matted, grayish-brown fur of a not so recently deceased opossum. I couldn't let Jim down; he was truly excited to present me with this unique and scientifically appropriate gift. So I squealed with obvious delight, "This is just what I needed. Thank you *so* much!"

You might think I'd be repulsed or angry with my gift. Instead, I merely realized that I would have one more pressing task to perform. I didn't have much longer before my present would become quite a stinker. However, once the formalin was prepared and this guy was successfully bottled, ours was the only classroom sporting a beautiful and local marsupial sample. Can you see God's mercy and abundance through the road kill of your life?

PRAYER: Don't let me be deceived. Let me see all that you give me as good and perfect.

115
God Helps Those Who . . . ?

SUGGESTED SCRIPTURE READING: Hebrews 4:13-16

VERSE DU JOUR: *"He will reply, 'I tell you the truth, whatever you did not do for one of the least of these, you did not do for me.'"* (Matthew 25:45)

"Thanks for helping me again. It's already dark out, so be careful getting home," Tommy cautioned as he packed up his books. For awhile, it felt like nearly every after-school tutoring session included Tommy, the young man classified as "special ed," who needed so much extra attention and help. While I tutored him, Tommy seemed like other students and presented himself as a sensitive, intelligent boy who could eventually comprehend even difficult concepts. So I couldn't understand why he would consistently fail tests and written assignments despite demonstrating complete understanding of the tested material the afternoon before. Did he forget to study, could he possibly forget the work we'd done together twelve hours before, or was he not trying?

Helping Tommy, I tried to ignore the voice in my head repeating the old adage: "God helps those who help themselves," My co-teacher, Lonnie, and I worked together with Tommy and finally figured out the problem. Despite making it to the eleventh grade, Tommy could not read!

The concept that God helps those who help themselves is not a biblical concept. Nowhere in the Bible will you find the phrase, and you will find example after example refuting the idea. Looking at the life of Jesus, we find a man who, instead of insisting that the needy find a way to help themselves, responds to the helpless by offering immediate and practical help. Jesus does seem to give highest priority to assisting the helpless who are willing to admit their helplessness. He tends personally to those who ask for his help; we see Jesus heal the blind, counsel the seekers, and defend an adulteress. He not only was moved to help individuals but also was able to feel compassion for crowds of people. "When he saw the crowds, he had compassion on them, because they were harassed and helpless, like sheep without a shepherd" (Matthew 9:36). Throughout the course of his ministry, Jesus lived up to the psalmist's prophesy: "For he will deliver the needy who cry out, the afflicted who have no one to help" (Psalm 72:12).

After Tommy's reading deficit was discovered, Lonnie spent even more time teaching Tommy to read than I did teaching him biology. He quickly caught on, and his work improved greatly. Tommy was so appreciative of our help and so happy to be reading that working with him was a joy. Of all the certificates and plaques displayed in my office, the most precious was one that read, "My Favorite Teacher," with my name filled in and Tommy's name printed on the bottom.

If we choose to emulate Jesus, we will take up the job of helping the helpless. Jesus promises that what we do for the least of these we do for him. We, who are God's children rescued by grace, are instructed to share that same gift by helping those who cannot help themselves. Will you help someone today?

PRAYER: Lord, let me not grow weary of helping my students. Remind me that you are in each of them and that I am serving you as I serve them.

116

Slandered!

SUGGESTED SCRIPTURE READING: 1 Corinthians 4:1-21

VERSE DU JOUR: *We work hard with our own hands. When we are cursed, we bless; when we are persecuted, we endure it; when we are slandered, we answer kindly.* (1 Corinthians 4:12-13)

After working with A. J. for more than four months and showing her every consideration I could offer, she turned on me. I'd given her special chances to make up late assignments, had individually tutored her after class, and answered each basic question. A. J. had an aggravating behavior of laying her head down on her desk and either sleeping or feigning sleep while I taught. Day after day, I'd told her to sit up, only to see her slip back down mere minutes later. Although she never professed to like me, she turned against me the day I told her that she had to sit up and stay awake or leave class. She decided to avenge this directive by spreading lies about me to anyone who would listen. "Mrs. Drake is evil. She is possessed. Ms. Drake is a racist," were some of the rumors that I heard about through several sources at school, friends who were concerned for my reputation and safety.

I guess I should feel honored that I was accused of some of the same things of which Jesus was accused. People said that he was possessed, too. The religious leaders considered him evil and spread lies about him. Jesus occasionally offered words of explanation in response to such accusations, but he never became defensive or nasty. When the disciples asked Jesus why they didn't fast, a question driven by rumors that the Pharisees raised about Jesus' lack of spirituality, Jesus responded, "How can the guests of the bridegroom mourn while he is with them? The time will come when the bridegroom will be taken from them; then they will fast" (Matthew 9:15). More often than not, it seems that Jesus ignored the rumors and went along on his way. Since I figured that there was no way I could argue away A. J.'s accusations,

I ignored the rumors and hoped for the best. I cried out to God about it plenty, too.

Strangely, A. J.'s lies never seemed to hurt me. In fact, after they started, I seemed to become more popular. Kids started asking me for hugs after classes; maybe they were testing me or feeling sorry for me. Although such dangerous lies worried me, nothing came of them. Whether A. J. ever publicly recanted or her gossip was discounted by her own reputation, I'll never know. And who knew that two years later A. J. would become one of my strongest supporters, even part of the devoted cadre of young women who would show up for after-school field trips? Or that she would be the one student waiting for me in the hallway on April 3, with a birthday card. Let us not tire of answering kindly even when we are slandered; life in God holds many surprises that time will unwrap.

PRAYER: Let me rest in your goodness. Lord, let me answer slander with truth and a smile.

117

Antz!

Suggested Scripture Reading: Proverbs 6:6-11

VERSE DU JOUR: *Go to the ant, you sluggard; consider its ways and be wise!* (Proverbs 6:6)

Sir Thomas Blunt once said, "Every flower of the field, every fiber of every plant, carries with it the impress of its maker." I couldn't agree with him more. It was while preparing a lesson on insects, of all things, that I was overcome with the truth of Sir Thomas's statement and the power of my Lord. Did you know that some entymologists have spent their lives observing ants? We can benefit from the information others have gleaned:

- Ants can easily carry ten to twenty times their weight. Amazonian leaf-cutter ants, which gather leaves and cultivate fungus in well-organized underground farms, carry their leaf burdens more than 100 yards, and in the course of nine days can carry 400 pounds of leaves.

- Ants rely on groups to make up for what they individually lack. In leaf cutter colonies, the smaller ants are the farmers, since they can easily move among fungus without causing damage to the fungus. The larger ants take on jobs more in line with their body design. Some act as soldiers (protecting the colony), workers (manual laborers), or reproductives (the "egg factory" queen).
- Army ants form bivouacs made up of their bodies, and they remain in the bivouac for twenty days while new young are raised. Once the young are raised, the army resumes its nomadic existence, a march that doesn't end until it is time to raise new young. When they raid, army ants are violent and search for prey by following chemical trails set down by their scouts. They can converge on any creature and by sheer numbers can kill and consume large (even human) prey.
- In a well-documented case of ant-aphid mutualism, ants domesticate aphids, which suck plant fluids with their piercing mouth parts. The aphids are moved from plant to plant by the ants, while the ants collect the high-nutrient plant extract that leaks from each aphid.
- Ants are diligent, ingenious, strong creatures that work mutually with other ants and work hard for the survival and benefit of the group.

Busy? Yes. Ingenious? Yes. Sluggards? Not on your life! Jesus used analogies and metaphors taken from nature in his teachings. The Scriptures encourage us to learn from God's creation, and the ant is specifically mentioned. How can we learn wisdom by considering the ways of the ant? Although ants may be considered cute, they seem like nothing but trouble. There is a lesson here; what is it that God wants us to learn from ants?

PRAYER: God, thank you for being a creative scientist who gives us a glimpse of yourself through your many and varied creations. Let me look with amazement at your world, and let me learn from all that you show me.

118

Power in Silence

SUGGESTED SCRIPTURE READING: Proverbs 17

VERSE DU JOUR: *One who spares words is knowledgeable; one who is cool in spirit has understanding.* (Proverbs 17:27, NRSV)

It had snowed the day before, so the students were somewhat ticked that they were in school, yet I had no major discipline issues. In fact, it was one of my best teaching days ever. My students were quiet and attentive; they waited to see the instructions that I would write on the overhead projector. Before I had completed the sentence "Read pages 105–110 in your text," they lined up to grab textbooks. Even my laboratory classes went smoothly. I distributed written lab procedures and wordlessly demonstrated several techniques. The few verbal instructions I gave were whispered, and the students, mimicking me, whispered to each other as they heated samples over the Bunsen burners.

My vow to relative silence was working in my favor. By lunch time, I was so serene that my co-workers must've thought I'd been drugged.

Jesus was the best example of silence under pressure. His silence said more than any words ever could. Consider the power and poise demonstrated by Jesus in the following scenario: All day, Jesus and his friends have been hiking the hot, sandy roads. As the sun starts to set, they are more than ready for a rest, a good meal, and a clean bed. Fresh off a stint of teaching to crowds and performing miracles, Jesus was, no doubt, exhausted and stressed. As they approach the nearest town, Jesus sends two disciples ahead to make arrangements for the night's accommodations.

The two disciples return sweaty and riled. The Master has been refused! Who do these people think they are? The disciples ask Jesus to send down fire from heaven to destroy the arrogant little town. Not only does Jesus refuse to take vengeance on these people, but also he refuses to complain or comment. He puts on his shoes, picks up his gear, and plods on down the road, looking for another place to stay. The disciples (no doubt grumbling and exhausted) watch and follow Jesus as he silently moves on. "What kind of man is this?" they whisper.

The reason I'd barely spoken on the great teaching day was because I was experimenting with a new classroom control technique. I was also sick as a dog. It was too late to call in a substitute on that morning when I awoke to find that I couldn't speak. It was my first bout of true laryngitis, and I thought that as the day wore on, my voice might return. It didn't. The day's events did serve to teach me a valuable lesson: Sometimes a teacher's greatest power is wielded by saying nothing. The urge to say something, to react, to speak to the problem, is one of the occupational hazards of teaching. Yet, great resolve and self-control can be shown through silence. How often my words can cause me trouble; what great witnesses we could be if we followed the advice of Proverbs and the example of Jesus.

PRAYER: Lord, let me know the situations in which I should say nothing. Do not let my words get in the way of your work. Let the words I do say be pleasing to you.

119

No Class!

SUGGESTED SCRIPTURE READING: Matthew 16:24-28

VERSE DU JOUR: *"For those who want to save their life will lose it, and those who lose it for my sake will find it."* (Matthew 16:25)

Impossible! The entire class of students was gone. I had left the room for two, maybe three minutes. But when I came back into what had been a bustling biology lab session, you could've heard a pin drop. The quiet was eerie—until I started to run and shriek, "Where is my class? Don't mess with me, you guys." I searched under lab tables and behind doors. What would the board of education do when they found out that I let an entire class walk away, disappear, be abducted, or whatever happened to them? My fear and surprise gave way to panic as the reality of my situation hit me.

Jesus came to save the wandering and find the lost. He did not come to earth to catch us in our sins or to punish us. Instead, the Scriptures portray Jesus' visit to earth as a rescue mission to save his friends. Jesus' came to seek and save the lost. Jesus taught using parables of the lost sheep, the lost coin, and the lost son. His use of these stories demonstrates an understanding of loss; Jesus knows what it is like to lose something precious. Yet Jesus tells us that if we want to live full lives, we must first lose our lives. Perhaps the loss he speaks of is a figurative release of our own control.

Shortly before losing my class, I'd been worried about a lot of little things: my upcoming dental appointment, the papers I hadn't yet graded, my weekly lesson plan sheet, the ink spot on my new taupe sweater, the supply order I needed to complete. I'd briefly left the classroom because a student told me that he wanted to see a book that I kept stashed in my office. What a fool I'd been. I allowed my worries and this student to distract me from my class.

As soon as I heard giggling coming from the lab prep room, it hit me. I'd been set up! Two of my more seasoned and apparently bored colleagues decided that it would be fun to organize a full-class desertion. In the short time that they'd arranged to get me out of the room, they had quickly briefed, shushed, and herded my students into the adjoining prep area and under the prep tables, where I finally found them. On that day, it wasn't until losing and then finding my class that I was able to focus on the most important part of my job: my students.

PRAYER: Jesus, I do want to follow you. I hand over the control that I think I have to you. Replace my worries, distractions, and fears with your joy and grace.

120

Relativity

SUGGESTED SCRIPTURE READING: Matthew 5:1-12

VERSE DU JOUR: *But do not forget this one thing, dear friends: With the Lord a day is like a thousand years, and a thousand years are like a day.* (2 Peter 3:8)

Ready to start the meeting, our group leader, Mark, looked around for the planned speaker, although the speaker was obviously not yet present. Mark took time to tell a humorous story and didn't look too worried. Finally, the scheduled speaker rushed in and apologized for his tardiness. Mark's response was a quick one that offered both forgiveness and perspective: "Compared with the endless stretch of infinite time, you're not late."

Jesus taught that although earth and heaven will someday pass away, his words would remain. There is no record of Jesus ever chastising his disciples for being late or slow to move. Nowhere in the Scriptures is it mentioned that Jesus was uptight about time or angered by another's tardiness. Instead, we are presented with a Jesus who thinks before he speaks and who generously invests time in others.

Knowing his true identity and the importance of his mission, Jesus was able to keep a balanced and eternal perspective. Does Jesus share the details of earth's creation so that we, too, might acquire this perspective? Might Jesus want us to recognize that earth and all of time are governed by his power?

I get so freaked about time. I hate to be late for anything and dread rushing around trying to accomplish more than time reasonably allows. And I can't stand to wait. Even worse, I detest being inconvenienced by someone else's tardiness, such as when I have to interrupt class to mark yet another student "late." I often lose sense of perspective. Perhaps I need to remember that I can follow through on necessary disciplinary procedures without carrying around associated anger. We ought to remember that compared with the endless stretch of infinite time, student tardiness is an inconvenience and possibly a disciplinary issue but is not worthy of our angst. No one but our infinite God holds the power that controls us.

PRAYER: Jesus, you have created time; let me use it wisely. Allow me the perspective that lets me relax even when my students are late for class.

121

Grief to Joy

SUGGESTED SCRIPTURE READING: John 16:17-22

VERSE DU JOUR: *"So with you: Now is your time of grief, but I will see you again and you will rejoice, and no one will take away your joy."* (John 16:22)

"You help me learn this, teacher? I no understand," Maria quietly whispered as I sat down beside her. The new girl seemed so skittish and shy, yet her physical beauty was remarkable. Her silky black hair fell in waves down her shoulders, and her model-perfect face topped off a proportioned, tiny body. But my eyes could not be drawn away from the sores that covered her forearms. Yellow pus oozed from the swollen, reddish-pink, open wounds that started at her wrists and ended at her elbows. Interspersed with these wounds were similar sores, some scabbed over and others healed to scars. Unsettled by the wounds, I tried to refocus on the earth science worksheet.

Jesus was particularly burdened by the state of humankind. He felt compassion toward people and went out of his way to help the needy. Being one with God, he felt great offense toward all sin and must have experienced great grief while observing the degradation of his creation. Prior to Jesus' arrest and crucifixion, Jesus warns the disciples of coming grief, yet he also explains that their grief will give way to great joy. This is good news but implies that we will experience grief through our journeys.

All day, I mentally replayed Maria's tutoring session. The wounds on her forearms haunted and baffled me. Finally, I found Maria's school counselor and shared my concern. "Those are cigarette burns. Maria has been in some abusive relationships, and we're unsure of her living situation," the counselor responded. "These kinds of burns are quite common; I'm surprised you've never seen them before." Sickened and stunned, I stumbled back to my classroom. How could this happen to a sweet, beautiful child? The pain must have been unbearable. No wonder Maria seemed skittish and shy.

It is easy to be disgusted by the self-destructive and cruel behavior that we see and the foul language we hear. To remain sensitive to sin and yet be able to peacefully exist in a world where it is the norm can become a tiring and difficult job. No wonder Jesus reminds us that we are not of this world but that we belong to the kingdom of heaven. As God's emissaries here on earth, we will witness and experience evil and its pain. But joy is also coming. Someday soon, God's love will triumph and good will prevail. We are part of bringing about this good news!

PRAYER: Let me see that the sin around me will not take me captive. Let me see the larger picture, and let me look forward to the joy that you have in store.

122

Be a Sheep?

SUGGESTED SCRIPTURE READING: John 10:1-18

VERSE DU JOUR: *"My sheep listen to my voice; I know them, and they follow me."* (John 10:27)

"Stop it, now! Just because she is different from the rest of us is no reason to torture her! Leave her alone, already!" I couldn't believe my ears. Apparently, things were not going well back at lab table four. Yet, Sandy had taken a stand. No longer would this usually shy and quiet young lady stand by while her lab team demeaned and belittled their less-than-brilliant and unpopular lab partner. Sandy risked being ostracized and belittled herself when she spoke up for someone less fortunate than herself. I didn't even try to stop her when, red-faced and near tears, she uncharacteristically stomped away from her group and out of classroom.

Jesus called himself "the good shepherd" and likened his people to sheep. Jesus used this analogy to explain how he protects his own and cares for each one of us. However, his audience was agrarian enough to know the metaphor about sheep could be far from flattering. As cute as sheep might be, they are generally stupid. If left to choose between standing in the rain versus going inside, they choose to stay outside, thereby risking the development of fungal infections that decompose their feet. Sheep lack any defensive mechanisms and don't even make a great run for it when predators are on the chase.

If Christians were to behave like sheep, timidly and mindlessly meandering, they would no more resemble their shepherd than a bovine would look like a milkmaid. I don't think that Jesus intends for us to use this analogy as a call to become senseless, defenseless individuals. Jesus wants us to follow him but warns us against following any leader that comes along. Jesus developed a knack for bucking authority, making risky choices and rejecting the crowd mentality. He stood up for what was right, even when the authorities said otherwise.

I found Sandy crouched in the hallway, right outside the room. Breathing deeply, she held her head in her hands, and a beam of light from a nearby window illuminated her hair. Finally she spoke: "Isn't it easier sometimes to just follow the crowd—to do what everybody else is doing? Why did I do that? Now they're all going to pick on me! But what they were doing to Samantha was just wrong!" "You did the right thing" was all I could say.

If we are to model our lives after Jesus, we need to question, search ourselves, and pray for guidance before proceeding on any given course. Sometimes we need to be different from the crowd. Rather than following blindly, we need to decisively follow our Shepherd instead of the crowd around us.

PRAYER: Let me stand away from the crowd for you. Please do not let me comply with the demands of this world, but let me follow the standards that you have set.

123

Waiting

SUGGESTED SCRIPTURE READING: Isaiah 26:1-9

VERSE DU JOUR: *Yes, LORD, walking in the way of your laws, we wait for you; your name and renown are the desire of our hearts.* (Isaiah 26:8)

All I'm buying is this little bag of ginger root for the anaerobic bacteria lab, and the express line is closed. I had plenty of time to get this done before school, but traffic was heavy, and now this. It's only sixteen minutes before my next class starts, but the shopper ahead of me in line turns out to be a coupon queen. My life is so hectic, and yet all I seem to do lately is spend time waiting in traffic, on hold, in the lunch line when there are only twenty minutes left to eat, for my turn in the doctor's office, for my students to get it. Did the writer of Genesis forget to add "waiting" to the list of curses following the Fall?

Perhaps it's just part of the human experience, this needing-to-wait thing. If so, then Jesus must have also done his fair share of waiting. He probably needed to wait for the right piece of wood to carve that special-order bench. Jesus waited to grow up. He waited for what must have seemed an eternity to be returned to his rightful place in heaven at the right hand of God. He waited to be recognized as the Messiah. Jesus waited in line for food and for his turn near the fire. And down to his last night on earth, he waited for his friends to get it. Jesus waited for Judas to deliver him to the authorities and for the pounding of the first nail into his hands. He also waited for God's will to be done. Jesus waited for an end to the agony of the cross. He continues to wait for me to become the person that I should be.

Waiting requires patience. In order to get patience, I need to be ready for the trials and aggravations that develop it. I don't want to pray for patience in any area, least of all in the area of waiting, since I expect that acquiring such virtue may necessitate even more waiting. Maybe it would be safer to pray for strength; mental and physical!

Knowing that Jesus understands the waiting game makes it more bearable. Also, I might consider using those aggravating wait times as prayer times (as long as I'm not praying for patience).

PRAYER: Lord, remind me that you have done it all. Help me to wait with grace and style. Let me show your love and remind me to talk to you even while I wait. Of all the things I wait for, I gladly and expectantly wait for you.

124
Free Protection

SUGGESTED SCRIPTURE READING: Psalm 91:14-16

VERSE DU JOUR: *"Because he loves me,"* says the LORD, *"I will rescue him, I will protect him, for he acknowledges my name."* (Psalm 91:14) *(Substitute your name for the pronouns.)*

The two girls who practically tumbled into my office were flustered and distressed. "It was terrible, teacher! They were punching Clay and pounding his head against the locker. We didn't know what to do. The boys told us to get lost or we would be next. We heard them yelling something about Clay missing his protection payment. As soon as they told us to get lost, we did. What should we do?"

God promises us free protection. Good thing, because most of us can't afford to pay for it. Did you notice that God doesn't promise to rescue us and protect us only if we are doing something great? God did not say, "Because my servant is a great evangelist and packing out the largest stadiums" or "Because my child

has left all she knows to go far away to a squalid mission field."
God's provision and protection are not tied to our performance.
In Psalm 91, we learn that God wants our love and responds to it
by giving us whatever we need. And what kind of parent would
deny protection to a child?

Besides reporting the incident and offering Clay some ice packs
for his battered head, there wasn't much we could do for him. It's
not every day that you hear of students paying for protection or
witness the effects of nonpayment. Apparently it does happen, and
the payments aren't always affordable. How fortunate that all
those who love God are offered free protection. And don't doubt
that God has a heart that melts with pleasure when we express
our love for him. We are designed in God's image. Why would
God not feel the same concern for offspring that loving parents
have toward their children? We don't love God because we are
rescued and protected. Because God loves us, we receive these gifts
at no charge.

PRAYER: God, I love you. Please give me your protection as I go
out to do my work. And be with those students who need your
protection today.

125
Taste and See

SUGGESTED SCRIPTURE READING: Psalm 34:1-22

VERSE DU JOUR: *O taste and see that the LORD is good; happy
are those who take refuge in him.* (Psalm 34:8, NRSV)

Each student was required to orally present research, provide
some sort of audiovisual to the class, and assess class comprehension on their chosen topic; in preparation for our next dissection
laboratory, all topics related to frogs. Today was the second day
for student presentations, and Nan, clearly excited, explained that
she needed to leave her presentation in the refrigerator until she

needed it. Nan had been adamant that she be allowed to present about the anatomy of frog legs.

Following a thorough yet somewhat quiet and haltingly presented instructional period, Nan brought out and uncovered the plate. "I have here for you some frog legs so that you can understand them better. Please enjoy," she said before personally serving a leg to each student. Then Nan explained that she had brought extras for me.

Jesus asks his followers to experience a new kind of life, a life in which the old rules are thrown out the window and a focus on loving God and others can begin. Jesus invites us all to experience this new life; he wants us to understand the depth of his love and the mercy of God. Psalm 34 lists the many benefits available to believers, to the ones who fear the Lord. To fear the Lord God involves a deep, respectful approach and a search for understanding. God invites us to taste what is good, to experience personally the truth that can connect us to blessings beyond compare.

Why did Nan bring in forty frog legs? Perhaps there had been misunderstanding due to an English/Vietnamese language barrier, or perhaps Nan was hoping for some extra credit. I think that she wanted to share something from her culture and her experience. Regardless of Nan's motivation, I can bet that the price she paid for those legs was quite a bit more than she would have spent on the standard white poster board. She was proud to announce that she had fried them herself.

In a sense, Nan was right: unless we tasted the legs, we wouldn't have a complete understanding of them. We might be able to identify the anatomical parts of the frog's leg or recite specifics of the physiology of their motion, but we would have missed a personal and gustatory understanding of those legs. We needed to taste and see what everyone raves about. They *did* taste like chicken, only a little sweeter. If we make an effort to taste of God's goodness, perhaps we will experience a life that is a little sweeter, too. Are you ready to taste and see?

PRAYER: Lord, I want to taste of your goodness and how life can be lived in your love. I open my mind and my heart to you today.

126

The Undesirables

SUGGESTED SCRIPTURE READING: Matthew 9:9-13

VERSE DU JOUR: *While Jesus was having dinner at Matthew's house, many tax collectors and "sinners" came and ate with him and his disciples.* (Matthew 9:10)

My empathy for the geeks, the uncoordinated, the ostracized, and the unaccepted is not born of will but of circumstance. I was not a popular child. My thick glasses and love of reading (perhaps related entities) did not enhance my athletic ability or my popularity. I preferred schoolwork to the playground and was unable to chat about the latest television show. Early in my elementary years, my mom had discarded our one working TV set. She decided that my dad and I wasted way too much time watching it, so it had to go. That issue alone marked me as a definite oddball. I was not delicate or petite, not beautiful or perky, and seriously not cool.

The popular kids shunned me. Because they were my sole social option, I hung out with other kids who were like me. I remember desperately wishing for acceptance, hoping for better days, and vowing that someday I would show those exclusive snobs who I really was.

Contrast my childhood social situation with the habits and social status Jesus experienced. We know little about Jesus' childhood, but as an up-and-coming young prophet, Jesus was a sought-after and popular man, chased by crowds eager to hear him speak. Jesus had a tough body and a sharp mind. He entertained well-connected and learned men as well as beautiful women. He was in demand. And yet, one had to question the company he kept. Jesus, who could have socialized with any group of his choosing, chose to hang out with the undesirables. He hung out with the outcasts because he wanted to, not because he had to. Jesus spent time with lepers (people who experienced the mother lode of discrimination and prejudice), shepherds (who were considered religiously unclean), tax collectors (for obvious reasons, unpopular and often unscrupulous folks), prostitutes, and poor people. He filled his social register with needy and sick people. Jesus dined with the down and out. He knew the ills of society because he was there with them.

Jesus didn't care what everyone else thought about his friends and acquaintances. He made a habit of sticking up for his oppressed and unpopular friends. Jesus praised the woman who poured expensive perfume on his feet and lovingly wiped his feet with her hair. He then immediately issued a verbal sting to the Pharisee who had witnessed and criticized her gift giving.

Jesus taught, through words and actions, that in the kingdom of God there are no undesirables. Every person is of great worth, a valuable part of God's creation. We are to defend the plight of the outcast and welcome them into our lives. By accepting and loving the so-called unlovable, we will teach our students a new kind of tolerance and will simultaneously share God's love with those who need it.

PRAYER: Let me boldly love those who are hard to love. Let me show as much concern for the outcasts as I do for the kids who make me look good. Let me see everyone through your eyes, Lord.

127
The First Irishman

SUGGESTED SCRIPTURE READING: John 3:1-22

VERSE DU JOUR: *In reply Jesus declared, "I tell you the truth, no one can see the kingdom of God unless he is born again."* (John 3:3)

At the back of my closet I find the one green blazer that will protect me from a day of pinches. I don my St. Patrick's day protection, remembering Sunday's sermon. Our minister had enlightened us on details of the first Irishman mentioned in the Bible—Nic O'Demus.

Have you ever wondered why this account has been included in the Gospels or why Nick came to Jesus at night? Some theologians postulate that Nick came to Jesus at night so that no one would know of his visit to the controversial vagabond. After all, Nicodemus had a reputation to protect; he was an upstanding member of the Jewish community and a Pharisee. He was even a member of the Jewish ruling council. Perhaps he did sneak over to meet with Jesus at night to avoid the certain gossip and rumors that would follow his visit. However, Nick also had a searching heart and a desire to know truth.

In addition, Nicodemus may have visited Jesus at night because he knew that as the day drew to a close and the crowds dispersed, he would have the best chance to catch Jesus alone. Nick wanted and needed a private meeting with the master teacher. The time was right, and Nicodemus got what he wanted (and perhaps more than he'd planned). Nicodemus asked the questions, and Jesus gave answers that made Nick's head spin.

After one meeting with Jesus, Nick became a changed man. In John 19:38-42, we find Nicodemus helping Joseph of Arimathea move Jesus' body to a tomb for proper Jewish burial. They were the only Jewish officials who were there to tend to Jesus' body. Not even Jesus' own disciples were around. Doesn't seem that Nick was afraid anymore!

Besides the many spiritual truths to be gleaned from the "Nick at Night" account, we can also learn about the teaching style of Jesus. He was just as good with one person as he was in with a large group. Jesus was willing to meet privately with his students (seekers) and was not intimidated by their status outside his circle. Jesus apparently reveled in the chance to give a private lesson. He probably wanted to go to bed, but he took the time to repeat his lesson one more time in a way that Nick could better understand. Jesus did not treat Nick's visit as an interruption or an intrusion but as a life-changing opportunity. And his time was well spent. Can you recognize that the time you spend with your students is also valuable and time well spent?

PRAYER: God, bless the time that I spend with my students. Remind me that the extra time I give them is important. Protect me and encourage me as I serve your children.

128

Empty Vessels

SUGGESTED SCRIPTURE READING: 2 Corinthians 5

VERSE DU JOUR: *So if anyone is in Christ, there is a new creation: everything old has passed away; see, everything has become new!* (2 Corinthians 5:17, NRSV)

One of my favorite mentors and colleagues often had his classes filled with the students considered most difficult and challenging. The reason? John's years of experience with often hostile and unmotivated students had made him an expert in dealing with such youth. So, why not load up his roster with the kids no one else wanted? John could handle them! Rather than becoming angry or disheartened by his situation, John took an interesting perspective. He seemed to rely on humor and the response of earned wisdom. After teaching a particularly tough bunch, it was not unusual to see him shaking his head and with a small smile, muttering, "They're empty vessels." When asked to expound on his utterance, John simply said, "My students are empty vessels, just waiting to be filled." And of course, knowing that it was he who was charged with filling those vessels, John walked slowly, but with purpose and conviction, to his next class.

Jesus allowed God to fill him and use him. "Not my will, but yours," was a recurrent theme throughout his life. If Jesus hadn't continually practiced giving over to the will of God, he could never have spoken those very words as he neared his final hours. Jesus also recognized that people could be filled with either good or bad. When approaching a man possessed by demons, Jesus wasted no time in driving them out. Unless the demons were exorcised, there would be no room left for Jesus' own healing and grace.

As it turns out, *you* are also a vessel for God's use and a channel for his power. On your own, you are empty, but when God fills you up and sends you into the world—*watch out!* God can work good through you, giving you the abilities and gifts to help others. As the school year drags on, you may think those empty vessels entrusted to you are ready to crack. Just don't lose sight of the fact that the universe itself will obey the commands of its Maker. Are you willing to be used by the Lord of the Universe to touch the lives of the people around you?

PRAYER: God, please use me today. I ask you to fill me with your power, grace, wisdom, and creativity. Use me as your vessel today!

129

Serving a God of Power

SUGGESTED SCRIPTURE READING: John 11:3-44

VERSE DU JOUR: *Great is our Lord and mighty in power; his understanding has no limit.* (Psalm 147:5)

"See that line between the hallway and this classroom? Once you cross that line, you are in the land of Drake. Everything is different in here than it is out there. Once in here, you are mine. Gone are the behaviors of the hallway. Gone are your friends. In their place, I reign supreme (like a big burrito!). I make or break your life." On and on I would rant, trying to make a critical point to the freshman intro class that survives on raging hormones, caffeine, and who knows what else. I drilled like a Marine sergeant with a new group of recruits.

One of the most almost amusing public demonstrations of God's power is shown in the account of Jesus raising Lazarus from the dead. If "Lazarus, come out!" is not enough to give you goose bumps, consider the conversation that precedes this miracle. First, we hear Jesus saying that Lazarus is asleep. Later, Jesus speaks clearly to those who had misunderstood him. "Lazarus is dead, and for your sake I am glad I was not there, so that you may believe. But let us go to him" (John 11:14). Jesus speaks plainly to his hearers, so that they can get a clear grasp of the situation. He takes extra time to explain things to them. Just like our God in heaven, Jesus is powerful and patient.

Power is everything, we are told. In biblical days, even servant status was dependent not only on the role you might have in a household but also the power wielded by the master you served. A servant of a king had more power than the servant of a small-time businessman. The same unwritten rules still apply. We see it all around us. The attorney who works for the firm Smith, Jones and Associates seemingly has more power than the waitress working at Dewey's Diner.

But this world occasionally throws us some illusions; we know it isn't where we work but for whom we work. Aren't you glad that you work for a Ruler who has the ultimate power over this world? Whether you choose to try to convince your students of your power or not, one compelling and comforting reality remains: you do serve a God of power, a God whose power extends even over death!

PRAYER: Your power is truly beyond my comprehension. How nice to know that one day you will enlighten me to your understanding and your perspective. Until then, I praise and serve you only, my powerful and almighty God!

130
Wake-Up Call

SUGGESTED SCRIPTURE READING: Psalm 39:1-13

VERSE DU JOUR: *Show me, O LORD, my life's end and the number of my days; let me know how fleeting is my life.* (Psalm 39:4)

Why, oh why did I listen to that naive instructor in the latest teacher seminar? "Give your students your e-mail address and contact phone numbers," he said. "If you give your students your home phone, they'll rarely misuse it and will feel more connected to you. It's the right thing to do."

Now I'm regretting my open door/open phone approach, pretty sure that it is associated with a recent string of hang-up and heavy-breather calls. I can screen calls with the answering machine, but the crank calls are annoying and sometimes spooky. So, when the phone rang early one morning, I tentatively reached for it with one hand, wearily rubbing my eyes with the other. The caller was not a student but a dear friend, Carol, who called to remind me that every day is a gift from God. Carol is a nurse who's been doing volunteer hospice work. In addition to working with hospice patients, she's been watching as a good number of friends face life-threatening illnesses, some of them preparing to die.

Jesus lived a dynamic and Spirit-filled life. His access to an eternal, heavenly perspective must have allowed him to embrace risk, love deeply, and live vibrantly. All accounts of his life indicate that Jesus lived with the attitude encapsulated in the e-mail quote my mom recently sent. Someone once said, "What goes around comes around. Work like you don't need the money. Love like you've never been hurt. Dance like nobody's watching. Sing like nobody's listening. Live like it's heaven on earth."

As our conversation continued, Carol said that she had called for other reasons, too, but that she wanted to remind me that every day is a gift. And she's right. It's not just the starry romantic nights and the smooth, problem-free days that are gifts from our Maker. Every day that God allows us to suck air in and out, every day we are with people we love, and every moment that our hearts keep beating—it's all a gift from the Life Giver. Carol and I determined to live life this day to its fullest, knowing that what lies ahead should change our attitudes now.

PRAYER: Thank you for giving me another day. I want to live it well and appreciate every moment. Help me live it for you.

131

Can't Find It?

SUGGESTED SCRIPTURE READING: 1 John 4:1-6

VERSES DU JOUR: *Dearly loved friends, don't always believe everything you hear just because someone says it is a message from God: test it first to see if it really is. For there are many false teachers around, and the way to find out if their message is from the Holy Spirit is to ask, "Does it really agree that Jesus Christ, God's Son, actually became man with a human body?" If so, then the message is from God.* (1 John 4:1-3, TLB)

"Cleanliness is next to godliness," I called out cheerfully, attempting to console my faithful student assistant, who is washing yet another sink full of dirty test tubes. "God helps those who help themselves," I heard a colleague yell another day, distraught with his current class.

Then one day, I tried to find both of these passages in the Bible. Guess what? They weren't there! All my life I thought these were Bible verses or at least biblical concepts, but they're not in the Bible.

Jesus warned his disciples about false teachers. He urged his followers to carefully test and discern the source of their beliefs. The Scriptures urge us to carefully and constantly monitor ideas that spring from anywhere but God's Word. How often is my belief system altered by things I think I have read in the Bible, and yet those ideas or dictums are not there? How many times do I believe something because someone I trusted or someone I considered to be smart told me so?

I have become aware of this problem since I started to write these daily missives. On several occasions I've written about an issue I believed to be an important aspect of the Christian life, only to experience problems in finding Scriptures I was convinced were popular or significant biblical texts. The reason I can't find these Scriptures is not because I lack decent resources. The concordance I use is comprehensive, and my stack of Bibles is intact, but the Scriptures I am seeking don't exist. Even some things that I attribute to the teachings of Jesus fail to show up when I search the Scriptures.

This dilemma demonstrates not only that we must constantly return to the Scriptures to find our plans for daily living but also that we must beware of ideas and beliefs that we assume are inspired by God. We must constantly be aware of the influence that the world has on us and be ready to check our beliefs against the Word of God. People love to comment on what they think is in Scripture, but often ignore what is actually there. Don't be fooled by the flawed concepts and strange beliefs that surround you. It is hard enough to live the Christian life, without adding misinterpretation or extraneous ideas.

Was it Jesus who said that the early bird gets the worm?

PRAYER: O God, your Word alone is perfect and worthy of my attention. Help me follow only what comes from you.

132

Royalty

SUGGESTED READING: 1 Peter 2:1-12

VERSE DU JOUR: *But you are a chosen people, a royal priesthood, a holy nation, a people belonging to God, that you may declare the praises of him who called you out of darkness into his wonderful light.* (1 Peter 2:9)

Queen Elizabeth II (the royal personage, not the ship) once waved at me—and several hundred other people. Other than that, my closest brush with royalty was the way I felt at my wedding. There I was covered in ivory pearls, tulle, and sweat (It was August in New Jersey. Need I say more?), while the huge pipe organ blasted the wedding march from *The Sound of Music*.

As I walked with my dad down the long aisle, out of the corner of my eye, I saw my students craning their necks to get a better view of me. Yes, I invited all of my students. The ones who made it were crammed together into two rows of the stone cathedral. Despite my nervousness and excitement, I couldn't help looking over to see them.

Despite his earthly appearance (dusty hair, dirty feet, and all that), Jesus carried himself and conducted himself like the royalty he was. How else could Jesus confound those who sought to attack him? How else could he mesmerize the crowds and righteously deal with the desperate ones who swooned in his presence? How else could he teach in the temple at age of twelve or display the confidence that attracted a dozen die-hard followers? Jesus changed the history of the world, in part, because he was confident in himself and in his royal standing. Jesus wants us to understand that we have that same source of confidence and possess the same royal heritage; as God's chosen people, we also are part of a special family.

Several years after my wedding, I was driving our daughter, Riley, home from day care. Looking intently out the truck window, she blurted, "We are like windows, Mommy. I think that we are the windows and God is the building." Wow. Where did she get that one? Riley also likes to hear about how she is a child of the King. She figures that means that she is a true-to-life princess. Come to think of it, I kind of like the idea too. But this princess thing is not just a Halloween dress-up event or a fantasy; Christians are indeed royalty. And like earthly royalty, our family connection bestows both privilege and responsibility. Jesus sends his royal ones into the world. He charges us with the task of glorifying the One who has rescued us from the grave. We go out into the world as his emissaries. Walk tall!

PRAYER: God, please give me the confidence and vision that I need to continue my mission. Let me remember that I am your child and as that I represent you. Help me act and live accordingly.

133

Can't Reciprocate

SUGGESTED SCRIPTURE READING: Psalm 106:1-5

VERSE DU JOUR: *Praise the* LORD. *Give thanks to the* LORD,
for he is good; his love endures forever. (Psalm 106:1)

I still remember the gifts I received on my birthday, April 3, 1991:
a rousing version of happy birthday sung by my entire class and
led by one of my rowdiest students, a card delivered by two girls
who previously confessed to hating me, two peanut-butter cups,
and two homemade birthday cards left on my desk by my faithful student assistant. Those gifts might seem little to you, but they
seemed huge to me and made the difference between feeling appreciated instead of forgotten. By contrast, I have several friends and
family members who give me so ridiculously much. So many of
their acts of kindness and their gifts to me go unreciprocated, not
because I am ungrateful but because I feel that I cannot match
their generosity. Sure, I send out a thank-you note or attempt to
verbalize my gratitude, but sometimes words don't seem to cut it.

Once my dear friend, Kelly, sent plane tickets for me and my children to fly up to visit her in Maine. She had decided that we needed
to visit and knew that we couldn't afford it. She had asked me when
I could come and then mailed three round-trip tickets! You may
also be fortunate in this way—to have people in your life who have
given so much to you without expecting anything in return.

Jesus, God's Son, took time out from a hectic schedule to pray
and worship. He retreated to the wilderness to communicate with
God; Jesus rose early in the morning to go outside alone to pray.
With no earthly riches to offer, it was his body, his time, his intellect, and his praise that Jesus offered up to God. Jesus modeled
King David's advice: He gave thanks to God. Jesus taught that God
is not only good but also God's love endures forever. Jesus made
concerted efforts to pursue the will of God. The life and teachings
of Jesus were a sacrifice of praise. Jesus taught his followers that by

expressing thanks and worship to God, they, too, might please their heavenly Maker.

How can you thank people who do so much? How can words express the gratitude that is due? Words are not enough! Likewise, how can I properly thank the God who supplies me with every breath I take and every blessing that comes my way? How can I thank King Jesus for the sacrifice he made for my soul? He knew that words were not enough to rescue me.

Thinking of those birthday gifts from my students, I consider that perhaps I do have something worth giving God. I don't have great riches or plane tickets to send God; he doesn't need those, anyway. But I can give God thanks, a heart of worship, and songs of praise. Perhaps small offerings, like those candies, cards, and birthday songs, will show God our love and appreciation. We must continue in our quest to thank Jesus through our words, our lives, and our worship—not because we can repay God's generosity but because we can't. We will never be able to reciprocate God's mercy and kindness, but we can offer praise because God is good.

PRAYER: I praise you, Lord. I will thank you with my mouth and my deeds. You alone are worthy and good.

134

Focus and the Rat

SUGGESTED READING: Philippians 3:12-14

VERSE DU JOUR: *I press on toward the goal to win the prize for which God has called me heavenward in Christ Jesus.*
(Philippians 3:14)

Rolan was a tall, athletic high-school junior, with an easy smile and an impressive flat-top. To my great annoyance, Rolan developed an unusual affinity for our class pet, a sleek white rat named Swede, who lived in the yellowing glass aquarium at the back of the room. Rolan spent much of the class time playing with and antagonizing the tolerant animal.

Throughout every lecture and even during lab sessions, Rolan was constantly reaching into the aquarium to touch Swede, poking him, grabbing his tail, rubbing between his ears, or slipping him potato chips. When I moved Rolan's seat, he found a way to wheedle his way back toward Swede's corner.

Not surprisingly, Rolan's activities were distracting to his fellow students. What was surprising was the way that Rolan's playful misbehavior drove me, a battle-hardened disciplinarian, to utter distraction. How could we all stay focused on the task at hand?

Jesus was an incredibly focused man. Paul's writings indicate the importance of focus for Christians. The immensity of Jesus' mission must have been overwhelming at times. How many times might Jesus have wanted to just be a normal person? Jesus endured stress, temptation, poverty, and heartache, yet somehow he managed to keep everything in focus. Jesus never gave in to sin and never wavered from his mission. How easy it is for the rest of us to be distracted from our missions by any number of things: material possessions that we think we need, financial propositions that we think we must find, minutia that plague us (grading, administrative issues, failing photocopiers), and difficult students.

Following prayerful focus, Rolan and I worked out an agreement, and eventually he became one of my favorite students. I came to appreciate him for the genial and intelligent young man he was (albeit with a penchant for rodents). In addition to becoming Swede's protector, Rolan became my advocate. I felt honored when this popular young man would wade through crowds of unruly students in the hallways to greet me and say, with great respect and admiration in his voice for all to hear, "Hi, Mrs. Drake!" The next time a student drives you to distraction, why not try whispering a quick prayer to ask God for focus and redirection? Later, when you are more relaxed and focused, you can work out a plan to resolve the problem.

PRAYER: Lord, I am doing this job for you. Please help me to focus on what is important and on the task you have given me. Please give me clarity of focus.

135

Rich Kid, Poor Kid

SUGGESTED SCRIPTURE READING: Proverbs 22:1-16

VERSE DU JOUR: *Rich and poor have this in common: The LORD is the Maker of them all.* (Proverbs 22:2)

Did you ever go to New York City and visit the Trump Towers? Visiting the towers, I tried to imagine what it would be like to live there. Checking my reflection in the huge windows, I held my head up a little higher than usual. I walked along, pretending to be one of the residents. Out of my way, tourist! I'm going downstairs to lunch!

You don't even need to visit the city; all you have to do is open popular magazines to realize that our culture teaches us to revere the rich and the beautiful. The tabloid publishers think that we can't wait to read what the latest movie star served at her most recent wedding or learn the cost of an idol's new house. When you hear about their antics, it's hard to understand why we should care.

Jesus was not naïve about money; he knew of its powers and gave strong instruction regarding it to his followers. Jesus never let a person's money or lack of it cloud his perception of that individual. Jesus also protected himself against money-related prejudice; he had no campaign contributions to repay, no mortgage to weigh him down, and no income to fritter. His opinions were not influenced by money. In the eyes of Jesus, all were considered equal. Jesus showed no preferential treatment and seemed not to care whether a person looked rich or ragged. It seems Jesus never changed his opinion or attitude toward people based on their financial portfolio, age, health, class, race, or gender. He said, "Let the little children come to me," not, "Bring over the children of my strongest supporters." He was equally likely to accept a dinner invitation from a homeless wanderer as from a rich businessman. Regardless of people's social or financial status, Jesus met each person with interest and respect.

Sometimes teaching and working with students in a poor school is easier than teaching rich kids. At least you don't have to listen to tales about how their parents make much more money than you do. And some of the lower-income kids will respect your decision to come into their world. Another set of problems plague the poorer schools, but that's a topic for another day. Teaching any students, rich, poor, or in-between, is hard work. Regardless of our student body, we must remember that it is the Lord whom we serve, and God is the Maker of them all.

PRAYER: Please keep me from the lure of money. Protect me from its grip and from the fear that I won't have enough of it. Do not let money make choices for me or influence how I treat others.

136

Bad Crawl

SUGGESTED SCRIPTURE READING: Hebrews 12:1-12

VERSE DU JOUR: *Therefore, since we are surrounded by such a great cloud of witnesses, let us throw off everything that hinders and the sin that so easily entangles, and let us run with perseverance the race marked out for us.* (Hebrews 12:1)

I don't need to tell you that teaching is a grueling job. We need to stay healthy and strong to do our jobs well. So there I was, working hard to simultaneously clear my mind and strengthen my body. I was diligently stepping up over and over on the Climber 2®, an evil cousin of the more familiar Stairmaster®.

Searching for distraction from my current discomfort, I blankly stared through the glass panels and into the huge pool below where people of all shapes and sizes were swimming. One fit-looking young man was stroking like crazy but hardly moving anywhere. My staring morphed into sharp focus, and I immediately diagnosed the obvious source of the sinking Adonis's trouble. For every two crawl strokes he took with his arms, this guy barely managed to pump out one weak flutter kick. At first I thought that perhaps this was a cruel drill designed to strengthen his stroke, but as he continued, I had to fight the urge to run downstairs to the pool and yell, "Kick, good man, kick!" This man had a really bad freestyle, and he probably didn't even know it. Of course, I hate to think what observers might want to yell to me when they see me swimming . . . or living.

I wonder how many times God has to watch me flounder around through life when I should be swimming skillfully through it. Are there sins, bad habits, friends, or material possessions that prevent me from moving ahead? Do I forget to use or do I disregard the resources and gifts that God has given me? Is the effect of my Christian life hindered by my disregard of God's plans? Do I know God's plan for my life? Have I asked?

If I am swimming like crazy and getting nowhere, maybe something is wrong. My plan or my technique may be awry. Sin of the mind or of the body may be slowing or stopping my spiritual progress. Just as the swimmer should continually reassess his stroke, so should the believer assess his or her spiritual growth. Perhaps I am merely crawling along when I should be running. I might even need to take the advice of an unbiased observer who can diagnose the problem with my stroke. You've got to love the directness and applicability of Hebrews 12:12: "Therefore, strengthen your feeble arms and weak knees."

PRAYER: God, reveal to me my weaknesses and any outstanding sins. I am open to your healing and to your redirection. Please let me grow in you and your plans.

137

Duty to Defend

SUGGESTED SCRIPTURE READING: Proverbs 31:1-9

VERSE DU JOUR: *Speak up for those who cannot speak for themselves, for the rights of all who are destitute.* (Proverbs 31:8)

In an interview, Erika Howard, Miss America 2002, recounted the painful verbal and emotional harassment that she endured in high school. Erika shared the experience of not fitting in and of enduring cruelty from students who taunted and intimidated her. They threw food at her and even broke a window at her house. Her teachers did not punish the troublemakers for their obvious abuses. Ms. Howard now speaks out against schoolhouse hatred and has launched a national campaign against this all-too-common problem. But how many abused kids never get the chance to share their pain or do anything about it?

Jesus always defended the underdog; He chose to defend the sad and the helpless. He showed them love and acceptance through his words, his healing, and the honor of his company. It must have taken great courage to defend an adulteress against the powerful authorities who were itching to execute her. It took chutzpah to lunch with the outcast Zaccheus, too. It usually takes me quite awhile to gather my courage when I must stand against the often overwhelming crowd. Sometimes I fail to follow Jesus' example and then am ashamed. After all, it only takes a few words to offer defense for another person.

For a moment, imagine that you are worshipping in glory when you spot a clear-skinned being who looks over to you and smiles—ah, you sense a spark of recognition. Wasn't that Jeremy, the kid from your first-period biology class way back when? Didn't he endure months of harassment from the other kids because his clothes were dirty, his hair was always matted with oil, and his face covered with pimples and scars? Back then he was sloppy and overweight but a genuinely kind and sensitive boy. What was your response to his situation? Did you reprimand Jeremy's tormentors, or did you turn the other way?

We don't know where our students will end up, but we do know that each and every one under our care and tutelage is precious to God. Even if they don't become Miss Americas, those who are God's children will someday be transformed into heavenly bodies of perfection. Even now, each one is valuable and loveable to our God. We are in a position to assist the destitute. We can represent Jesus when we defend those who are taunted and abused. God will give you—and me—the courage, wisdom, and words to defend "those who cannot speak for themselves."

PRAYER: God, help me to be brave as a lion when I need to defend your children. Help me to boldly speak for others. Thank you for trusting me with the care of your children.

138

Biting My Tongue

SUGGESTED SCRIPTURE READING: Luke 6:37-38

VERSE DU JOUR: *"Do not judge, and you will not be judged. Do not condemn, and you will not be condemned. Forgive, and you will be forgiven."* (Luke 6:37)

If I bit my tongue every time I should, it would be full of holes. "What did you think of today's lesson?" escapes my lips. The students who had been on their way out the door shoot each other conspiring looks before they turn to me. I sense that I will not like their answer. Or, I ask my husband, "How do these pants really look on me? Do they make me look fat?" How can he possibly win on that one? Maybe I shouldn't have asked.

Jesus understands us better than anyone else. He knows that sometimes we have trouble accepting truth. Jesus was sensitive to the feelings of the humans with whom he interacted. The biblical record makes it clear that he made a comment only after he was asked to do so. Even then, he was careful with his answers.

Before Jesus advised the Samaritan woman he had just met at the well, Nicodemus, or the rich young man, they had asked him for truth and advice. It wasn't until after Jesus was asked that he offered the sometimes unpleasant truth to each of these people. He clarified the Samaritan woman's situation: "You are right when you say you have no husband. The fact is, you have had five husbands, and the man you now have is not your husband" (John 4:17). His comment to Nicodemus was a question: "You are Israel's teacher, and do you not understand these things?" (John 3:10). And of the rich, he observed, "I tell you the truth, it is hard for a rich man to enter the kingdom of heaven. Again I tell you, it is easier for a camel to go through the eye of a needle than for a rich man to enter the kingdom of God" (Matthew 19:24). Jesus told the truth, did not sugarcoat his statements, and gave accurate advice when asked to do so.

Sometimes I don't want the truth but would prefer a less honest, kinder response to my questions. "That lesson was b-o-r-i-n-g," or "Yes, you look a bit large!" might be truthful responses but not ones that I would welcome. So, perhaps I do need to bite my tongue and not ask unless I'm ready to hear the answer. And when it comes to my opinions and the driving desire to share them, sometimes I need to consider carefully my responses before allowing my tongue to wag. Jesus, who had all the right insights and instincts, did not travel around the countryside randomly criticizing and judging the people he met. Jesus never avoided confrontation, but, when asked for the truth, he always spoke it.

PRAYER: Keep me from a judgmental attitude. Help me to be tactful yet honest when approached by another. Keep me sober to my limitations and my need for grace.

139

A Tasting Party

SUGGESTED SCRIPTURE READING: James 5:7-11

VERSE DU JOUR: *As you know, we consider blessed those who have persevered. You have heard of Job's perseverance and have seen what the Lord finally brought about. The Lord is full of compassion and mercy.* (James 5:11)

Until I obtained Howard Hughes grant funding to take an Entymophagy for Educators class, I didn't know the meaning of the term. It turns out that entymophagy is the study of eating insects. The fact that this was funded by Howard Hughes, the eccentric and reclusive billionaire, was not lost on me.

The class started with a basic introduction to the history and advantages of eating bugs, followed by insect preparation guidelines. Finally, we went into the kitchen to cook and sample the recommended recipes. I have to admit that the cricket fajitas were tasty, but it was alarming to feel and see the dark spindly legs caught between the gaps in our teeth. The garlic-marinated, fried mealworms were my least favorite. There was nothing to camouflage the plump, somewhat mushy larvae. But as long as I didn't look too closely, the chocolate chip mealworm cookies were almost like the standard treat. You can cover almost anything in chocolate and I'll not only eat it but also rave about it, which is what I did the next day.

My students were curious about my bug-eating experience, and I couldn't wait to share with them. My enthusiasm to share those insects and my knowledge with my students that day was sincere and contagious. But sometimes I'm less enthusiastic about my role as a teacher or less motivated in my Christian walk. Jesus wants disciples who are willing to follow him for the long haul. He wants believers who persevere in the faith long after the novelty of their new life has worn off. When he calls his disciples he does not say, "Follow me for a while and when you tire of my plan, you can go home and catch up with your old life." Instead, Jesus says, "Follow me." For most of the disciples, the response was a to-the-death decision. In today's Scripture, James uses the example of Job to remind us that the Lord rewards perseverance with compassion and mercy.

The students flocked to my desk when I first offered mealworm cookie samples. Seeing the building crowd and hearing the crescendo of excited squeals, I calmly asked the students to form a line: first come, first served. The cookies ran out before the line did. But to my knowledge, none of the students went home to whip up their own batch of these babies (I offered the recipe), and none of my students switched to insects as a main protein source. Once the novelty wore off, so did this particular craving.

Once the novelty of our Christian lives or of our teaching mission wears off, do we do the same thing? Do we get out of line and forget the excitement of life's tasty alternatives? I challenge you to remember your commitment and act accordingly.

PRAYER: Jesus, help me to remember the joy of life in you. Don't let me lose the taste for excitement that you bring me. I'm in for the long haul.

140

Sweat of the Sale

SUGGESTED SCRIPTURE READING: Judges 16

VERSE DU JOUR: *No temptation has seized you except what is common to man. And God is faithful; he will not let you be tempted beyond what you can bear. But when you are tempted, he will also provide a way out so that you can stand up under it.* (1 Corinthians 10:13)

I left school early yesterday. Well, I left at the time I'm scheduled to leave every day. Several students had been discussing a big sale at a store downtown. "Why not go find a few bargains?" I thought as I pulled out of faculty parking lot. Maybe I'm just a little insane about a bargain.

Does this ever happen to you?: You ride a little farther than you expected to go, finally become part of the throng in the store, and begin to scope the sale items. You see the 50-percent-or-more-off signs and dive toward the merchandise in a frenzy that sets you into a sweat. You feel the excitement rising as you see things that you only now realize you need. By the time you make it through the ridiculously long line at the register and gulp in some fresh air as you leave the store, the adrenaline rush starts to wear off. You empty your bags at home, assess the monetary damage, and realize that you've done it again. Although the rush of the sale was fun, you spent more than you expected to spend, stayed a lot longer than you'd planned on staying, and bought something that you don't need or want.

I am not a pathological shopper, just an average one, I think. Yet, looking at my packages, I considered how participating in a sale can be analogous to participating in a sin. When the excitement of the sin lures us and we are tempted, we need to follow Jesus' sin-avoidance plan. When tempted, Jesus considered the holiness of his Creator. And when Peter suggested that Jesus should not suffer, Jesus rebuked, "Get back, Satan!" Jesus knew that he was being tempted, even through the words of a best friend. And he responded decisively! Jesus also quoted Scriptures relevant to his temptation. That we know of his words implies that Jesus quoted the Scriptures aloud. Jesus also consulted with God; he prayed for help and asked for the power to surrender to God rather than to the sin. So, our perfect teacher, Jesus, used his voice and his prayers to fight sin's temptation.

Careful study of the life of the biblical hero, Samson, shows us that God uses even imperfect people. Samson is recorded as Israel's strong man and prophet. His weakness for women and taste for revenge led him lose his strength, his eyesight, the respect he'd held in the community, and his freedom. The man who started out as Israel's hero ended up as pathetic entertainment for his torturers. His sin cost him much more than he'd expected. Worse than getting caught by his weaknesses, Samson was slow to repent and change his ways. Because he stayed longer in his sin than he would have if he had quickly repented, the problems that resulted from his behavior became harder and harder to escape. Is there some sin that you need to avoid? What change can you make in your life?

PRAYER: Lord, help me remember that although I am imperfect, you will still use me. When I am tempted by sin, please give me the words and the strength to turn away and follow you.

141
Paralytic Interruptions

SUGGESTED SCRIPTURE READING: Mark 2:1-12

VERSE DU JOUR: *And we know that in all things God works for the good of those who love him, who have been called according to his purpose.* (Romans 8:28)

The girls are shrieking and jumping onto the lab tabletops. Streak, the fastest of the wild, school-dwelling rats (*not* a teacher's pet), is once again making his fifth-period appearance. He runs through the maze of desks and sends most of the girls into a panic, which makes the boys laugh hysterically. The ensuing mayhem is hardly conducive to learning, and the lesson is invariably and irreparably shot. This rat is a big, shiny-gray, energetic intruder, who is roaring to run right after lunch. He enters through a crack near the cabinet in the back of the room. Even before Streak's visitations started, this was my wildest class. I now chase him until he exits the room through my supply closet near the teacher's desk. I figure if I try to turn this daily fiasco into a game, perhaps we can eventually go on with the lesson. I wonder how that long tail will feel like if I ever catch him. The whole situation is unnerving.

Jesus was not flustered by interruptions. In fact, he seemed to welcome interruptions, managing to translate them into teachable moments. Jesus did this so well that certain events almost seem staged. Consider for a few moments the scene in which the paralytic is lowered through the roof and lands in front of Jesus as he is lecturing to a packed house. Do you think the shards of plaster banging the top of Jesus' head interrupted his train of thought, or did the powdery stuff falling remind him to redirect his lecture topic? Instead of being agitated, Jesus is impressed by the diligence and faith of the paralytic's friends. Perhaps Jesus understands the desperation that has driven these roof-busters to such measures and is moved to heal the man. The healing is not complete, however, until Jesus proclaims that the man's sins are forgiven. Jesus strategically uses an otherwise aggravating interruption to showcase his divinity and his mercy. By keeping a cool head, Jesus manages to deftly incorporate an educational healing into the context of his latest lecture series. Jesus continually focused on people and their needs rather than on the pressing desire to check one more item off on his to-do list.

By the time I finally learn to keep a cool head in the presence of Streak, it's too late. Returning from winter break, I find him dead, stretched out long and lean, next to my desk, looking as if he had calculated his final goodbye. Perhaps Streak succumbed to starvation during the break, losing his main food source—the potato chips that students drop in the hallways. I was surprised to find myself mourning the rodent as I deposited his carcass in the school dumpster. The next time you are unnerved by a seemingly needless interruption, try to remember that like Streak's relatively short lifespan, your interruptions will eventually disappear, too.

PRAYER: Lord, please teach me to calmly think and creatively redirect when those unavoidable interruptions cross my path today.

142

Winning Team

SUGGESTED SCRIPTURE READING: John 16:17-33

VERSE DU JOUR: *"I have told you these things, so that in me you many have peace. In this world you will have trouble. But take heart! I have overcome the world."* (John 16:33)

Judging by the decibel level, consequent ear pain, and the wild antics at today's pep rally, you'd think we had a winning team. Our students love the excuse to get a little wild. They chant and scream, gyrate and boogie. The noise of almost seventeen hundred students pulsates through the gymnasium while our mascot works the crowd into a frenzy. A high-pitched whine from the PA system precedes the introduction of the football team. Each starter makes his own signature appearance—they run out pumped and hollering, waving fists in the air and punching each other after joining the team huddle.

It could almost move you to tears . . . or to a quieter location. Despite the large and diverse crowd, the players are rarely booed or required to dodge flying foodstuffs; these guys are presented as heroes even before the game begins.

Jesus had an unusual attitude about life on earth. His boldness, his healing love, and his desire to be connected to God must have been reinforced by his knowledge of an unseen spiritual world. Does it sometimes seem that evil is pervasive all around you? Those who participate in evil seem to benefit and those who do good appear powerless. The kids who are dealing drugs flash around more money than you have in your bank account. The fear that surrounds those who carry the guns feeds them power. The good kids are scorned as geeks, and even among your colleagues, honesty is not rewarded but might be a deterrent to success. Take heart, my friend, for despite all appearances, we are on the winning team. No matter how things look in our limited vision, the spiritual world is busy and at work. We are part of the team that will prevail and win.

The students returned as usual from the pep rally. They were wound and wild. The assembly might have been an amusing distraction for the students, but it was ultimately ineffective; the team lost the Friday night game, further depleting an already dismal record. But, regardless of their past performance, the football team members continued to hold their heads high, laughing off their losses with jaunty taunts. "Just wait till next year when we have our full line again! We so ROCK! We will get them ALL!" Those boys swaggered around like they already had a winning season.

You, by the way, are connected to the true King of the universe, who has already won the biggest battle. You are linked to the Almighty God who has a guaranteed winning streak. When you're tiring of the good fight and are feeling your will and your confidence slipping away, can you turn to the Savior who has already overcome the world?

PRAYER: Help me to remember that I am on your winning team. When I see evil all around me, help me to remember that you have already overcome. Let me find confidence in you.

143

Spring Signals

SUGGESTED SCRIPTURE READING: Mark 13:28-36

VERSE DU JOUR: *"Be on guard! Be alert! You do not know when that time will come."* (Mark 13:33)

The lilacs displayed on my desk emit a heady fragrance. The weather is nice enough that we can all go outside to run so that the students can measure a before- and after-exercise pulse. In an effort to set a good example and to share my enthusiasm for the cardiovascular health unit, I've decided to run with them. As I round the last lap of the path that borders the smoking area, I see some students who are purposely slacking. "My grandma moves faster than you two," I yell, between my own gasps. Glad that I wore flats today and thinking that I can count this as part of my daily workout, I chuckle as we run for the door. We're now all more comfortable in our roles; the students know what they can and can't get away with, and I've finally figured out how to balance the disciplinarian-to-friend ratio. I am having so much fun, and it looks like they are, too.

What is it about spring? There is newness in the air, an expectation of things to come, yet we also bask in the satisfaction of making it this far. There is the promise of nearing change and the hope of better days. Everyone seems at least a little bit excited. In our spiritual lives, the coming of spring can remind us that something even better approaches. Those who belong to Jesus know that a new and improved world awaits them. Our pain, disappointments, and challenges will be transformed into relief, joy, and reward when we meet Jesus.

Doesn't that change your perspective? Although we know the date that our next school vacation will arrive, we do not know the date of our spiritual deliverance. Most of the things that stress and disappoint us now will seem insignificant in heaven. The lesson plans and headaches will be forgotten as we crowd around his crystal throne. Our attitudes and our work can reflect that eternal hope, the hope that brings us a healthy and balanced perspective as we follow Jesus in the here and now!

PRAYER: Lord, help me to keep your perspective. Don't let me worry about the little stuff, and please help me to know that my life here is only for a season.

144

Borrowed Things

SUGGESTED SCRIPTURE READING: Psalm 50:1-11

VERSE DU JOUR: *Know that all lives are mine; the life of the parent as well as the life of the child is mine.* (Ezekiel 18:4, NRSV)

Last Sunday, I bought a cute potted African violet for my daughter's Sunday school teacher. Unable to deliver the plant to the teacher, who has been absent for a couple of weeks and rumored to have been hospitalized, I've been trying to preserve the appearance and life of this thing. Although I'm a biology teacher, my thumbs are far from green; I kill most plants that find their way into my home or classroom. This one, so far, has been different.

Because this plant is meant for someone else and because I'd be embarrassed to present a dead gift, I have been ridiculously attentive to this plant. I put it on the window sill every morning so that it gets some light during the day, then move it away from the cold window at night so that the leaves don't freeze onto the pane. I mentally debate the proper watering schedule and frequently check the leaves and deadhead the flowers. I hope I can pass off this gift soon. If I had bought this plant for myself, it would have been long dead by now.

During Jesus' teaching recorded in Matthew, he said, "Seek first his kingdom and his righteousness, and all these things will be given to you as well." This statement implies that all is available to God and that God freely gives to his children. Jesus called the synagogue "my house." Jesus' words focus on a God who is the Creator and owner of all things. My obsession with this plant has led me to consider the other possessions in my care that are not my own. The book that I borrowed from my girlfriend has been properly stored on my night table, and I cautiously turned the pages so as not to break the binding (a fate met by many of my own books). When my husband loans me his cell phone, I carefully tuck it into a soft spot in my purse. I obsess over the possibility that I might've dropped it or lost it, so I constantly check my purse to see that it is still there. My own cell phone, by contrast, can be heard ringing in the middle of the night from the dark recesses of an abandoned and cluttered gym bag.

Why does this attitude and behavior operate with material goods borrowed from other people, when it doesn't always follow with things borrowed from God? My body is a loaner from God. My home, my family, and all my possessions are not really mine anyway. The students who supply me with a job, the place where I teach, the supplies I use, and my classroom—all these are not my own. Perhaps I should be more mindful about how I regard and how I care for all of these borrowed things. Yes, all the blessings bestowed on me by God are to be used by me (for divine purposes), but I am also responsible for the proper maintenance and use of these blessings. Everything that surrounds me is on loan from God. Even the air I breathe and the lungs that do it for me are borrowed from the Giver of life.

PRAYER: Thank you, God, for the amazing loans you have sent me. Help me to properly care for your people and your things.

145
Exposed!

SUGGESTED SCRIPTURE READING: 2 Corinthians 7:2-7

VERSE DU JOUR: *I have great confidence in you. I take great pride in you. I am greatly encouraged; in all our troubles my joy knows no bounds.* (2 Corinthians 7:4)

I was feeling pretty pulled together; I *did* have on my coordinated business suit jacket paired with the maroon silk broomstick skirt, matching hose, Aigner shoes, the works. My hair even looked good. I was ready to teach! I'd run out the back door to the rest room and then had plenty of time to sashay back through the halls toward my classroom. And all went well, until I turned my back to the class to write a simple punnet square on the chalkboard. What was that twittering I heard? A few giggles?

I turned toward the class and looked over at the far left row to see Tina, a serious girl not taken to passing notes, holding up a scrawled paper sign. "What the heck is she trying to do?" I thought. "What *does* that sign say?" Stepping closer and squinting, I finally made out the words "Your skirt!" ("Yes, it is a *fine* skirt," thought I, before considering her unusual format for a compliment.) Reaching back to smooth my skirt, I felt exposed pantyhose and a balled-up skirt. Turns out I had caught my pantyhose in my skirt and never knew that I was prancing around with my underwear exposed. I scampered behind my desk and pulled everything out and down. I tried to act like nothing happened and never did have the nerve to ask the students how bad it all had looked.

Jesus spent a lot of time talking about and promising his followers joy; the New Testament accounts reference "joy" sixty-two times. And Jesus knew the history of joy; the Old Testament accounts reference the word *joy* a full one hundred times. I believe that Jesus holds the patent on the special brand of joy that allows us to truly laugh at ourselves. How could someone who makes such a big deal about joy have been without it? And would crowds really gladly follow an uptight, stone-faced, and overtly pious Jesus through the dusty countryside?

Psychologists advise us to laugh long and often. We are told that the ability to laugh at ourselves is evidence of a healthy ego, and medical evidence supports the validity of laughter's healing properties. I'm laughing now, but I can't say that I was laughing then. I was worried about my image and was embarrassed, to say the least. The next time you are embarrassed or feel flustered, don't forget that healthy humor is often hidden in the oddest places and situations. I wonder what Jesus would have laughed at?

PRAYER: Lord, please stay by my side today and open my eyes to see the humor around and in me. Please laugh with me and show me your joy.

146

Olfactory Clues

SUGGESTED SCRIPTURE READING: 2 Corinthians 2:14-17

VERSE DU JOUR: *For we are to God the aroma of Christ among those who are being saved and those who are perishing.* (2 Corinthians 2:15)

My devoted student assistant was bent over and gagging while I stood dizzily, expecting to pass out any moment. The stench from the Petri dishes was overwhelming. We were emptying into the dumpster the agar from dishes that had been filled with overgrown bacterial samples. Although the dishes had been heated and pressurized to kill the bacteria, the reeking smell of death was prevalent. It didn't help that the plates had been sitting in a makeshift autoclave for four days after they'd been sterilized.

It seems that a colleague had used the plates filled with agar for a bacteria growth lab, pressure-cooked the plates, and then forgotten about them. (The "forgetful" teacher had disappeared. We never again saw him after he deserted those dishes. But that's a story for another day.) I needed the plates for an upcoming lab and had no alternative but to retrieve and clean them.

Dead things really stink. The odor of death is distinctive and repelling. Try to contrast the smell of death to the aroma of Christ. What is the aroma of Christ that we are supposed to carry with us? The Scripture tells us that it is the fragrance of life. A life smelling like Jesus must include the aromas of self-sacrifice, empathy, servanthood, and positive thinking. Like ingredients in a fine perfume, the essence is blended to create an alluring bouquet of attractive scents. The fragrance of life, like a costly perfume, must be pleasant and exciting—it cannot be offensive, repulsive, or nauseating. If God can sense in us the aroma of Christ, others will sense it, too.

How fortuitous that as my student assistant and I were emptying those plates, preparing to wash them, (if we could possibly hold out that long), I noticed a clustering of hall monitors. "Hey, guys! Any chance we have any students deserving some work duty? I've got a humdinger duty here," I called. One monitor pulled out his walkie-talkie and in less than two odiferous minutes, the dean of students appeared with two recently apprehended class-cutters in tow. We happily turned over our repulsive job to the two boys, who despite their groans and complaining finished the job somewhat quickly. I overheard them blaming each other for their fate: "If we hadn't ditched class, we'd be *in class* right now instead of smelling this stuff!"

All is well that ends well. The ditchers learned a lesson, I had clean Petri dishes ready for my next lab lesson, and the air in the prep room eventually cleared. Let's sniff out a lesson here. We *can* attract the unsaved to Christ's aroma, draw them in with a sweet smell, an aroma that can overcome even the stench of death. How will *you* smell today?

PRAYER: I want to permeate each room I enter with the aroma of Christ. Jesus, please fill me and direct me today.

147
Greater Than Jesus?

SUGGESTED READING: John 14:5-14

VERSE DU JOUR: *"I tell you the truth, anyone who has faith in me will do what I have been doing. He will do even greater things than these, because I am going to the Father."* (John 14:12)

My mother looks at me in disbelief and horror. "Susan, what happened to you?" she asks as she surveys my bedraggled appearance. My skirt is ripped, my leather shoes are stained with some nasty yellow paint, and my stockings are run in three places. My ankles wobble with fatigue, and my hair is pulled out of its bun. I just want an icepack and my warm bed.

"Substitute teaching in an elementary school is what happened to me," I answer. "You don't have to go back to *that* school again if it was too much for you," my wise mom counsels. I decide to take Mom's advice but seriously question the wisdom of my plan to pursue a teaching career.

Jesus was a *great* teacher. "But," you say, "he wasn't dealing with the likes of the kids making up my classes." Jesus probably had worse to work with (if the twelve he chose as his finest gives any indication of what the worst must have been). But whatever our comparative teaching conditions, it matters not. Jesus promises that he will petition God in heaven to send help to us so that we can accomplish great things for God. The next part sounds heretical, but Jesus also said that we would use God's power to do things that are greater than what he did. What an incredible promise from the Lord! Notice, however, that Jesus tells us that our ability to accomplish greater things than he did is dependent on our asking him for help and on having faith in him. Also, the wording implies that our intentions for doing great works would be to bring glory to God, not to ourselves. Jesus does not give us a time frame for when we will accomplish these great works, miracles, or whatever. Jesus tells us that we will do greater things than he did, yet he doesn't tell us when these achievements will come to fruition. I might not receive the Teacher of the Year award anytime soon. In fact, I might not even attain classroom control tomorrow.

It is truly amazing that after the trauma of substitute teaching in third grade, I ever became a teacher. May God doubly bless every elementary teacher! Even once I became a "real" teacher I often felt that the job was too difficult. I sometimes questioned my ability to survive, let alone succeed. Today you have a promise of great hope from the master Teacher. Notice, the text does not say, "You must believe that you can do it!" or "Believe in yourself." That isn't the instruction given here. You must believe that the power of God, requisitioned through Jesus, will allow you to succeed—even in your current situation, with these kids, in this school, and against all earthly odds. I challenge you to access God's awesome power: Ask, believe, and you will achieve.

PRAYER: Lord, send me the power I need to bring glory to God.

148

Rich in Every Way

SUGGESTED SCRIPTURE READING: 2 Corinthians 9:8-15

VERSE DU JOUR: *You will be made rich in every way so that you can be generous on every occasion, and through us your generosity will result in thanksgiving to God.* (2 Corinthians 9:11)

At the ripe age of thirteen, my life did not seem good; I was not pretty enough, thin enough, or popular enough. "Enough" for what, I have yet to know. But my status, or lack of it, depressed me. When I look back at that time, I can quickly muster pity for any young person approaching that terrible and confusing age.

Things seemed pretty grim for me until one dark and stormy night when a tentative knocking lulled us from our cozy family dinner. There at our door, with hair dripping wet and a noticeably protruding abdomen, stood our teen neighbor, Cybil, and her boyfriend. The boyfriend spoke for Cybil, explaining that in a violent rage, Cybil's stepfather had literally kicked her out of the house; he'd become physically and verbally abusive. The boyfriend explained that he feared for her life and for the safety of their unborn baby. She needed help, and they wondered if Cybil could stay with us for awhile.

Scripture reveals a generous and a thankful Jesus. Jesus habitually offered praise and thanks to God. Jesus also spent great time and energy helping the unfortunate, the sick, the blind, and the unloved. In the second letter of Corinthians, Paul teaches that we are to recognize the many gifts that God has given to us and that we are to sow those gifts generously. Paul teaches that in helping others less fortunate than ourselves, we are not only helping them but we become part of a positive feedback loop, investing in thanksgiving raised to God.

That night Cybil moved in, with not much more than the ill-fitting clothes on her back. Her acne-covered face looked so frightened and lonely. Cybil had nowhere else to go, not even the house of a friend. Suddenly, I saw things in a different light. I was the lucky one. Relative to Cybil, I was so richly blessed. I had a home, a family, a room of my own (well, before that night it *had* been my own), lots of nice clothes, a few good friends, and I wasn't pregnant. Despite the seeming inconvenience of an intruder into my space, I felt an impressive sense of shame and a flood of thanksgiving. Even in the throes of my thirteen-year-old hormones, I knew I was rich in every way and that I had no right to feel sorry for myself. It wasn't until I opened my eyes to Cybil that I saw the many blessings God had given *me*.

Sometimes we need to honestly count our blessings and, as my parents modeled, share those blessings with those who are less fortunate. As we generously share with others, we gain the advantage of seeing our lives in a different light. Will you honor and offer thanks to God as you share your knowledge and time generously with your students?

PRAYER: Thank you, God, for the blessings you have given me. I am blessed beyond belief. I am saved by your grace, rich with your provision, and honored by your presence in my life.

149

Chaos Theory

SUGGESTED SCRIPTURE READING: John 19:25-27

VERSE DU JOUR: *When Jesus saw his mother there, and the disciple whom he loved standing nearby, he said to his mother, "Dear woman, here is your son."* (John 19:26)

The intercom interrupts my lesson and the new student, a boy with attention issues, distracts half the class from the lab activity that I'd set up. Five kids are simultaneously at my desk asking me something. Their requests range from bathroom passes and homework to an emergency room visit. I wonder how I will make it through this class so that I can finally run out of here. Talk about chaos!

Jesus endured the incredible agony of dying on a Roman cross. Despite the incomparable physical, emotional, and spiritual pain, Jesus managed to notice his mother and his friend John standing nearby. At this terrible moment in history, Jesus was more concerned about his mother than he was about himself. Jesus uses the little time and the few words he has left to conceive and carry out a plan that will provide for the woman who loves him so much. He blesses his mother with a surrogate son who will care for her in his absence. At the same time, Jesus honors his beloved friend, John.

So, I guess my distractions are nothing compared with what Jesus was going through when he overcame chaos. Jesus chose to ignore unparalleled pain for a few moments so that he could respond to the needs of another. Even in his final hours, Jesus continued to show us that it is *people* who matter. The things of this world and the chaos that seem to rule this place are irrelevant. The people around us are irreplaceable and of utmost importance. Can you look past the chaos surrounding you, so that like Jesus, you can see and respond to the needs of the people around you?

PRAYER: Jesus, please help me to remember that you are the Ruler of the universe and that the chaos around me holds no power over me. You rule over everything, including apparent chaos. Take control of my chaos, and help me to see through it so I can tend to the needs of the ones you love so dearly.

150
Keeping God "On Hold"

SUGGESTED READING: Isaiah 30:18-20

VERSE DU JOUR: *Yet the LORD still waits for you to come to him, so he can show you his love; he will conquer you to bless you, just as he said. For the LORD is faithful to his promises. Blessed are all those who wait for him to help them.* (Isaiah 30:18, TLB)

Utterly exasperated, I slam the phone down and growl through my sesame-seed laden teeth. I just spent my entire lunch break on the phone. I crunched and munched my way through twenty-two minutes of muzak "on hold" before I was allowed to speak to a fellow human. I'd called my current insurance company with what I thought was a quick question. Of course, my wait was made even more frustrating by the fact that I couldn't even relax, because every fifty-nine seconds, a recording calmly told me some interesting information about how I could access the web to get my answer more quickly. I was repeatedly told, "Please continue to hold, and we will be with you momentarily."

The moments continued to tick away as I pondered any relationship between this situation and possible spiritual connection. I was hoping for insight on patience, or some other profound realization, but instead I began to feel guilty.

Just how many times have I put the Lord God, maker of heaven, earth, and even the maker of me, on hold? How many times have I failed to pray or forgotten to ask God for direction? How many times have I sent my Creator bad music instead of real praise? Too often, I've sent pathetic recordings instead of real communication. I keep God waiting and waiting and waiting, saying, "Please continue to hold. I'll be with you momentarily." I could start up some communication and wait for an answer. Perhaps God has allowed humankind the ability to develop the technology that depersonalizes and separates us from each other so that we can see what we are constantly doing in our spiritual lives.

I would have been much happier if someone had come on the line and simply spoken to me before I was forced to wait such a long time. My ire would have been greatly lessened if, when the real human finally picked up, she would have apologized for my extended wait. But no one apologized. And I didn't even think to use that time to pray . . . Perhaps I should apologize for my rudeness. My God has been waiting to talk to me, to help me become a better person and teacher. God has been waiting to answer my questions and wants to solve my problems. How about you? Have you ever kept God on hold?

PRAYER: Forgive me, Lord. Consider the line open. Let's talk to each other today.

151

A Better Place?

SUGGESTED SCRIPTURE READING: Matthew 13:44-45

VERSE DU JOUR: *"The Kingdom of Heaven is like a treasure a man discovered in a field. In his excitement, he sold everything he owned to get enough money to buy the field—and get the treasure too!"* (Matthew 13:44, TLB)

The students across town are expectantly packing their bags with clothes and their brains with last-minute verb clauses before they head out for their European studies. I remember leaving my home town to do the same thing. Before leaving, I believed my New Jersey home to be one of the greatest places in the world. We lived within commuting distance to New York, the mountains of Pennsylvania, and the beach. New Jersey was, by my adolescent standards, pretty much perfect. Before long, I was witnessing ancient cathedrals, the grandeur of the Alps, the beckoning blue of the Mediterranean, and the opera house in Vienna; the excitement of it all was incredible.

Jesus compares the kingdom of heaven with a treasure; a treasure for which a person would give anything. I sometimes wonder how we will perceive heaven upon arrival. Once we settle in, will we grow bored with it? Will we miss earth? Are streets paved with gold preferable to single-track bike paths or talus slopes? Will we have enough to do, and will it be any fun? When such questions occur to me, I think of the phenomenon I experienced upon returning home from my European studies. The houses and the towns of my childhood seemed smaller and less impressive; the ski slopes of my youth failed to impress me; and even my favorite beach hang-out seemed dingy and run-down. How had so much change occurred in such a short time? When I tried to communicate my observations with hometown friends, they resented my negative observations—they did not want to hear that our little piece of the world no longer held the patent on coolness.

When I think now of how the beauty and excitement of Europe and the Mediterranean altered my view of New Jersey, I expect that once we've been to heaven, the world as we now know it will seem dingy and unremarkable. The activities that consume us now and the wealth and status we so strive for here will all seem stupid and passé. Any work done other than for God's kingdom will have been a waste of time. And the beauty of the place and of our lives there will be beyond today's imagination. Only the firsthand observer can aptly comprehend such a treasure. Jesus has seen it and tells us that heaven is a treasure of a place; I'll take his word for it and try to remember that the earth is not my true home. How about you?

PRAYER: I trust you in everything, Lord. I know that you have prepared a place for me. You know me better than I know myself. Please begin today to prepare me for your kingdom.

152

A Very Bad Day

SUGGESTED SCRIPTURE READING: Matthew 10:11-20

VERSE DU JOUR: *"If anyone will not welcome you or listen to your words, shake the dust off your feet when you leave that home or town."* (Matthew 10:14)

Something was wrong. As I hurried in to teach my first morning class, it was too quiet. Although the late bell was about to ring, several students lingered outside the door. Others sat in their seats, blank expressions on their puffy faces. I questioned three boys before I got the whole story: a local pizza restaurant had been the site of a horrible shooting spree the night before. Shortly before closing, a disgruntled robber had sprayed the place with bullets.

People had been shot. At least one was already pronounced dead with plenty of others injured.

No one was sure of the status of our students; quite a few of them worked the night shift at that very location. Students were worried about their friends. We were all stunned, and it didn't seem right to launch directly into our lesson on plant biology. This was not going to be an easy day.

Jesus experienced some good days, some bad days, and some *very* bad days. On one good day, Jesus helped his new disciples haul in tons of fish, and on another, he healed ten lepers. Jesus probably had a few memorable and relaxing days hanging out on the beach with his followers, grilling fish over the campfire at night and gazing up at the stars on cool desert nights. Sometimes people crowded at his feet, hanging on his every word. But on other days his teaching was unwelcome and people threw rocks at him. One day, Jesus rode on a donkey into town while the crowds applauded and cheered him. The next day, he was betrayed and sentenced to death. Most likely, there were days Jesus was on the road and sick; he probably had a few bad cases of sunburn, sore feet, and nasty infections with no antibiotics to be found. Jesus experienced grief, the loss of friends, painful hunger, threats of grave danger, and frustration with the government. Yet, Jesus taught his disciples to shake off the bad and look forward to better times.

As news filtered in about the shooting, we discovered that a few of our students were injured but stable, traumatized but alive. It was a sad, frightening, and tense day, but we comforted each other and felt closer because of our shared concern. I must admit that I was happy when the day was done, and I made a point to not stop for any pizza on the way home. We will experience good days and bad days. Yet, if we see each day as a gift and recognize that a better day is coming, then perhaps we can develop a healthy, Jesus-like perspective.

PRAYER: Jesus, help me to shake off the bad days and remember the goodness and mercy that you have shown to me. Let me continue on in my mission, and do not let my spirit be broken when the tough days appear.

153

The Cup

SUGGESTED SCRIPTURE READING: Matthew 26:36-46

VERSE DU JOUR: *He went away a second time and prayed, "My Father, if it is not possible for this cup to be taken away unless I drink it, may your will be done."* (Matthew 26:42)

I have the coolest biology teacher mug in the business. And I'm not referring to my face, but rather to a real mug, as in a cup from which I drink. In fact, I have two noteworthy liquid holders: one is a glass beaker with a mug handle, and the other is off-white porcelain shaped like an oversized vertebrae. I drink from either one of these mugs nearly incessantly, as I'm a dry-mouth person who needs constant hydration. It's a wonder I haven't been poisoned yet; my partially filled mugs are always out and about.

My attachment to my liquids and their holders got me to thinking about why Jesus prayed for some sort of cup to be taken from him. What was he talking about? I'd always thought that this cup to which Jesus referred was a figure of speech, a figurative reference to the physical agony that he was about to endure. Recently another teacher pointed out some Old Testament references to the "cup of God's wrath." In Isaiah we read that the cup refers to God's fury and that the cup sets people to trembling and staggering.

It seems that Jesus dreaded God's anger and the separation from God that such anger would induce more than he dreaded the physical torture of the cross. In anticipation of the cross, Jesus knew that the emotional torment of "the cup" awaited him, and he pleaded with God to remove it. If God were willing to grant the request of a sincere prayer, wouldn't it have been for Jesus? And yet, God allowed Jesus to suffer and let history play out. God did not send hosts of angels to assist Jesus, did not create a display of power that would set humankind straight, and did not allow Jesus to defer his torture for a later time. And yet, for our sake, Jesus was willing to endure even this; he was willing to drink the entire cup, down to the dregs.

I have occasionally felt the wrath of one student or another. I once had a student throw a chair at me, many a student has thrown unflattering epitaphs my way, and a young man once bit my leg. But I have never drunk from the cup of God's wrath—and thanks to Jesus, I never will. I would prefer to drink from my beaker facsimile and bone-like cups, thank you very much. The next time you take a drink of anything from any cup, I urge you to consider the price that Jesus willingly paid for you. Jesus paid the price for you, and you weren't cheap.

PRAYER: Thank you for taking the cup for me. Today, let me say "not my will, but yours."

154

Teacher Love

SUGGESTED SCRIPTURE READING: Colossians 3:1-17

VERSE DU JOUR: *And over all these virtues put on love, which binds them all together in perfect unity.* (Colossians 3:14)

"I won't leave until I get my hug," Ralph suddenly announced after class one day. Other students were clustered around me, with various questions or requests; they all turned to see what I would do. Panicked, with a crowd of witnesses, I stiffly embraced the boy, offered a motherly pat or two on his back, and tried to avoid any close contact. Was I compromising my reputation? It's not that I feared lice or skin infections, although those would've been reasonable concerns. I also didn't want to give Ralph the wrong idea or indulge any bizarre fantasies.

The other students looked on in horror, "Gross! She's touching *him!*" they no doubt thought. Or maybe it was more like, "Gross! He's touching *her!*" Day after day, we went through this somewhat strained routine. I wanted to help this boy and wanted him to feel welcome in my class but wished at the same time to get him out of my classroom. The whole situation made me nervous. If I wanted to do something illegal for which I'd be fired, I'd choose something else.

Jesus taught that we are to love one another. Jesus couldn't possibly demonstrate his love to everyone alive; at any point in history, it takes more than one person to love the whole world—which might explain why Jesus made disciples. As disciples of Jesus, we are instructed to share his love. But, as teachers, it is usually inappropriate to show love by kissing or even hugging our students. We need to find appropriate ways to share Jesus love, a special kind of teacher love. Teacher love need not make you a wishy-washy person or a pushover. If anything, sharing the love that Jesus has given you will make you a stronger and more effective teacher! My teacher love is not the same as your teacher love, but the effect is the same.

If, like me, you are uncomfortable hugging your older students, how can you effectively share Jesus' love? What does your teacher love look like? Teacher love might appear by holding a tough line with one student or be shown in the willingness to listen to another. Teacher love might require pushing a student beyond that student thinks he or she can do. It may drive you to discipline that student who needs direction or to compliment the child with the damaged self-image. Teacher love may inspire you to give up your free period to work with a struggling student, or it may be revealed because you show up each day. Teacher love remains flexible to change its face for each student and is shown in various ways to different recipients. Some days, we can love only by making a conscious decision to do so, one person at a time. To whom will you show Jesus' love today?

PRAYER: Lord, I am yours. All the days of my life you have shown me nothing but mercy and love. My goal is to pass on some of your love to at least one of my students. Please make it clear to me who it is you have in mind and help me to follow through. Thank you.

155

Influence

SUGGESTED SCRIPTURE READING: Proverbs 3:1-12

VERSE DU JOUR: *My son, do not forget my teaching, but keep my commands in your heart.* (Proverbs 3:1)

For awhile, Pete's mom would call to update me on his progress at West Point. I was so proud of him and thought back to our times together: watching him master biology, chatting at the copy machine, hearing him play the "Maple Leaf Rag" on the old upright piano while his mom danced circles through their living room. It all seems so far away now that Peter is off learning to lead the free world!

In much the same way that God knows the influence each teacher will have on the future, God knew the power that Jesus held over the future of the world. Jesus lived as a laborer and as a poor itinerant teacher. His lifestyle was not glamorous, nor did he appear to be influential. And yet, it is his life that changed the course of all history. Jesus recognized that the future of the humankind was in his hands, so he actively sought the power of God in is daily life. It was the only way that he could carry out the tasks that lay ahead of him. If Jesus needed help in fulfilling his mission, you can bet that we need it, too. We also have access to that same power.

In our culture, teachers are not highly esteemed, highly paid, or considered highly influential. And yet, the students who pass through our lives may well greatly influence world history. The students whose lives we touch can be found all over the world. Some have become doctors and lawyers. Some have become missionaries, and others, pastors or youth group leaders. Some are fighting crime, while others are committing it. At least one of mine is performing autopsies for the county sheriff's office, while several others serve as commissioned military leaders. Some care for children or staff cancer research laboratories and educational posts. Eventually our students may hold government offices and positions of economic power. Who knows the influence we wield in our seemingly low positions? Only God knows. God wants to guide us in our teacher roles and promises the benefits of divinely inspired wisdom and protection.

PRAYER: God, you have given me material blessings, and now you have given me great responsibility. I know that what I do today will touch tomorrow. Please go with me and give me your power. Let me influence the future of your kingdom though the students that I teach.

156
Be at Peace?

SUGGESTED SCRIPTURE READING: Romans 12:9-21

VERSE DU JOUR: *"Blessed are the peacemakers, for they will be called children of God."* (Matthew 5:9, NRSV)

Tanks are closing in on refugee camps somewhere in Palestine. The war on terrorism rages on, and people drive like maniacs around the rotary circle on my commuting route. Kids talk when I'm trying to teach, and they laugh at my efforts to be creative. While I'm at a conference on cooperative learning, an administrator confides in me; perhaps she senses that I'm disheartened with conditions of our schools or my current students. "Last year I almost gave up the ghost myself," Connie whispers. Wondering what she's talking about, I smile and nod. "In the course of two to three months, I took nine guns from nine different students. The dangerous nature of my job kind of freaked me out, and I nearly quit." Simple mental math led me to a feeling of panic and despair. If she disarmed nine students and there are four other administrators . . .

Despite our surroundings or the era in which we live, Jesus urges us to become the bearers of peace. Jesus modeled the role of peacemaker, not in a political sense but by bringing healing and wholeness to shattered lives. He taught about peace in the lesson known as the Beatitudes. The sermon was delivered in a natural setting, during a time of great political turmoil and social unrest. The status of the Jews under Roman occupation was uncertain: people were waiting for a Messiah, an uprising, religious suppression, or a war. In the New Testament, we find information on how we can be blessed as peacemakers. We are to try to get along with everyone and not seek revenge. Jesus told us to love everyone, even our enemies. These instructions run counterintuitive to our human nature and appear as risky behaviors for those living in a violent and unstable culture. In more than two thousand years, some things haven't changed.

If my calculations are correct, today there could be more than forty-five students carrying firearms around my school, so the subject of peace becomes a practical issue. But how do educators double as peacemakers? Jesus doesn't teach us to acquiesce in the face of moral questions or in defending others. Perhaps we can initiate peace by overcoming evil with good. Words of affirmation and moments of selfless giving can be the tools that overcome evil. Showing acceptance and sharing God's love with the bearer of a firearm might keep him or her from using it. Since we can't be sure who is carrying a dangerous weapon, the scriptural advice to try to live at peace with everyone makes perfect sense. Might peace come as the result of keeping our emotions in check, our connection to God strong, and our expectations high?

PRAYER: Lord, help me to love your children. Let me keep my emotions, especially my anger, in check, even when I feel offended. Please show me your peace today.

157

Outside Ourselves

SUGGESTED SCRIPTURE READING: Matthew 10:5-8

VERSE DU JOUR: *"Heal the sick, raise the dead, cleanse those who have leprosy, drive out demons. Freely you have received, freely give."* (Matthew 10:8)

Five or six girls are gathered in the elegant, pristine living room of our favorite third-grade teacher. We are an unlikely assortment of girls, yet we are all dressed in our finest with freshly scrubbed faces, our look complete with missing teeth, pig tails, and nervous smiles. As our teacher serves us refreshments, she compliments each girl individually. Balancing plates of snickerdoodles and glasses of homemade lemonade, we expectantly look toward the door. We can hardly believe that we're with our favorite teacher on a Saturday or that we've been considered worthy to visit her home in Princeton. Yes! Here comes Mrs. Bond's husband. It's time to walk over to the natural history museum, where we will see real dinosaur bones.

Jesus tells his followers to heal the sick, raise the dead, cleanse those with leprosy, and even drive out demons. In a way, he tells us to step outside of ourselves. When we serve others, taking risks by going outside of our comfort zones, we honor our Creator. Additionally, the Scriptures teach and earthly models confirm that God has designed us in such a way that we will feel most alive when we serve others. Since teachers rarely see leprosy, let alone need to tend it, could educators extrapolate and synthesize Jesus' words to our worlds? We can tend to the depressed, raise those who feel dead, affirm the broken-hearted, cleanse those who have fallen into the wrong crowd, and drive out the demons of ignorance and hatred.

Do you suppose that Mrs. Bond went outside her comfort zone when she invited those girls into her home? Was she anxious that morning, wondering why she was letting a group of clumsy, pre-adolescent girls know where she lived? Did she worry that we might damage the Persian carpet or embarrass her at the university museum? Perhaps—but it didn't stop her from inviting me and the others to her home. And I can say that based on her attitude that day, Mrs. Bond seemed alive and happy. I don't know if Mrs. Bond invited all the girls in the class and we were the only ones who showed up or whether she gave up multiple Saturday afternoons to entertain. But I do know that by showing acceptance and hospitality, she made a huge impression on me. For years, when I doubted myself or struggled with the demons of adolescent angst, I was comforted with memories of that visit. "Mrs. Bond invited me to her house. She told me that I'm charming and smart; I must be okay," I often thought. Are you willing to step out of your comfort zone to affirm or heal someone?

PRAYER: Jesus, I thank you for giving freely to me, for giving me gifts that I can share with others. Let me gladly help those you place before me.

158

Enemies?

SUGGESTED SCRIPTURE READING: Matthew 5:38-48

VERSE DU JOUR: *"But I tell you: Love your enemies and pray for those who persecute you."* (Matthew 5:44)

It's bad enough when I see my students emotionally hurt each other, but it breaks my heart to see the unfairness that makes my daughter cry. My six-year-old girl, Riley, is sniffling and purposely averts her eyes from mine when I pick her up from school. Once we're away from the crowd, my dear girl cries all the way home. Eventually I get the story: Anna (not her real name), a mean-spirited and unhappy little girl in Riley's first-grade class, is systematically ostracizing my daughter. Despite Riley's attempts to befriend the other girls in the class, Anna has been advising the other girls to "stay away from Riley, or else!" The unfairness of this world starts early—and it makes me angry.

Pray for your enemies. Bless those who curse you. Turn the other cheek. Pray for those who persecute you. It seems I've always known of Jesus' commands, yet these particular ones often seem abstract, if not downright absurd, at least by the world's standards, and abstract because I don't think I have any serious enemies.

"Enemies" seems like such a strong term. I envision enemies as evil, cackling, twisted villains who exist in action movies or cartoons; they don't seem to fit in the modern world. So, I've been conveniently pushing these commands under the rug, along with a fair amount of Cheerios and other archeological snack items. Practically, however, enemies might be people who steal ideas from you, those who purposely hurt you, or those who secretly speak against you. They may be people you don't know very well.

Why then did it take a moment of epiphany for me to realize that we, my daughter and I, need to be praying for Anna? I finally realized that my dear Riley had an enemy and I'd been wasting valuable time. Instead of teaching my child about the power of prayer or doing some, I'd been inert and whiny.

The next day, as we walked down the alley on the way to school, we prayed for Anna. We asked God to make her a happier and a nicer person. We prayed that Anna might see Jesus in Riley and asked God to watch over Riley. My daughter left the alley with a spring in her step and a smile on her face. Later, I thought of those whom I curse instead of bless: the guy who cuts me off at the light, the students who roll their eyes at me, the rude cashier, the competitive colleague, and sometimes even my tired, grouchy spouse. Perhaps, for even just a moment, these people become my enemies; they become the ones for whom I am instructed to pray. In praying for them, I am distracted from my anger and frustration. I am able to act instead of react, and my action leads to something that is good for them and me. Is there someone for whom you need to pray?

PRAYER: Forgive me my sins as you help me to forgive others who have sinned against me. Please bless those who are my enemies.

159
Something Missing

SUGGESTED SCRIPTURE READING: Matthew 5:13-16

VERSE DU JOUR: *"You are the salt of the earth. But if the salt loses its saltiness, how can it be made salty again?"* (Matthew 5:13)

I arrived home from a hectic school day to find my husband sitting on the living room couch, blankly staring into space, apparently awaiting the arrival of his dinner. On this particular evening, the concept of the feminist movement eluded my inert and hungry husband. Amazingly, I had remembered to set out chicken to defrost earlier in the day. There were plenty of eggs and green onions in the fridge. Unsalted peanuts sat waiting on the counter, along with the magical pad Thai kit that would help me make my new favorite Asian meal. Knives chopped, pots flew, and less than forty-five minutes later I was calling everyone to dinner.

Excited for the first taste of culinary delight, I wasted no time after saying grace to sink in my chopsticks. The delectable olfactory sensations I expected did not match the disappointing taste. Then I remembered to add just a little salt. Ah, much better! My wild preparation was worth it, after all!

Jesus likened his believers to the "salt of the earth." We are here to spice up this sometimes drab planet. Without us the world is missing something. It's not just that we are to be different from everyone else, but the Scriptures instruct that in each believer is dwelling the living presence of the Holy Spirit. This great Comforter resides in and assists those believing in Jesus' name. If all believers were removed from this world, it is possible that the Holy Spirit would vanish as well. How much worse would our world become if the Spirit of God were to disappear?

You are not only an instrument of God but also a vessel carrying the Holy Spirit. As a Christian teacher, it is not just your actions that are a force for good, but it is the Spirit of God who accompanies you. You carry the Spirit who, like the once missing salt in my pad Thai, can transform this often weary, bland world into a more bearable and even delightful place. Wherever you go today, the Spirit also goes—God's presence accompanies you through the hallways you walk, into the classrooms where you teach, and even to the corner desk where you may plan, eat, and visit. It is impossible for us to know how much evil might be diverted by the presence of God in you.

PRAYER: Please send your Spirit through me into my world. Go with me today, Lord, and bless those with whom I interact. Let my students feel your presence.

160

Never Give Up!

SUGGESTED SCRIPTURE READING: Luke 18:1-8

VERSE DU JOUR: *"And will not God bring about justice for his chosen ones, who cry out to him day and night? Will he keep putting them off?"* (Luke 18:7)

Tito must really want an A this semester. He was waiting outside my door yesterday morning, and this morning he must have been here well before seven. Like a stalker, he's chased me down the hallway twice this week. I'm not feeling threatened, but the boy's persistence is a bit unnerving. Now someone is pounding on the door of the science office. Since I'm the only one on prep this block, I pull myself away from my papers to pull open the heavy wooden door. What now? "Do you think I have a chance for the A?" the boy at the door asks me breathlessly. It's Tito yet again. He wants me to check the lab questions that are due tomorrow. And there's something about the reading that he wants to discuss.

Jesus told his disciples the story of an ungodly judge and a persistent widow seeking justice. The judge doesn't fear God or even care about the good of the people, but he finally does dole out justice. The judge eventually grants the widow's request, not because he cares about her or about her cause, but because he is tired of hearing the widow's pleas. He sees that the widow will keep bothering him until she gets the justice she seeks. Jesus then goes on to explain that if the persistence of a needy widow can influence an uncaring judge, how much more will our loving God respond to our persistent and unending prayers. Jesus says, "And will not God bring about justice for his chosen ones, who cry out to him day and night? Will he keep putting them off? I tell you, he will see that they get justice, and quickly." Luke's foreword to this passage tells us that Jesus told this parable to teach his disciples to "always pray and to never give up."

When it came time to issue semester grades, I found Tito one point short of the elusive A. Thinking back on Tito's persistence and his deep desire for the grade, I added the missing point so that he could receive what he so deeply desired. I had the authority to award an unearned point or two but wouldn't always use the option. In this case, I have to admit that Tito was beginning to wear me down. I also realized how important the grade must have been to Tito, and I didn't want to see him disappointed—not when I could do something about it. Do you have a need that is not yet met, an issue that needs resolution, or a situation in which justice must be served? The biblical message is clear: Keep praying and don't give up.

PRAYER: Merciful God, thank you for hearing me every time I come to you.

161

Listen to Me!

SUGGESTED SCRIPTURE READING: Mark 9:1-8

VERSE DU JOUR: *Then a cloud appeared and enveloped them, and a voice came from the cloud: "This is my Son, whom I love. Listen to him!"* (Mark 9:7)

We were on our way to watch our friend, Paul, box at a fight club in Jersey City. As my Dad drove north on the New Jersey Turnpike, we got to talking. Probably because we were distracted, we missed exit 14B, and the sparkling lights of Manhattan were all too quickly approaching. Now, how would we avoid going over the bridge and being hopelessly trapped in the city? We had to find a way to turn around and get back so we could get to the armory before Paul was set to fight. The chances of doing a legal U-turn were slim, so we took the next exit in hopes of getting turned around. When we stopped to pay our toll, my dad leaned out the window to ask the toll collector how we could get back to Jersey City. The toll taker started to give us very intricate instructions to help us maneuver back the way we'd come. Suddenly, he rocked us out of our glassy-eyed nodding as only a New Yorker can do: He looked my dad in the eyes and sternly barked, "Now, listen to me! You're *not* listening to me!"

Jesus knows all about us mortals. He knows that we often ask for help but haven't learned to listen. He knows that we haven't trained ourselves to take the advice we get. We fear that God's advice might require us to make changes or maneuvers that turn us around completely. After three decades of trying to get people to listen to him, even Jesus needed a helping hand. In Mark's Gospel, we read about God delivering confirmation to Jesus in the form of a dove along with a heavenly voice, projecting from the skies with an unmistakable message: "This is my Son, whom I love. Listen to him!"

Until that New Yorker admonished us to listen, my dad and I had been in that kind of lazy-minded daze where only half of the directions register and you drive away hoping that half directions and half luck will get you to your destination. And sure enough, the man did get us to wake up and listen. We did get correctly turned around and made it to the fight on time. Clearly, that guy knew that most people who ask for directions rarely pay close enough attention to get any real help.

Try not to be too discouraged when your message seems ignored or when your efforts at educating don't seem to get through. It is maddening when you work so hard and your students don't seem to be listening. At least you are in good company. Like Jesus, we have to keep on saying what must be said and doing what must be done. And don't forget that sometimes we need to listen, too.

PRAYER: God, please give me the presence and authority so that my students will want to hear what I say. Please help me to remember that like them, I must listen.

162

Raising the Bar

SUGGESTED SCRIPTURE READING: Philippians 2:1-18

VERSE DU JOUR: *For it is God who works in you to will and to act according to his good purpose.* (Philippians 2:13)

Imagine my conflicting emotions when Tyrone, a seventh- or eighth-year senior, walked across the podium and proudly accepted his diploma. Happy that he'd finally made it through but curious about how he'd completed his science requirements, I applauded as loudly as anyone else—he had been at Midway at least as long as I had. Years before, Tyrone had taken my earth science class and failed. He'd taken my general biology class and failed. His second attempt in my biology class ended in failure as well. Every time he was in one of my classes, Tyrone seemed to enjoy himself and even appeared to understand most of the material, but he would forget to turn in major assignments and missed many classes. Although Tyrone was always respectful and pleasant and I gave him extra help, he consistently flunked. I was tempted to pass him and be done with it, but my conscience wouldn't let me. I continued to hope that Tyrone would eventually meet my expectations.

Looking at the teachings of Jesus and at the standards he set for his behavior, we see that raising the bar is essential. Jesus promises us the help of God in developing us into godly people, but Jesus never lowers the standards to accommodate our weaknesses. Instead, he raises the bar in order to improve us. In the Book of Philippians, Paul gives specific directives on how to live a godly life. His instructions on how we should think and live begin as challenging goals and then progress to the nearly impossible. Paul does not give us vague, easy-to-attain guidelines, but like Jesus, Paul continually raises the bar toward perfection. The fact that I won't ever reach perfection in this life is obvious, yet forgiven. But I'm expected to attempt to strive for that goal—the attempt is an imperative. We see in the reading that we are to strive toward good purpose, to work out our salvation, and to be one with Christ. But as the instructions continue, the going gets even tougher. We're supposed to be like Christ, quit the complaining and arguing, and become blameless. Talk about some high standards!

Three days after graduation, while classes were still in session, I was working with several students in my laboratory when I looked up to see Tyrone standing in my doorway. He greeted me and then walked toward me. I thought, "He's mad and here for revenge. I was the one who held him back for so long." As he reached for me, I remember thinking, "This is it. Tyrone's going to put me down." Instead of the blow I expected, Tyrone delivered a big hug and whispered in my ear, "Thank you for failing me." "Excuse me," I answered. "Why are you thanking me for that?" Tyrone smiled and replied, "Thank you for failing me, because failing made me work harder, and now I'm off to business college." Thrilled for him (and relieved for myself), I congratulated Tyrone. "You will be a *great* businessman! You could sell a drowning person a drink of water."

Prayer: Lord God, help me to keep my standards high. Whether working with my students or on my own, allow me to use failure as a teacher.

163
Getting "Used"

Suggested Scripture Reading: 1 Corinthians 1:26-31

Verse du Jour: *But God chose the foolish things of the world to shame the wise; God has chosen the weak things of the world to shame the strong* (1 Corinthians 1:27).

Trouble was brewing, and a curious crowd was quickly gathering in the tenth-grade hallway. Bags were flung down, books slid across the polished floor, and an energized throng surrounding the two agitated girls whistled and whooped. "You are so pathetic. I can't believe you let him use you like that," one girl yelled. The other replied, before jumping the first, "He loves *me*, you fool." Although I couldn't see over the crowd, I heard the evidence: clawing, curses, pounding purses. Rather than making room for the fight, the crowd gathered closer and the pandemonium increased as I ran for a phone. No way was I going to offer my face as a punching bag, accidental or otherwise. My policy on student fighting is a straight R&R approach—run and report.

Jesus called to his disciples, "Follow me," and they did. Samuel answered the voice of God when he heard his name called out in the middle of the night. "Here I am . . . Speak, for your servant is listening." Samuel, who in his waking hours had already committed himself to the Lord's service, seems to have naturally answered God's call; he then shook off his sleepiness and asked for the God's instructions. If you are one of God's own, chances are that you, too, want to be used by him. But I would venture to guess that most of us are a little afraid of what might happen if God uses us. We also may be unclear about how it happens. God is looking for available workers and plans to bless us. He is willing to use you in miraculous ways, but only if you make yourself available. Scripture instructs us to clearly answer God: "Here I am, Lord. Please use me." God uses mightily those who seek to be used.

I breathlessly called the office to report the fight, which left two unhappy teens even more miserable. Their fight focused on a negative view of being used. Although our fears and insecurities may make us uncertain about what God wants us to do, God has already chosen us and placed us. God will give us the wisdom and strength we need to complete our assignments. The ball is in our court, so to speak. Have you told God that you are ready to be used? Ask yourself if you are up for the challenges, the excitement, and the rewards that God has planned for you.

PRAYER: God, here I am. Use me today.

164

When You Fall

SUGGESTED READING: 1 Peter 2:18-25

VERSES DU JOUR: *To this you were called, because Christ suffered for you, leaving you an example, that you should follow in his steps. "He committed no sin, and no deceit was found in his mouth."* (1 Peter 2:21-22)

To this day, I cannot pinpoint any one accident that caused my broken bone, but I can vividly recall the embarrassment suffered at the X-ray table. "You're here for a film of *what?*" the technician asked incredulously. "My coccyx. My tailbone. Just X-ray my butt, okay?" I replied, in an I've-had-enough-already tone. I'd already spent weeks hobbling from classroom to classroom, sliding my feet ever so slightly ahead so that I could ease my hips forward without jarring my spine. I couldn't sit comfortably on a lab stool for even a minute.

Like the parent of a newly toddling child, Jesus knows that we will inevitably fall. He also understands the consequences of our spiritual falls, sin, and the evil that wounds and kills. "But," you might be thinking, "if Jesus never sinned, how could he possibly understand the ease of the deed? Since Jesus was without sin, how could he understand how it feels to slip up or fall away?" Jesus was truly perfect and never committed a sin in his life. But the reality is that Jesus did experience the worst of sin's impact. While suffering the cross, Jesus experienced the consequence for all our sins. To say, then, that Jesus doesn't understand the shame and ugliness of sin is not true. Jesus experienced ultimate pain, with complete separation from God, when he took on all our sin. Even in our worst moments, God never forsakes us. Jesus also promises that if we have a repentant heart, we will be forgiven; our sins can be erased, and once they are, healing can begin.

My broken tailbone was later blamed on several ski falls and the contorted twisting of a yoga pose. There was no therapy available, just the hope of slow healing with the tincture of time. You can imagine the fun my students had teasing me about that one: "No. I do *not* need a cast, thank you very much," became my new mantra.

In the same way that I broke my bone through a fall, I am capable of damaging myself and others when I spiritually fall. Following in the steps of Jesus encourages me to avoid the pitfalls that will cause such damage. Additionally, once I have fallen, I must be quick to seek forgiveness and work to heal the wounds I've created. I need to pick myself up, seek forgiveness, and move on. Time is short, and forgiveness isn't worlds away but only words away. Is there a fall you need to confess so healing can begin?

PRAYER: Jesus, thank you for forgiving me when I fall away. Help me walk in your footsteps. I want to spread the light of your love and the mercy of your forgiveness to my students today.

165

Do Something

SUGGESTED SCRIPTURE READING: James 2:14-17

VERSE DU JOUR: *In the same way, faith by itself, if it is not accompanied by action, is dead.* (James 2:17)

Nearly every day, Starr, the sophomore brunette with a serious face and a matching attitude, is late for class. And she leaves early, too. But I don't mind. The first day that Starr explained to me the reason for her tardiness, her face was flushed with excitement and happiness. Starr explained that she was now an assistant to Sara. It was Starr's job to push Sara's wheelchair to class. Since Starr's and Sara's classes were not the same, the four minutes between classes would not be enough. Starr clearly enjoyed filling this volunteer position and not only took her new responsibility seriously but had begun to develop a bond with Sara. Starr refused to hear any taunts directed their way and took great delight in making Sara laugh.

Jesus developed an approachable personality that was other-centered, and he taught that by serving each other, we show God's love. Why is it that many Christians, myself included, are intimidated by the concept of good deeds? I know why I want to run when the faith-versus-deeds argument begins, because the deeds that I think are required to validate my faith seem outrageous. I envision actions requiring Herculean strength or heroic bravery. I think that I can't perform any worthwhile deeds until I've packed up to feed the poor of Calcutta or first give up my job to spend my life in some truly wretched locale. If there is a flush toilet in the vicinity, surely it's not sacrifice enough. Unless I leave all that is familiar, I figure I won't be doing anything that counts as a good deed. In actuality, God wants to use me where I am.

Although Jesus' life was far from normal, he gives us a realistic and practical model of faith in action. Jesus demonstrated faith and deep love through constant action. Some of that action consisted of miraculous deeds, but many of his deeds, considered noteworthy enough to be included in the Gospel accounts, were small acts of kindness, displays of empathy, and demonstrations of genuine and common courtesy.

Perhaps in the future, God will want you far away from where you are now. But today you can follow Jesus' example and teaching, demonstrating your faith through small acts of kindness and service. Perhaps rather than Calcutta, you've been chosen to serve in your own neighborhood or your own classroom. What seem to be small deeds may greatly influence the lives you touch—many small acts of kindness and sacrifice will mark you as one of God's own. It's not too difficult to give small offerings of love: a smile to a stranger, a song of praise on the way to work, a letter of gratitude written to a friend, or an honest compliment. You might design a particularly fabulous lesson, give a word of encouragement, gladly tutor the student who needs a little extra help, or encourage someone like Starr. Every act of kindness makes a difference in your small corner of the universe.

PRAYER: I want to show you that I love you. I am ready to do something today. Please go with me.

166

Jumpin' with the Monkeys

SUGGESTED SCRIPTURE READING: Philippians 4:1-8

VERSE DU JOUR: *Finally, brothers, whatever is true, whatever is noble, whatever is right, whatever is pure, whatever is lovely, whatever is admirable—if anything is excellent or praiseworthy—think about such things. (Philippians 4:8)*

Have you ever spent time watching monkeys? I mean real monkeys. And I don't mean glancing into their cage as you shuffle past at the zoo but taking a good chunk of time to sit and watch them. My dad and I have to be pulled away from the monkey cages at the zoo, we are so enamored of them. It doesn't matter which species you pick; they are wild fun to watch. We have spent hours watching them and can't imagine how much fun it would be to watch monkeys in the wild. Picture them frolicking way up in the banana trees: There's a lot of jumping around, the bananas are flying, the monkeys are hopping, and the party is on.

Jesus, being one with God, had the perspective and mind of God. We do not have this advantage but must strive to come closer to God's ways. That means, more or less, that unless they are tamed, our minds are like banana trees with a lot of monkeys jumpin' around up there! There's a lot of activity, but not much getting accomplished. Or, a teacher might make the analogy that our minds are a lot like an unattended classroom with too much activity, a lot of stuff flying around, and hardly any learning happening.

Unless we tend to our minds and carefully monitor what we allow them to absorb, we will accomplish no more than those monkeys up in the banana trees. Amid a great many instructions on how to live a godly life, Paul encourages us to guide the activities of our minds. Unattended and left to the reign of chaos, our minds will quickly stray from our goals and our God. Paul reminds us that we must make a concentrated effort to discipline our thinking regarding those things that will positively affect our mindset and, consequently, our lives. As a result of this effort, we are promised God's divine peace, which transcends human understanding.

PRAYER: I want to tame my mind so that I can become more like you, God, and know your peace. Help me to rid my mind of those negative things that do me no good. Let me think about things that are noble, right, pure, lovely, admirable, excellent, and praise-worthy because you are these things.

167

A Voice in the Wilderness

SUGGESTED SCRIPTURE READING: Matthew 3:1-17

VERSE DU JOUR: *In those days John the Baptist came, preaching in the Desert of Judea and saying, "Repent, for the kingdom of heaven is near."* (Matthew 3:1)

Today we couldn't get anywhere near downtown. The streets were blocked off, and traffic was rerouted. There were sharpshooters on top of the higher buildings, and police lined the sidewalks. Helicopters swarmed the skies, and the air buzzed with expectation. Everything was clean and polished, but it was safety that was of the utmost importance. The president of the United States was on his way! Maybe, if we were lucky, we could get past the barriers and get a chance to see him.

What happened when Jesus, God in human flesh, came to visit earth? This little dust ball of a planet made no special preparations. No hulking bodyguards or police teams were deployed. No reservations were made at the finest of hotels, and threats to his safety were not removed. Instead, one man, a special man, was given the job of preparing the way for the Master. This man, John, was selected to be a voice to the people. His voice would prepare the way for the greatest visitor in our history. Look at his specs:

Name: John the Baptist
Address: the wilderness
Phone/e-mail: none
Diet: locusts and wild honey
Wardrobe: clothes made of camel hair and
    a leather belt about his waist
Relations: cousin of Jesus Christ
Length of teaching occupation: six months
Favorite lesson/phrase: Repent!
Teaching finale: Ends career with violent death

John the Baptist (JTB) was willing to be a voice to the crowd. Knowing that he was born to fulfill this one mission, John was willing and committed to downplay his own importance. His sole role in life was clear: John would prepare the way for the Lord Jesus Christ. JTB announced to anyone who would listen that the Messiah had finally come; he was neither afraid to be different nor worried about the personal consequences of his message.

Are you willing to be a voice? You can be the voice preparing the way for the Lord. You don't need to be the loudest voice, the most convincing voice, the most intelligent voice, or the most dynamic voice. You don't have to eat bugs or wear funky clothes to be a voice to those around you (although this could be fun!). Perhaps, like John, you were born to be a voice for Jesus—to speak for Jesus and to prepare others for his arrival in their lives.

PRAYER: Lord, let me be willing to be a voice for you today. In my wilderness, let me speak for you. Let me use my voice for your glory and honor.

168
Laugh Out Loud

SUGGESTED SCRIPTURE READING: John 12:1-19

VERSES DU JOUR: *"If you obey my commands, you will remain in my love, just as I have obeyed my Father's commands and remain in his love. I have told you this so that my joy may be in you and that your joy may be complete."* (John 15:10-11)

When the blender exploded, precious puree flew out all over the kitchen. How would I clean up this mess? I'd finally had the time to prepare the slop from which my biology II students would extract DNA; now it was all over the ceiling.

After the mess was cleaned up, I had a good, long laugh. Describing this event would add an exciting finale to the tale of my latest exploits: First the furtive pick-up from the local castration center, the storage of gauze-wrapped dog testicles in my freezer, and now this. I knew it would make for a great story. I found all of this rather amusing and told the sordid tale to anyone who would listen.

Jesus was in great demand as a guest. He was invited to dine with reigning politicians, social outcasts, and even the Pharisees who claimed to loathe him. Celebrities and commoners alike clambered over each other for his company. Jesus accepted their invitations and dined with them. He was a man in demand for a reason. He had raised Lazarus from the dead! Apparently Jesus was not only an interesting personality but also had somehow conquered death. The attraction that people felt toward Jesus was not caused by some supernatural spell but may have been based on the character of Jesus—a confident, compassionate, youthful leader. Part of his personality clashed with his social affability. His open smile and easy laugh must've seemed incongruous with his dangerous, challenging words. Jesus was both joyful and intelligent, a man of mirth and of serious thought.

How much fun are you? Can you tell a good story, do you laugh easily, and can you express genuine gratitude? Once word of my blender accident got out, the number of guests accepting invitations to dinner at my house dwindled considerably. Oh, lighten up, people! We are not good witnesses for our Lord if we become like the Pharisees. If we get caught up in our religious laws and forget to enjoy people and their differences, we will have missed the mark. Teaching is tough work, but we must take time out to relax, enjoy, and emulate the attitude of our Lord.

PRAYER: Let me take on your attitude and your joy. Help me to smile and relax as I enjoy life and its ups and downs.

169

The Mystery of Time

SUGGESTED SCRIPTURE READING: Ecclesiastes 3:1-22

VERSE DU JOUR: *Whatever is has already been, and what will be has been before, and God will call the past to account.* (Ecclesiastes 3:15)

Yesterday morning, my husband, Chuck, was taking our son, Wolfie, to school. Because I usually drop the Wolf at school, Chuck, unsure of the routine, asked Wolfie what time he had to leave for school. Wolfie responded with, "I don't know. I don't know time." What he meant was that he didn't know how to read the clock and was not aware of what time means in the context of his life.

After hearing the account of this father-son conversation, I pondered the innocent wisdom of Wolfie's remark. I also recognized that Wolfie is not alone. I, too, really don't understand time. Sure, I can read the clock, although I might not do so often enough. And I generally know when and where I am supposed to be, assuming that I remember to check my date book. But in the grand scheme of things, I don't have a handle on time either.

Jesus had a unique understanding of time. "The right time for me has not yet come," he said (John 7:6). "Repent, for the kingdom of heaven is near" (Matthew 4:17). "Heaven and earth will pass away, but my words will never pass away" (Matthew 24:35). Jesus obviously knew that while he was in human form, his time was precious and limited; a gift given by the Creator. The number of good works, humanitarian efforts, and self-sacrificing acts crammed into his relatively short life demonstrate this wisdom. As the Creator, Jesus understood time in a way we can't. Able to state prophetically that his time had not yet come, Jesus shows that he had always known his time here would end and only what was done for others would matter.

I often forget how valuable time is. How easy it is to waste time, to misspend time, or to ignore time—my most valuable commodity. It is time that makes up my life and time that limits it. It is time that is given to me from God, and it is time that God has ordained from the "get-go" of the universe. We have only one life in which to serve our Maker. Seasons come and go—spring changes to summer, and summer changes to fall. Fall quickly turns to winter, and then death takes us home. Our lives pass quickly, and few of our activities here will count for much if we are not watchful. We have only one life in which to serve, please, and praise our Master, Jesus Christ.

PRAYER: God, I don't understand your view of time, but I know that you are in charge of it. Please let me use my time in ways that are pleasing to you.

170
Christ's Servants

SUGGESTED SCRIPTURE READING: Luke 12:35-40

VERSE DU JOUR: *"There will be great joy for those who are ready and waiting for his return. He himself will seat them and put on a waiter's uniform and serve them as they sit and eat!"* (Luke 12:37, TLB)

"Here's your orange juice. Would you like me to bring over some extra bacon?" our eager waitress asked. "Of course, we'd *love* more bacon," I quickly answered to the parent volunteer who was serving our table at the annual teacher appreciation breakfast. These parents had worked so hard; they had been up late last night making casseroles, up in the early morning baking coffee cakes, and now they were cheerfully serving us. I knew that for some of these parents, working on this breakfast was a pure labor of love, a sacrifice they made in an effort to show appreciation to their children's teachers. I was humbled by their devotion and their humility but was still willing to inconvenience this dear mother further. We're talking about bacon, after all.

How will you feel at the great banquet that Jesus hosts? It seems unbelievable that Jesus himself will seat us and serve us. Imagine, Jesus putting on a waiter's uniform to serve us. How ludicrous it seems; the Savior whom we are supposed to serve will turn the tables, so to speak, when he serves us. And, unlike the teacher appreciation breakfast, I won't be able to feel that I've done anything to deserve the service of my waiter. After all, Jesus has already done everything for us, including reserving our seats at this feast. Can you imagine feeling comfortable with Jesus waiting on you? Yet, Jesus promises that he will do just that! It doesn't appear that we will have a choice in the matter—and that's okay. But we do have a choice now—the choice to serve him.

If I was slightly embarrassed by the attention of the waiters and waitresses at the teacher appreciation breakfast, imagine how we will feel at Jesus' feast. We cannot earn our way to that table, yet those of us who are connected to Jesus through faith and trust will be in attendance. What a crowd! Perhaps if we take on the attitude of servants of Christ's servants now, we will be better prepared to sit at that regal table. This is our chance to serve Jesus as we tend to his children. Let's serve Jesus before he comes to serve us. Will you be ready to party with Jesus and the saints? Will you hear, "Sit down and eat, my good and faithful servant"?

PRAYER: I can't earn my way to your table, but can you please help to mold me into a faithful and willing servant? Thank you for your grace, Jesus. Thank you for the invitation to access your power today and to feast with you tomorrow.

171

The Widow

SUGGESTED SCRIPTURE READING: Romans 13:8-14

VERSE DU JOUR: *And do this, understanding the present time. The hour has come for you to wake up from your slumber, because our salvation is nearer now than when we first believed.* (Romans 13:11)

She showed up in the chemistry lab, tickling a young man's neck. The chemistry teacher knocked her down, captured her, and claimed her as my prize. The tickled boy arrived in my classroom, sheepishly holding out the unusual gift. I could tell almost immediately, by her markings and size, that the beauty in the jelly jar was a female black widow spider. What a prize: a local and a lethal specimen! Determined to find a way to preserve this rarity, I took her home, carefully taped her jar shut, and waited for her to succumb.

After almost a week of waiting, the spider was as vibrant as ever. Not wanting to a squash her but unwilling to keep her indefinitely in the same kitchen where my two-year-old wanders, I chose the humane death-by-cold method, popping her, jar and all, into my freezer. Three days later, the widow looked less lethal and most certainly dead. But because black widow spiders are nothing to mess with, just to be safe, I gave her one more day in the deep freeze.

Jesus was God's permanent solution to evil. His once-and-for-all victory sealed the deal. Jesus' life, death, and resurrection transformed the realities of hatred and sin. In 2 Corinthians 5:17, Paul tells us, "If anyone is in Christ, he is a new creation; the old has gone, the new has come!" These vibrant words speak of new life in Christ. Once we have submitted our lives to God, we are reborn as God's children, protected and accepted through the blood of Jesus. Paul does not say that our old life may someday return or that our status as Christians may someday disappear.

After four days in the freezer, the widow's long legs were balled up. I checked the acrylic, the casting container, and the toothpicks that would be used to rearrange her legs once she was placed on the first acrylic layer. In the middle of the procedure, my mom called to chat. Figuring I could multitask easily, I poured the acrylic and held the phone under my chin—until the widow woke up!

"Gotta go, Mom!" I barely gasped before dropping the phone. I frantically poured all the remaining liquid over the widow. She was caught in the acrylic, but the look I captured wasn't quite like the specimens we buy commercially. The cold must've merely sent the widow into a hibernating sleep, and when the warm acrylic woke her up, she was as active and dangerous as ever. In somewhat the same way, once God takes you as one of his own, you remain one of God's own. Even if you've been a sleeper Christian, you are still marked as God's own. Jesus calls you to wake up. He can still move powerfully through you and is willing to use you. Will you answer him today?

PRAYER: Lord, thank you for considering me a keeper. Let me wake up to live in your grace and your love. I want to be vibrant and proactive for you.

172

Held to a Higher Standard

SUGGESTED SCRIPTURE READING: James 3:1-12

VERSE DU JOUR: *Not many of you should presume to be teachers, my brothers, because you know that we who teach will be judged more strictly.* (James 3:1)

Now I know what it feels like to be chased by paparazzi. I was almost halfway through my grocery shopping before I realized that I was being followed by two curious students. Each time I switched aisles, I saw them slip past the end aisles and peek around the corner. Finally, I approached the giggling duo. After greeting them, they offered an explanation, "We just wanted to see what you have in your basket."

I was glad that I wasn't on a junk food run that night. We were in the middle of a nutrition unit at school, and I'd been lecturing on better food choices. Relieved that my cart contained mostly whole-grain bread, vegetables, fruit, and salad greens, I wondered if they could see the corner of the doughnut box that peeked out from under the toilet tissue.

Jesus knew that he was held to a higher standard. Every now and then I cop out from my responsibilities by saying, "Well, I'm not Jesus!" The reality is that God does hold us, Christian teachers, to a higher standard. We will be judged not only for our thoughts and behavior as humans but also for our performance and behaviors as teachers. Jesus said that to whom much had been given, much would be expected.

You have been given the resources and intellect to capture your subject matter, and as a teacher, you have already made the decision to share your knowledge with others. But your decision to share carries with it added accountability. Therefore, let us be respectful of God's children and mindful of these added expectations while we rely on God's expert assistance.

Ever notice how when your students see you in any nonschool setting, they are so amazed? You aren't carrying a textbook! Maybe you're getting your hair cut or are shopping. Perhaps you are working out at the gym. Students might follow you to find out who cuts your hair, what you're buying, or evaluate your workout routine. You might feel like a bit of a celebrity. I know I did the day after my shopping expedition. Every student in my biology class could recite the contents of my grocery cart. Perhaps you enjoy the attention, or perhaps it feels like an invasion of privacy. No matter what your reaction, the fact is that because you are a teacher, you are a leader. Your students will look to you for more than purely academic information. God will help us as we strive to keep our standards high.

PRAYER: Lord, please give me your expert advice and assistance as I seek to be honorable, consistent, truthful, and just. Let me be a model of your love and strength. Help me to serve you in ways that will make you proud.

173

No Regrets

SUGGESTED SCRIPTURE READING: Philippians 4:6-7

VERSE DU JOUR: *Do not be anxious about anything, but in everything, by prayer and petition, with thanksgiving, present your requests to God.* (Philippians 4:6)

"That kid is dumber than a bucket of hair," I overhear as I enter the teachers' lounge. I laugh at the image. Then we really get down to business; it is time to gripe and complain. I have a captive and sympathetic audience. Sometimes the content covered when I'm with other teachers goes beyond reasonable limits. "I have to let off some steam or I'll lose my sanity," I reason. Later, I think back on my conversations and know that my reasoning is faulty. I regret my words and think that the tension released is hardly worth the guilt I feel. Then I wonder if, at the end of my life, I'll look back and have other regrets. I may wish I had done many things differently.

Jesus modeled an attitude of constant thankfulness. He habitually turned difficulties into opportunities. The lepers who asked for Jesus' help were not just another hassle along his travel route but rather an opportunity to show God's healing touch. The death of Jesus' friend Lazarus was not a senseless tragedy but a chance to showcase God's power over death. We never find evidence that Jesus complained about or made fun of anyone. Paul, in his letter to the Philippians, reminds us that we should ask for help in all our struggles and challenges and do so with thankfulness. Praying for wisdom and/or strength is fine and good, but perhaps we should preface our prayers with a little introductory thanksgiving. This action would be especially meaningful if we can thank God for the students who are driving us to distraction. Then we could ask God for help in dealing with those students. Who knows, in time we might begin to feel thankful for those very students.

I already regret that I'm rarely thankful to God for the difficult students who come my way. I am ready and willing to ask God to help me manage them, but I'm not often truly thankful for them.

(Unless you can count muttered statements such as, "Thank God I am not that child's mother," as prayers of thanksgiving.) Instead of muttering, complaining, and grumbling, I can thank God for each and every challenging, difficult, rude, and unnerving student. I can recognize that each one comes wrapped in opportunities—after all, they give me a chance to hone my skills. Each tough student is a chance to make me a better teacher. I don't have to share all my worries and frustrations with my colleagues; I can turn those concerns and those kids over to God. Can you thank God for each and every student? We can remember to thank God especially when we don't feel like it and allow God to give us blessings that we will never regret.

PRAYER: Thank you for _____. (Insert the name of one student who threatens your sanity.)

174
Big Fun

SUGGESTED SCRIPTURE READING: John 15:1-11

VERSE DU JOUR: *"I have told you this so that my joy may be in you and that your joy may be complete."* (John 15:11)

Sometimes during lunchtime, students and teachers stop by the science department office just to look inside; they are curious to know what is causing the racket. The cackling and uproarious laughter, which can be heard in the hallway, seem incongruent to the setting. People open the door and stare in. That makes us laugh all the more. I am blessed to be part of a department that not only sticks together but also uses humor as an outlet for stress. We discuss the morning's events and most recent challenges while shoveling down our lunches. Then we critique and comment. This activity usually leads to insights that we find quite amusing.

Jesus, the master Teacher, taught an unusual lesson to the roughest class on earth. He was surrounded by doubt, ignorance, and vindictiveness. Untrue rumors, catty lies, and physical inconveniences must have made Jesus' teaching career even harder. And yet Scripture shows us a Jesus who managed to have a good time. Not only did Jesus enjoy his job, but also he emitted a joy that attracted others. Of what significance would a promise of his own joy be, if Jesus displayed none? Jesus' joyful and positive attitude extended beyond mealtimes and weddings; he was a lot of fun to be with because he truly enjoyed people.

Today we all had a great laugh. Seems the administration is looking for a new place to designate as the student smoking area. The vice principal came down to the science department to share the idea of moving the smoking area to the courtyard directly outside our office door. He thought it was a good idea to relocate it there because, in his words, "We might as well move it there since the science department is a bunch of smokers themselves." One of the twelve of us smokes, but that hardly accounts for the whole group.

Kevin, a biology teacher and ex-smoker, was semi-insulted that we had been pegged as "a bunch of smokers," and he told the VP so. "I thought you still smoked," the VP quipped. "I quit in 1979!" Kevin replied.

And we think the administration is informed about our personal lives. We all guffawed accordingly. Are you able to laugh at something, maybe even yourself, daily? I pray that you will be blessed with the joy of Jesus and that you can laugh as you fulfill the mission God has given you.

PRAYER: Master Teacher, please show me something funny today. You have promised to give me your joy, so please let me revel in it with you.

175

In My Weakness

SUGGESTED SCRIPTURE READING: 2 Corinthians 12:9-10

VERSE DU JOUR: *But he said to me, "My grace is sufficient for you, for my power is made perfect in weakness." Therefore I will boast all the more gladly about my weaknesses, so that Christ's power may rest on me.* (2 Corinthians 12:9)

"So, do you want to know who's packin' in here?" Jerome asked as I stood gazing at my somewhat new class. "I probably should tell you, for your own protection, you know," my ex-student and self-proclaimed protector continued.

I was torn between the protection this knowledge might offer and the allure of blissful ignorance. *Did* I want to know who was carrying a gun? I didn't want such knowledge to alter my teaching or my dealings with these students. I have to say that the decision, along with the need to make such a decision, was overwhelming, and I started to feel powerless and small. It's not everyday that a woman of my size feels small.

When Jesus came to earth, he was willing to work with his hands as a skilled tradesman. He did not put his faith in wealth, appearances, education, or physical appearances. Jesus could relate to the common man because he was a common man. Perhaps calling Jesus common is a bit of a stretch, but God does delight in showing divine power and might through regular men and women. God does not want anyone to confuse human strength with heavenly power.

Even Israel's great judge, Gideon, felt too insignificant and weak for the task that God had given him (Judges 7). Gideon was charged with the job of delivering the people of Israel from the Midianites. Here was Gideon, a pretty common guy, with plenty of fears and the need to be continually reassured of God's promises. He was a small man, physically weak, and came from an unimpressive family. God told this fearful man with low self-esteem to take three hundred men to fight the Midianites, most likely tens of thousands of warriors. Worse yet, God ordered Gideon to send his men into battle with nothing more than torches, jars, and trumpets. They were to surround the camp of sleeping Midianites and blow trumpets, shout, and break jars—a strange battle plan, don't you think?

I finally refused the information Jerome offered. I figured it was better for all of us, but I still wonder if I made the right decision. Blessedly there were no tragedies that made me regret my choice. God had ordered me there, and I wasn't leaving soon anyway. As for Gideon—following God's seemingly absurd orders resulted in unprecedented victory. The Midianites were stunned, fought against each other, and were consequently conquered. If Gideon had chosen to put his faith in the force of his army or in his own planning, the victory might not have been realized. Since he considered himself neither cunning nor strong, Gideon put his faith in God. Then, God delivered the victory. If you are an average or unimpressive individual, you can rejoice. You are the type of person God loves to employ to showcase divine glory and power.

PRAYER: Lord, teach me to accept what I can't change. Use my weakness and my frailties to show off your power. I am yours. Please stay with me, use me, and protect me!

176
What You Need

SUGGESTED SCRIPTURE READING: 1 Samuel 1:1-20

VERSE DU JOUR: *Then Hannah prayed and said, "My heart rejoices in the LORD; in the LORD my horn is lifted high. My mouth boasts over my enemies, for I delight in your deliverance."* (1 Samuel 2:1)

Just this weekend, our trusty vehicle with 140,000 miles to its credit tried to blow up. I know that's not the correct term for the dramatic loud pop that was followed by a racket sounding like a helicopter coming out of its hood. Of course, we were off in the hinterlands of Pennsylvania. We were on a deserted dirt road, and it was a three-day holiday weekend. By the time we got to a shop, I was close to tears. The coming repair might cost thousands of dollars. We were clearly at a disadvantage: 250 miles from home, ignorant of local lore, kids in tow, and already stretched to the edge financially. I started to panic, adding up the numbers that would certainly plunge us deeper into debt.

I started to doubt myself and my judgment: Why don't I have the money to pay for this? I'm too old to be this poor. Why don't I have more savings? Did I somehow damage the truck? On and on it went. The questions continued to plague me as I pursued rest. I couldn't sleep, so I started to pray. "Lord, please make sure that whoever looks at our truck is a good mechanic who can fix this. Please make him feel the desire to be honest and fair. I leave this in your hands."

Jesus taught his followers to pray without ceasing and to bring their requests to God. I don't know how anyone can pray unceasingly—it's hard enough to breathe and walk at the same time. Perhaps Jesus means for us to keep a mindset that is constantly attuned to God and a rightly focused inner dialogue. I *do* know that although my prayers aren't always answered the way I want them to be or the way that I expect, they are always heard. Hannah, the mother of Israel's greatest judge, Samuel, was able to smile at her mockers. She had been given the son she had asked for, and through that son, she was assured of God's provision and blessing. She knew that she was accepted by God and that God had heard her prayers. God knew Hannah's deepest desire and understood her needs and insecurities.

I prayed the same request over and over until I fell asleep. The next morning was the same. Whenever I started to panic or obsess over the problem, I began to pray again. I felt such peace. The situation was out of my hands and in God's control. Of course, when the truck was finished on the same day that we were scheduled to leave and when the bill came to only forty-two dollars, I was joyful in the outcome and joyful because God had heard me. Like God had heard Hannah, God had heard my cry. God had answered my prayer and had given me peace. Our God has power over our minds, money, and mechanics. God knew my need and heard my request. God will hear you, too. Will you turn over your needs and your worries to God?

PRAYER: Thank you for hearing my prayers. Thank you for knowing my needs before I ask.

177

Flee!

SUGGESTED SCRIPTURE READING: James 4:1-10

VERSE DU JOUR: *Submit yourselves, then, to God. Resist the devil and he will flee from you.* (James 4:7)

"Get back, Satan!" Serina shouts firmly, as she pushes away the handsome young man who is seductively rubbing her back and whispering in her ear. I hear the students around the two laugh, but I get to thinking about Serina's order and consider her wisdom. Serina is one of my few Christian students, and she appears to be trying to be obedient. How many times in the Scriptures have we been warned to flee from evil, to turn away from wrong, to resist temptation? It is clear that those who believe in Jesus Christ are to make a true effort to avoid evil and to guard against the evil one. Sexual sin is one form of evil, though there are, of course, others.

The Lord's Prayer teaches us to pray, "Lead us not into temptation, but deliver us from evil." Jesus was familiar with temptation and the necessity to avoid yielding to it. Jesus not only was tested in the wilderness for forty days but also must have struggled constantly with temptations to abandon his mission. "Why," the devil must've whispered, "should you, the Son of all power, be here living the life of a poor, filthy wanderer? Your uncomfortable life will only end with horrifying death." Jesus never sinned, so we can surmise that Jesus was the master of fleeing temptation and evil. Instead of speaking of our flight from evil and temptation,

James explains how we can get evil to flee from us. James follows his advice with a vivid picture of the consequence of our obedience. We are told that if we will resist the devil, he will flee from us. The word *flee* implies a hasty exit. It's not the same as a person who knocks and knocks diligently at your front door, only to sullenly trudge away after receiving no answer. Instead, we see a diligent enticer, hastily running from his intended victim. According to this Scripture, we have a way to send Satan packing. But Satan's fleeing is dependent on our action and on our attitude. We must first give ourselves humbly to God. Once we draw close to God, God promises to draw close to us. When we are connected with God, the Evil One abhors our presence.

Serina was right on the mark. Satan is real and powerful, yet God is greater and is our rear guard. How many times during your day must you rely on the goodness of God to guard you from evil? Do you realize that you do have a powerful protector, all day of every day?

PRAYER: Lord, I lift you up. You have taken me as an imperfect vessel and are using me even now. Thank you for your forgiveness and for making me strong. You alone make me worthy and protect me from evil and harm. Please stay close by my side today.

178

Too Close to Home

SUGGESTED SCRIPTURE READING: Matthew 13:53-58

VERSE DU JOUR: *And they took offense at him. But Jesus said to them, "Only in his hometown and in his own house is a prophet without honor."* (Matthew 13:57)

We sat together at the piano, the tea kettle whistling in the not so far distance, birds twittering outside the window. The birds weren't the only ones twittering. What had I been thinking when

I decided to save a piano lesson slot for my daughter? Riley appeared unable to concentrate on the lessons that seemed to work fine for my other students, and even the smallest thing distracted her. Why wouldn't she listen to what I was trying to teach, and who put on that stupid kettle?

Jesus found it difficult to reach many of those whom he came to save, and the hardest to teach were those from his own hometown. Although they had heard all about Jesus and recognized the extent of his impressive fame, the hometown crowd wasn't moved. Perhaps they saw no reason to respect a man who was all too familiar. Despite Jesus' wise teaching and reports of his miraculous powers, those unappreciative homies refused to honor the Master. How difficult it must've been for Jesus to restrain himself. Wouldn't it have been fun to amaze the doubtful crowd? And yet, we read that Jesus did not perform many miracles while back home in Galilee.

I'm embarrassed to admit that when an experienced piano teacher moved to our neighborhood, I was one of the first in line to enroll my dear daughter. It wasn't with pure defeat that I moved from writing lesson plans to writing checks. Riley eventually transferred her musical interest from the piano to the trumpet and later, to the clarinet. And the same daughter who zoned out during those early piano lessons listened intently to my clarinet instruction and mimicked my somewhat rusty playing all too well.

PRAYER: Lord, let me realize that when those closest to me fail to heed my instruction, I am not alone. You've been there and done that. I beg you for patience, fortitude, and your everlasting wisdom.

179

Involved Learners

SUGGESTED SCRIPTURE READING: John 9:1-15

VERSE DU JOUR: *"He put mud on my eyes,"* the man replied, *"and I washed, and now I see."* (John 9:15)

You can imagine my surprise when I found seven students waiting outside my classroom door on the first day of summer vacation. They were not there to argue about grades, to turn in late assignments, or to harass me. They wanted to do one more lab.

At the end of the last quarter, we didn't have time to fit in the amazing cow-eye-dissection laboratory. I jokingly told several classes that if they wanted to do the lab, they could see me during the summer. And there they were! How blessed I am to teach a subject with hands-on activities that appeal to the students and to me. After scrambling around to find enough dissection pans and tools, they settled in to work.

In only sixteen recorded instances did Jesus teach utilizing pure didactics. If the master Teacher knew that didactics stimulate learning and retention, he would have spent his three years of ministry following a strict lecture plan. Instead, we observe that Jesus expertly wove his message into many formats. He drew on the experiences and knowledge of his students. He consistently modeled the behaviors and attitudes that he was trying to teach. Jesus actively involved his students in the learning process.

Jesus also knew that if his students were to be involved in their learning, particularly if they could experience learning with all of their senses, his lessons would stand the test of time. We see Jesus drawing in the dirt with a rough stick as he speaks to the Pharisees. Now he's pouring water over his disciples' feet and scrubbing calluses. He asks for a drink of water after a day walking in the hot dust. In the coolness of the upper room, Jesus breaks bread with his hands and passes around a goblet of wine. He touches the lepers, bounces the children on his knee, and shouts out the demons. The temple vendors scurry away when Jesus cracks a whip overhead. Even the recipients of Jesus' healing miracles are drawn into the process. In today's reading, the blind man feels mud on his eyes and the touch of the Master's hands. He hears Jesus speak to him, but it is not until the man follows Jesus' command that his healing is complete.

As my students honored me by showing up to do that lab, I want to honor Jesus by showing up each day ready to teach like him. Why not consider Jesus' methods to teach your students? The methods by which Jesus taught were ultimately so effective that in three years of teaching, Jesus changed the world. His students not only understood his message but also retained the information so that they could pass it on to others. His teachings were the foundation of the church. His teachings were the start of a new way of thinking and a radical way of living. His teachings continue to this day.

PRAYER: Jesus, teach me to become a great teacher. Show me effective ways to reach students with my subject matter and with your love.

180
Finishing Well

SUGGESTED SCRIPTURE READING: 1 Corinthians 9:19-27

VERSE DU JOUR: *Do you not know that in a race all the runners run, but only one gets the prize? Run in such a way as to get the prize.* (1 Corinthians 9:24)

By the last week of school, although the end is in sight, I can barely see it because my eyes are puffy and bloodshot. My patience has worn thin, and I'm feeling a special kinship to the big bad wolf. My main focus is the two-hundred-question final exam that waits, locked in my desk drawer, along with my growing collection of water guns. I've confiscated quite a diverse and novel collection. When I allow myself, I fantasize about the rewards ahead: sleep, freedom, and a chance to get away. But I also want to finish well. I want the last hours with my students to count for something permanent and would like to leave them with fond memories. I want some of them to leave me with fond memories, too.

Remember the biblical hero, Noah? Noah began his mission well but ended poorly. A man eager to obey God, Noah sacrificed seventeen years and his reputation to build an enormous ark in which humankind would be preserved. Toward the end of his life, Noah was involved in an incident that had severe repercussions for one of his sons. Judas began his life's mission by leaving family and wealth behind to follow Jesus. Judas sacrificed many human comforts to gain wisdom and knowledge straight from the Master. Yet Judas finished poorly, marking his name forever in history with betrayal and death.

In contrast to these men, Jesus began his mission with a flourish and ended it well. Jesus began his public ministry turning water into wine, and in his grand finale, he conquered the gates of hell. His appearances to the disciples and ascension into heaven formed the perfect closure for his followers and marked a perfect ending.

Wouldn't it be great to live well and to finish well—to say, "I stayed with God's plan and enjoyed his love to the finish"? We are all in the race not only so that we finish but so we win the prize of God's approval. "Well done, good and faithful servant" (Matthew 25:21) are the words to which we aspire. May we all find the nerve and the verve to finish well.

PRAYER: Lord, help me to begin well and to finish well. Please help to make this a day that I want you to see, a performance that gains your loving and grace-filled approval, even though I know you accept me always. Let my day be a sacrifice to you.